THE AMERICAN SCENE

LET ME SHOW YOU NEW HAMPSHIRE
by Ella Shannon Bowles

LET ME SHOW YOU VERMONT
WINTER IN VERMONT
by Charles E. Crane

OUR SOUTHWEST
by Erna Fergusson

DESERT CHALLENGE:
AN INTERPRETATION OF NEVADA
by Richard G. Lillard

CALL IT NORTH COUNTRY:
THE STORY OF UPPER MICHIGAN
by John Bartlow Martin

RED HILLS AND COTTON:
AN UPCOUNTRY MEMORY
[South Carolina]
by Ben Robertson

FARTHEST REACH: OREGON AND WASHINGTON
by Nancy Wilson Ross

CONNECTICUT: PAST AND PRESENT
by Odell Shepard

GEORGIA: UNFINISHED STATE
by Hal Steed

ಬಿ

These are Borzoi Books, published by
ALFRED A. KNOPF

Pine, Stream and Prairie

PINE, STREAM & PRAIRIE

Wisconsin and Minnesota in Profile

BY

JAMES GRAY

NEW YORK · ALFRED · A · KNOPF

1945

THIS BOOK HAS BEEN PRODUCED
IN FULL COMPLIANCE
WITH ALL GOVERNMENT REGULATIONS
FOR THE CONSERVATION OF PAPER, METAL,
AND OTHER ESSENTIAL MATERIALS

Published April 16, 1945
First and Second Printing before Publication

26689

CONTENTS

ॐ

THE PLACE AND ITS PEOPLE

1. Heartland: Theme with Variations   PAGE 3
2. "Here Is the Place—the Central Place"   11
3. Waves of Invasion   22
4. From Primitivism to Primitivism   36

WORK

5. The Farmer Is a Scientist   47
6. A Saga of Bread   58
7. Red Giant in the Earth   70
8. "Timber Is a Crop"   88
9. Fisherman's Luck   101

THOUGHT

10. Hearing from the People   109
11. Cows, Colleges, and Contentment   135
12. Voices in a Quiet Room   151

THE ARTS

13. Sing, Regional Muse!   175
14. The Creative Impulse Is Indestructible   192

15. A Day in Erewhon 205
16. Father of the Skyscraper 217
17. "Reject Me Not" 222

PLAY
18. Escape of the Old Adam 227
19. "Short Retirement, Sweet Return" 238

SOCIAL LIFE
20. The Hum of Cities 254
21. Main Street Revisited 282
22. The Old Complaint 288
23. Souvenirs of Pioneer Splendor 295
24. Ten Chimneys 303
25. Postscript and Prediction 310
Index follows page 312

ILLUSTRATIONS

&

Map of Minnesota and Wisconsin   FRONTISPIECE

FOLLOWING PAGE

Painted Rocks on the shore of Border Lake   20
Minnesota Tourist Bureau

Minnesota and Wisconsin meet at the St. Croix River   20
Minnesota Tourist Bureau

Post office, general store, and bar at Penasse, Minnesota   36
Northernmost town in the United States
Minnesota Tourist Bureau

The Mississippi River at Lynxville, Wisconsin   36
Dispatch-Pioneer Press

Open pit mine at Hibbing, Minnesota   52
Minnesota Tourist Bureau

Hibbing, Minnesota, was moved so that its site could
be mined (1919)   52
Dispatch-Pioneer Press

The largest iron-loading docks in the world,
Superior, Wisconsin   52
Dispatch-Pioneer Press

The ghost town of Trommald on the Cuyuna Range   52
Dispatch-Pioneer Press

Highway through the fields near Red Wing, Minnesota   84
Minnesota Tourist Bureau

Grain elevator at Superior, Wisconsin   84
Minnesota Tourist Bureau

Hungry gulls in the wake pick up scraps   100
Minnesota Tourist Bureau

FOLLOWING PAGE

Fishing through the ice   100
Minnesota Tourist Bureau

A twenty-pound pickerel caught through the ice   100
Minnesota Tourist Bureau

De-netting the catch aboard a fishing tug   100
Minnesota Tourist Bureau

They lit the fires of reform: 116
1. Victor Berger   *2. Floyd B. Olson*
   P. & A. Photo   Dispatch-Pioneer Press
3. Ignatius Donnelly   *4. Robert M. La Follette, Sr.*
   Dispatch-Pioneer Press   Underwood & Underwood

The University of Minnesota, Minneapolis, from the air   116
Minnesota Tourist Bureau

Frank Lloyd Wright and four of his disciples   148
Taliesin, Spring Green, Wisconsin
Dispatch-Pioneer Press

The Capitol (designed by Cass Gilbert), St. Paul, Minnesota   148
Minnesota Tourist Bureau

Dog team and sled near Gunflint Lake, Minnesota   180
Minnesota Tourist Bureau

Bringing a doe into camp near Ely, Minnesota   180
Minnesota Tourist Bureau

Paul Bunyan and Babe, the Blue Ox, at Bemidji, Minnesota   212
Minnesota Tourist Bureau

Modern logging near International Falls, Minnesota   212
Minnesota Tourist Bureau

St. Paul is on the Mississippi   228
Dispatch-Pioneer Press

Minneapolis is proud of its parks   228
Minnesota Tourist Bureau

Milwaukee takes advantage of its Lake Michigan shore   228
The Milwaukee Journal

FOLLOWING PAGE

Duluth and Lake Superior, looking toward Wisconsin   228
Minnesota Tourist Bureau

Rochester, Minnesota, is dominated by the Mayo Clinic   244
Rochester Chamber of Commerce

Sister Kenny demonstrates her method to Rosalind Russell,
screen actress   244
Dispatch-Pioneer Press

The Villa Louis at Prairie Du Chien, Wisconsin   276
Drawing-room
Library, with portrait of Hercules Dousman
Dispatch-Pioneer Press

The Capitol and Lake Mendota, Madison, Wisconsin   276
Dispatch-Pioneer Press

Ten Chimneys   292
Home of Alfred Lunt and Lynn Fontanne at Genesee,
Wisconsin
The Theatre Guild

Lynn Fontanne   292
at the kitchen door of Ten Chimneys
The Theatre Guild

Alfred Lunt   292
in the garden of Ten Chimneys
The Theatre Guild

Pine, Stream and Prairie

HEARTLAND: THEME WITH VARIATIONS

THE RETURN of a native is a scene in drama that is represented always as one of intense poignancy and passion. Stone and leaf, spire and winding road, great gray monument, and city high-way—all have special declarations to make to the heart of the wanderer. The mystery of the past is pierced by the clear white light of intuition. A man sees himself in relation to his place and understands both unmistakably, in a moment of illumination.

This passion of recovery is not available to one who has never left his own place for more than a few months (or at most a few years) at a time. His awareness of his environment is much less intense and operatic. It is composed of affection, indulgence, respect, and disesteem in very nearly equal parts. When a reasonably honest and normally critical man thinks of the region in which he lives, in contrast to regions that are clearly dissimilar in important ways, his whole community becomes an extension of the family group. It is an entity with which a man may have a private quarrel but which he will defend with spontaneous and even unreasoning ardor against any outsider. One loves the region to which one is used with an inclusive fervor that catches up even its shabbiness or flamboyance if those characteristics happen to be assailed by the unsympathetic. In private one may try to cover up (except in intervals of great energy or great desperation one does not try very strenuously to cure) the squalor

3

or the vanity. A pretty picture is hung over the ink spot on the wall; a desk is moved to conceal the worn place in the rug. Few men are willing to admit that their rooms, their towns, their communities are not essentially places of great charm. But as one lives in one's own place day after day, subject to many inconveniences and trials as well as to some modest pleasures, one's consciousness of it is not often stirred to passion.

Yet today we live in a moment when even the native who has never left his own place is likely to feel an occasional surge of intense feeling as he rediscovers what has always lain about him. Threats to security have a way of making the shaken world look fresh and fair. But it did not take a second World War to make us begin to think well of the land of our birth. Somewhere midway between the first and the second World Wars, Americans began to feel much more like Americans than they had ever felt before. The legend of the vast and immeasurable superiority of Europe in sophistication, in culture, even in landscape, began to lose its fascination for those who had had only a superficial knowledge of Europe. To others, the genuinely creative men and women of America, it became clear that they could not go on wistfully imitating forever. An American art and an American culture could have roots only in the American soil. The evidence that Europe was beginning to go to pieces yet another time merely accelerated the process of America's discovery of itself.

As a nation we had the psychology of a man returning to the place of his beginnings, eager to find the way back into the past, back into something that was distinctly his own.

Only in our time has American painting expressed America; only in very recent years has American music found out its own themes, its own tempo, its own style. And as for those most strenuous of explorers, the writers, they have scurried into every corner where some souvenir of our beginnings might be found; in the stories of wars, of building, of tearing down, in the quiet minds of teachers and in the stormy souls of demagogues. The impulse has been to get the American story told—told honestly and in its crazy, varied entirety.

The drama is as big and sprawling as an adolescent boy. It is difficult to discipline it into orderliness and to translate its stormy outbursts into intelligibility. As history, the record shows too many influences to be dealt with in any way other than piecemeal. So many fine, brawling creatures of so many different nationalities and cultural backgrounds have stomped through our various periods leaving behind their different codes and tastes, hates and loves, that it has been possible to cope with the richness of our heritage only section by section. The mixed blessing of Puritanism is still the theme that we have been trained to remember when our imaginations turn toward New England. The collapse of the aristocratic tradition gives the story of the South its meaning for us. The never quite completed Hispanic conquest of the Indian world and the Indian culture is a segment of the American story that our minds can encompass as we move into the beautiful purple haze of the Southwest.

We have needed the literary tradition of "regionalism" to break up the story of America into digestible fragments. But a region in America may still be too big for any but the most Gargantuan (or, to translate into a proper American equivalent, Thomas Wolfeish) appetite. The tendency of the less hearty is to nibble off smaller and smaller bits, as this book will try to nibble off bits of Wisconsin and Minnesota.

Of all the regions of America, the Middle West is probably the least self-conscious in its pride, perhaps the least certain of its entity. Many states of other sections have long had their traditions of uniqueness and special desirability. Vaudeville's literature of nostalgia records the plaint of many a prodigal son longing to go back to Tennessee, to Carolina (either North or South), to Virginia or Maryland. The austerity of the New England tradition overawed Tin Pan Alley so that it has never dared to indulge in any comfortable crying spell over the yearning to be returning to Massachusetts or Vermont. But it is always understood among the friends of exiles from New England that, as Touchstone said, when they were at home they were in a better place.

No such certainty has been expressed about the special charms of the states of the Middle West. This was not an accident, of course. Many natives of the Middle West consciously reject the idea that a place, as a place, has any claim upon the tender sentiments. The large urban centers of the country are full of former Middle Westerners who are afflicted with a curious ailment, the acute inability to remember that there is anything west of Pittsburgh or east of Reno. The Middle West which can trace its history back only a hundred years or so has not yet weathered long enough to be picturesque in the eyes of its restless children.

Yet Bernard De Voto has recently called it "the American heartland." He means, of course, that it is a place of abundance and fertility, rich in resources, rich in the means of transporting those resources to the rest of the country. For generations the vitality of the nation will continue to be pumped out of this heart.

He means something else as well, I think, when he calls the Middle West the "heartland." It is not by accident that he uses a term of geopolitics. Though anything that recalls the Nazi ideology must make one wince a little, it is necessary to overcome that aversion and examine the idea. Mr. De Voto believes that out of this heartland will spring also the beliefs, the convictions, the code of international relations by which our national policies will be formed. For better or for worse, the American future will take form in the mind of the Middle West.

This may or may not be true. But if it is even a possibility, all of the symptoms of that heart should be examined with curious attention.

In its physical as well as in its intellectual attributes the Middle West has been caricatured more often than it has been correctly painted. One of Minnesota's native sons is, in part, responsible. Sinclair Lewis's satiric steam roller has passed over the whole region, flattening it out into a broad and featureless enlargement of Gopher Prairie. Many people who have never visited Wisconsin and Minnesota know that these states lie on a plain as flat as the world of Christopher Columbus's contemporaries and much less interesting. The land is apparently capable of growing wheat for bread and should therefore be encouraged to make itself useful. But it should not be visited by those who have any liking for beauty, grace, or the lively interests of the heart and mind.

This, of course, is a sad delusion. No heartland could be so dull and dispirited. Wisconsin and Minnesota are not lacking in the attractions for which a hopeful man looks in choosing a companion. Age cannot wither nor custom stale their infinite variety.

Indeed it is the wild, improbable, and dramatic alternation of opposites that gives to the region its most noticeable characteristics. Having been the Yukon for eight or nine months of the year, Wisconsin and Minnesota whimsically become Tahiti. Weather, which is good for little more than small talk in most well-ordered corners of the world, is fit material for a whole succession of grand-opera librettos in this region.

The wilderness is never far out of sight in Wisconsin and Minnesota. It is ever ready to let its green encroachment slip back over towns and villages. Even in the larger urban centers its dark invitation is to be found just beyond the end of the pavement. Every sort of life that has ever been lived on American soil is still lived here. There are frontiersmen on the northern fringe of our lands, hunting, fishing, trapping, improvising a genial existence out of the simplest gratifications that man has ever sought. They would feel much closer to the *voyageurs* of a century or two ago than they would feel to the mink-coated, orchidaceous audiences that sweep into our great halls to listen to Beethoven, Honegger, and Shostakovich.

Wisconsin and Minnesota might well become a sort of sociological laboratory for the study of the development of a culture. The whole evolution lies exposed before the eyes of the investigator, passing from simplicity to complexity, from scarcity to abundance, even from primitivism to decadence, all in three generations and six easy lessons.

It is virtually impossible to live in Wisconsin or Minnesota without participating actively and personally in the variety and range of the region's social habits. The most devitalized of city dwellers cannot hope to be let alone to trudge between a cell in an air-conditioned, fluorescent-lighted office building and a slightly larger cell in an apartment house. Someone will resolutely drag him out to hunt or fish or swim or climb. It is the normal thing to have a farm to go back to—a parent's perhaps, or a relative's. If inheritance or neighborliness has not satisfied the need, the average man will pinch and save until he can buy land on which to dig and plant and build and struggle and curse and struggle again.

Everyone skis in winter in the hills, which have not, after all, been flattened out by Sinclair Lewis's steam roller. Everyone boats in summer on one or another of the thousands of lakes that punctuate the landscape with their sparkling exclamation points. Everyone has his favorite chain of lakes through which he paddles during the long, somnolent days of a vacation, feeling often that he is the first man ever to penetrate into this particular stretch of leafy mystery. Everyone has his favorite river, the frenzied rapids of which he likes to shoot or the wandering slews of which he likes lazily to explore.

The attraction that people of the Middle West find in the Middle West is the opportunity that it offers to live many lives in one. You may be a city man if you must or if you will. You may sit at a too heavy public dinner knotting your brow over the perplexities of a debate on foreign policy. But you do not have to continue to be that city man any longer than you wish. Within an hour you can have changed your mind, your costume, and your environment to become a primitive living among primitives. There is always the not unrewarding threat of danger in such a transformation. You may start out on a beautiful autumn day to spend a week-end hunting and suddenly find yourself cut off from civilization in the midst of a blizzard quite as thorough, quite as elemental, as any that you have read about in musty documents at the State Historical Society.

The truth is that it is an old habit with people of Wisconsin and Minnesota to vibrate between the civilized world and the world of the wilderness. The pioneers in the Wisconsin River Valley, those of St. Paul and those of Marine-on-the-St. Croix lived well, drank discriminatingly if not discreetly, had their race tracks and their urban pleasures. They were also completely at home among the Indians, the trappers, the farmers. The custom of inviting variety has never changed.

On the basis of what they did to exploit the riches of the heartland it would be possible to make a dismal case against the pioneers who invaded the region. The vigorous men who stormed through the wilderness came with no thought of their duty toward future generations, toward the grandchildren who would still need the resources of forest, stream, and prairie. They took "what they thought they might require" in the innocence of greed.

First the trappers rushed through Wisconsin and Minnesota to exhaust the resources of fur and then pass on. Treading on their heels came the lumbermen to exhaust the resources of pine and then pass on. Not far behind were the miners who dug for gold and found iron. Last of all came the large-scale farmers who exploited the richness of the soil by forcing it to grow more wheat than earth (which also tires if it is not treated well) should be required to grow. When they could no longer exploit the soil of Wisconsin and Minnesota, the exacting and selfish among the pioneers passed on to the Dakotas.

But the important thing about the history of Wisconsin and Minnesota is that these states had the hardihood to withstand the heavy, careless tread of the exploiters. They have survived each invasion and proved themselves, in the end, to be stronger than the trampling armies. To each loss they have adapted themselves cheerfully and successfully, finding new sources of abundance in their unexhausted store.

Wisconsin and Minnesota still have a fringe of wilderness on their northern borders, one of the few left in America where the conditions of the unexploited world still exist. Having been denuded of their pine, these states have found uses for the "weed trees" that early loggers scorned. From them they make pulpwood, insulation materials, and a hundred other commodities, the importance of which as industry very nearly equals, and promises presently to pass, the importance of logging in its most strenuous and roaring days. The deposits of iron have served America more significantly than ever before during these days of war need, while the vast quantities of low-grade ores remain inexhaustible, requiring only the new techniques, which will certainly be found, to make them commercially valuable. The soil, restored by diversification after the hysteria of the bonanza wheat-farming days, is richer than ever and is now intelligently dedicated to the indispensable interests that have made Wisconsin and Minnesota the "bread and butter states."

Each invasion of the exploiters has left behind permanent additions to the population, the sober and thoughtful men who have learned how to husband resources and to market their abundance wisely.

If this region is indeed the heartland, it is so not simply because it contains an abundance of physical resources. It is the heartland also because it contains within itself the memory of everything that America has been and the knowledge of what it may become. The memory is fresh and immediate. It can be revived at will simply by going into a corner where the memory is still an actuality. We could make Whitman at home here, I think, or Audubon or Lincoln or Tom Paine.

2

"HERE IS THE PLACE—
THE CENTRAL PLACE"

ʊ

THEIR FIRST GLIMPSES of this heartland woke in American and European explorers impulses toward prose poetry that any latter-day secretary of a Chamber of Commerce might envy. Jonathan Carver, sent by Major Robert Rogers to extend the geographical knowledge of the region in the interest of the fur trade, settled for quiet, unadorned superlatives. He wrote:

"The Country of the Nandowessee [the Sioux Indians] of the plains about the River St. Pierre [now the Minnesota] exceeds for Pleasantness and Richness of Soil all the places that Ever I have seen. . . ."

Beltrami, the Italian, undertook to foresee what sort of vivid, teeming, and dramatic society might in the future crowd into the silence of this wilderness:

"Nature seems to have lavished all her treasures on this beautiful valley; watered by the river St. Peter, it possesses a fertile soil, a salubrious climate, hills and plains adapted to every sort of cultivation, rivers and lakes abounding in fish, shellfish and game, richest fur and furnishing every variety of timber for building . . . and added to all these riches, magnificent stone which might be worked with the greatest facility and fitted for building barns, houses, temples, palaces. . . . When I woke from the dream of all that this favored valley might become, I was struck by feelings I cannot describe at its awful and desert stillness which perhaps no other scene could awaken."

The future which Beltrami imagined with awe has long since

overtaken the region, and though the temples and palaces may not be in all respects what he would have desired, the pattern of rivers, hills, and plains is still what he so exuberantly described.

But the look of the country changes greatly from section to section and season to season. The whimsical creative hand of the glacier folded the land into a variety of patterns. There is that of the gently undulant country that sweeps with repetitive but never monotonous rhythm over hill and into valley, each small detail of which offers some green assurance of fertility, some token of abundance.

This is perhaps the typical scene that a man from the region would see if, far from home, he were suddenly to hear someone say "Wisconsin" or "Minnesota." He would see a well-kept highway rising and dipping, leading past farmland under full, but not grimly or eagerly exhaustive, cultivation; he would see the wheat burning in the sun; he would see low-lying thickets of oak and elm, ash and poplar, maple and basswood, tangled over with vines of wild grapes; he would see the group of farm buildings, the tidy, unimaginative house, the much larger barn, swelling with the look of expected repletion, the windmill, the chicken sheds and corncrib—looking well cared for and in good order, all bearing the signature of competence; he would see the farmers riding their modern tractors across the fields, the older ones still muffled in woolens to neck and wrists under their overalls, the younger sons of the vitamin era bared to the waist and burned a deep brown; he would see innumerable tiny lakes with reedy edges, leading off into marshes where cowslips show their pleasant, plebeian stretches of yellow, and then on to diminutive forests strewn with violets and columbine, bloodroot, anemones, and lady-slippers.

This pattern of land and of living stretches across eastern and southern Wisconsin and on across central Minnesota. It is a quiet and confident region, one in which man seems to live with nature on a basis of complete connubial contentment. The tempo of the place and of the people is slow and patient; yet the look of everything about the land bespeaks a mood of persistent thoroughness. This is country that one can trust, a giving sort of land. It is not necessary to scratch frenziedly at every square yard of its area to make it give up its abundance. There is enough of everything, enough to provide even the luxury of unreclaimed marshland and the protection of wood lot.

There is nothing mean or meager about it anywhere. The farmhouses, charmless in themselves as architectural entities, are gracefully enfolded by green backgrounds that have made them seem paintable to many successive generations of artists. Want and fear seem never to scurry away at one's approach as one imagines they do sometimes in less fortunate places. A traveler in certain bleak stretches of America learns to avert his eyes from the sight of human habitations, not so much to protect his own sensibilities as because he dislikes spying on distress. Coming back to his own place after wandering through such other regions, the man from Wisconsin or Minnesota is conscious of drawing a sigh of relief. It is reassuring to know that he has not merely dreamed the abundance he thought he remembered. He stretches his eyes over the rise of the next hill and washes them in the Van Gogh yellow of wheat and the green of the forest fringe.

The pattern of rolling country is one pattern; that of streams is another. The good unconscious creativity of the glacier left us a glittering plan for work and pleasure, one which, though "writ in water," is still permanent. Five rivers, the Fox, the Wisconsin, the St. Croix, the Minnesota, and, of course, the great Mississippi, cut the region; and lakes of every size and shape, shading of temperature and temperament dot the central part.

The theme of water should perhaps respectfully be said to begin with Lake Superior, the largest of the inland seas. One's sense of immensity has already passed over some threshold of awareness when one looks at Superior. It would be useless for a body of water to be any bigger simply to impress humankind. Everything about Superior serves to justify its name. Man has made it useful, but Superior remains aloof and stern. The beauty of its north shore is that of untamed wildness; of rocks so huge that lighthouses are needed to warn of their threats to safety; of trees tormented by the weather so that they seem to come leaping out of the rocks in a wild impulse to escape; of dashing surf and tremendous storms. Superior is not hospitable to swimmers. Even in mid-August one enters it merely to be able to say pompously that one has done so.

Even trained sportsmen do not linger, for Superior grips them in what Rupert Brooke might have called "a rough, male" embrace. In the end this rugged meeting seems like an encounter with a Japanese wrestler who means to have one's life.

People who make lists of things and count them say that in Minnesota, officially "the land of the sky-tinted water," there are ten thousand lakes. From the rough majesty of Superior they grade down to the homely domesticity of little community models. Every neighborhood in the lake country has one or two of these, often several within walking range. They are, of course, the centers of social life, summer and winter. One learns the gossip of the streets while floating idly on one's back next to an equally relaxed neighbor. And when the water first begins to freeze, all of the enterprising boys of the community start to work on their iceboats. The pattern of life in Wisconsin and Minnesota takes its design from the checkerboard of lakes.

But the lakes are not all so easily tamed to the use of man. There are wild and unruly elements to vary the theme. Lake Pepin, a widening of the Mississippi River, collaborates each year in fine adventures for the gallant and foolhardy. Enticing and treacherous, Lake Pepin is the *femme fatale* among lakes. Even the most firmly realistic mind bends before its attraction and begins to invest its cold unconsciousness with feminine power and malignity quite in the manner of the Indian poets.

And in the north country there is certainly nothing tame about the lakes. They formed the fur-traders' route in an earlier day and they belong as much to frontier now as then. The theory that time flows in two ways and that it is necessary only to get started in the right direction in order to find one's way back into the past seems to be incontrovertibly proved in this strange land, which appears to have experienced nothing of the development of recent centuries. In its immemorial changelessness, the north country brushes off all the distresses and tensions and miseries that civilization has generally undergone and continues a way of life that was old before the coming of the white man.

You have only to provide yourself with a canoe, with provisions, with tenting equipment and start out on this chain of lakes in order to experience all those pagan pleasures for which the world-rejecting Wordsworth longed in his sonnet. Proteus and Triton do not belong to the picture, of course. They are the creatures of a mere modern heresy, no more than a few thousand years old, whereas the life of the north country has been rooted in the simple truths of reality for anywhere from 25,000 to 200,000 years. It is elemental, natural life itself that you see and hear as you move through this wilderness, past country where there is no sign of human life at all, past high overhanging cliffs on which there are traces of the pigments of ancient Indian paintings, past forests of pine so thick that, as Radisson said, "some places are as dark as in a cellar." Deer stand nibbling in the reeds along the shore. An osprey circles over the water searching for fish. A chipmunk sits on the edge of a cedar bough eating a prune seed. A bear scrambles up over a cliff, slips back into the water, and then climbs again. A family of deer emerges in sleek, fastidious elegance to bathe in the water. A porcupine cries in a cedar tree, its head between its paws. The only reminder that man belongs to this scene at all comes when a family of Indians passes in a canoe, one squaw sitting with a papoose strapped to her back. Unmodified by all of our latter-day love of intricacy, unshaken by our civilized passions, the way of life continues, in this alcove of time, to be exactly what it has always serenely and soothingly been.

The same variety in the theme of water shows itself in the rivers. The streams are by turn both tame and wild. The St. Croix, flowing between Wisconsin and Minnesota, first roars over rapids and then, near Stillwater, turns somnolent, forgetting the days when loggers lunged and lounged and swore and sweated along its banks. It has spectacular moments when it passes through the Dells between high rocky cliffs full of curious formations to which the prosy poets of our time have given such names as "the devil's punchbowl." But throughout its lower length it wanders placidly, running deep or running shallow just as the whim takes it, threading its way in and out of slews where cardinal flowers grow—the perfect place for a latter-day Thoreau to loiter through a long afternoon, filled with the tremendous trifles of discovery about fern and leaf and fish and reed.

The Flambeau in Wisconsin justifies its beautiful name by being always in a sputter or a roar over something. Its flame is that of youth as it rushes over hidden rocks, churning itself up into a foam of rapids at very frequent intervals and subsiding into quiet passages only long enough to catch its breath for another display of extravagant humor.

The Mississippi itself is many things at many different moments. Its beginning, at Lake Itasca, is completely mild. The "Father of Waters," without offering any prophetic suggestion of importance, appears in infancy as the most sluggish of brooks. Visitors like to patronize its mightiness-to-come by leaping from one reedy bank to the other. But even one who knows no more of rivers than how they look cannot fail to sense that the Mississippi earns its prestige. It is soon broad and impressive, flowing between high, wooded banks. There are those who have dared to say, perhaps in the interest of nothing more worthy than piquancy, that they find the Mississippi disappointing. If such men were willing to repeat that judgment under the most solemn pledge of honesty to all the divinities of beauty, then those of us who have lived our lives on the banks of the Mississippi could only say of them, more in sorrow than in anger, that clearly they are not river men. For it seems to us that the Mississippi is the great essential river, created after some rationale of rivers had been carefully worked out. It is broad and deep and useful; it is framed by terraces stepped gracefully back, or enclosed between cliffs of great height and ruggedness. If its waters run muddy, that is merely its token of service. If its waters are polluted by the ways of man, that has nothing to do with its dignity. The Mississippi is what a river should be.

To the pattern of lingering antiquity belong other scenes like that of the Gunflint Trail. Over this comparatively narrow highway tower the giant Norway pines, making a natural Gothic arch. Through the whole distance, traveling deeper and deeper into the wilderness, one has the impression of being in a serene and sacred place, dedicated to the contemplation of the divinity of nature.

It is the cone and the pine needle and the enveloping dark blue-green that one remembers with gratitude after being in the north country. The carpet of fallen pine needles silences the sound even of booted feet. The effect of movement without sound is so soothing that, as a party of people climbs a steep path into the wooded hills high above Lake Superior to look for the deer that may come down to visit the salt lick, it is hardly necessary to warn them to be quiet. Laughter and words seem not to belong to the swelling euphoria of the day and the place and the moment's mood.

The third pattern to be found in the region is that of prairie. The name was brought into our language by the French explorers who, when they spoke of prairie, meant "a tract of treeless grassland or meadow." They used it in place names left on our map, such, for example, as Prairie du Chien.

The line separating forest and prairie is an irregular one, crossing Minnesota in a southeasterly direction and nipping off a bit of southern Wisconsin. A forest map in James Truslow Adams's *Atlas of American History* shows the prairie country lying in an L shape along a narrow strip of western Minnesota and stretching eastward along a broader base.

If one were to try an experiment in association of ideas with one group of people who have lived in Wisconsin and Minnesota and with another group who know it only through exposure to writers of fiction, it might be found that the word "prairie" rouses two quite different images. The adjectives used by a native son to describe it would be "blooming," "rolling," "free." The words that have hacked a path of association into the minds of readers of farm literature at its most grim and virulent would be "bleak," "forlorn," "monotonous."

In Wisconsin and Minnesota the more benign adjectives fit the image of the prairie. The soil is rich and deep; great dramas of bonanza farming have been enacted on it. Even the characteristic of treelessness is neither fixed nor final. Scientists, who have their own attractive vein of poetry, speak of the way in which certain trees—the oaks and hickories, willows, elms, and cottonwoods—have "wandered away from the eastern forests and pushed up the streams" of the prairie country. Land, of course, does not suddenly stop being one thing and become another. It has its transition phases, and the strip of prairie in Minnesota never becomes fully convinced that it ought to be, by definition, treeless.

"The Prairie rolling free" is the description which occurs in a Minnesota hymn, and that is the image which satisfies the imagination of a native son. It can, however, be flat in its more decisive moments. This one realizes with a start of surprise upon seeing such a dramatic sight as that of Rochester, city of the famous clinic, raising its skyscrapers above the flat agricultural country that lies about it.

The look of Minnesota has still other variations. The mining country shows its own dramatic pattern. The harsh, strident clash of color found in the overturned earth of the open-pit mine offers a reminder of a significant theme in the story of the region. And the cocky towns of the iron range, wearing still the air of new-rich confidence, remember their riotous past. They look still as though they could be the setting of a story that is told with a kind of pride concerning one of them. A young citizen, tiring of his bachelorhood, went east to bring back a bride. Before returning he wrote to the town marshal plaintively suggesting that it would be pleasant if his inexperienced young wife need not be too violently disillusioned about her new home but might be initiated into ruggedness a little at a time. The town marshal saw the point and offered a pledge of special protection. He went himself to the station to greet and to shelter the newest citizen. So did all the miners go to meet the train, and in their eagerness to offer hospitality they crowded in, hot, voluble, and uninhibited. The town marshal, determined to keep his pledge that the bride should hear no unpleasant word, made himself a one-man guard of honor. And as he led the way through the crowd he shouted with fine chivalric fervor: "Listen, you bastards, I said gangway for the bride! Gangway for the bride, you goddam sons of bitches!"

But it would be untrue to suggest that life in Wisconsin and Minnesota is everywhere either cozy or strenuous or both. In the cities there are streets where people live in tragic slums. There are sections where the neglected live beside the rivers in constant danger of their rising waters. On the outskirts of the richest towns, in the midst of the most fruitful agricultural country, there live the failures about whom the community does not want to think too much. They survive precariously in shacks improvised out of tar paper and old boards and the refuse of other people's living.

The theme of insufficient thought for the failures of society find another characteristic expression in the bleakness of the cut-over and burned-over lands of the north. Partly concealed now by second growth, the ruins of this once magnificent forest country are still a sight to inflame the social planner with new enthusiasm for his work. Even where the stumps are hidden by the show of new green, the landscape betrays the meager and apologetic look of the ravaged girl in an old-time melodrama. The poverty of the scene is echoed in the houses and villages where the people, with a stubborn and often grimly cheerful loyalty, continue to live.

These are the dissonances to be found in the song of any people's living.

The look of the territory is one thing as it steams under the semitropical heat of summer and quite another thing when it goes to the other extreme and hibernates under a heavy blanket of snow. An epic of the region might well begin:

Temperature I sing, and the man. . . .

The hero would be just any resident, the extravagant exaggerations of whose behavior might be accounted for by the improbable exaggerations of the climate in which he lives. Marching valiantly up and down the Fahrenheit scale from one hundred and ten degrees above zero to forty degrees below, the people of these states have no chance to be other than adaptable creatures. And this adaptability in turn must show itself in temperament. The people are used to extremes and they have learned to be adept in the art of taking them calmly.

The tradition of the "dry, healthy cold" of Wisconsin and Minnesota is as old as the occupation of the white man. Some of the pleasantest people who have ever come into the region were sent in the first place because of the legendary faith that nowhere else could they survive the threat of tuberculosis.

Sometime in the 1840's a young captain of the medical service at Fort Snelling wrote to the bride whom he had left behind in Virginia, listing a dozen impressive reasons why the climate could be counted upon to make her a more radiant creature than ever before. He piled those reasons so high upon one another and with such an air of nervous zeal that a reader begins inevitably to look for ulterior motives behind protestations so ardent and insistent.

It is not difficult to catch a glimpse of a lonely young man on the snow-drifted frontier peeping wistfully through the explosion of enticements and hoping to heaven that his eloquence will bring his wife to his side. But he was a doctor, after all, and he lived to be a great one of unassailable integrity. So perhaps the reasons were not altogether of the heart.

There is another special character to the climate of these states. It is the impetuosity with which it leaps from winter to summer with no loose "lingering in the lap of spring." It is as though Wisconsin and Minnesota were reluctant to say good-by to the cold months, during which very nearly everyone skis, and then were suddenly in a great hurry to rush into the warm months, during which nearly everyone swims and boats.

The suggestion has been made (though not with perfect sobriety) that spring in our corner of the world should be declared a legal holiday. The buds on the trees of the region do not open "stickily," as Edna St. Vincent Millay says that hers do. They explode in the night, probably to a chime of bells. One whimsical lover of the region has insisted that if you could manage to stay awake all night on the right night you would see, hear, and smell spring happen.

Wisconsin and Minnesota ease off into winter from summer more reluctantly, and of that reluctance the most enchanting fragment of time is made each year. October in Minnesota is a season when anyone must see what the word "bounteousness" really means, and on Thanksgiving Day in Wisconsin it is easy to perceive the plenteousness of the earth and to touch the promise of good things to come.

In the pioneer period, when a conscious effort was being made to attract immigrants, the whole region became a sort of seminar for the discussion of climatic advantages and disadvantages, with the emphasis inevitably heavy upon the former. Editor Goodhue of St. Paul, who always made a violent issue of everything and finally got himself wounded in a street duel by doing so, declared without qualification that "the whole world cannot produce a climate more salubrious than that of Minnesota." Other less partial observers joined the chorus of praise and approval. A St. Louis writer, who seems not to have been in the ax-grinding business,

PAINTED ROCKS ON THE SHORE OF BORDER LAKE

MINNESOTA AND WISCONSIN MEET AT THE ST. CROIX RIVER

said that "the severity of the climate in this region, instead of operating as a hindrance to its improvement, constitutes the strongest argument in favor of its future prosperity." An English traveler supported this apparent paradox by pointing out that "crops produce more abundantly toward the northern limit of their range of growth." A committee of doctors made a cautious examination of all the claims that had been offered on behalf of the region as a kind of paradise of health, an Elysium for favored spirits who had triumphed over death, lurking everywhere else. "Owing to our geographical position," they wrote, "our altitude, the general condition of the soil, the temperature and comparative dryness of the atmosphere . . . the climate . . . is stimulating and curative to most chronic diseases of the lungs and air passages, except certain forms of catarrhal diseases of the inflammatory nature. . . ."

It was William H. Seward who put eulogy into its pithiest form. "Here is the place," he said, "the central place. . . ."

It is still the central place, and it still has all the stern and stimulating salubrity that it ever had. A former resident of Minnesota, striding down Park Avenue in New York with his overcoat open to the wind, was stopped by a paternal old gentleman. "Boy, do you come from Alaska?" he demanded. "No, sir, from Minnesota," the young man answered. "Same thing!" snapped the old gentleman, half in admiration, half in irritation.

A war correspondent, trying to describe weather conditions on the Russian front, wrote: "People from Minnesota would feel at home."

Certainly the people of Wisconsin and Minnesota have learned to make themselves comfortably at home whether the thermometer rises or falls. Men, women, and children who live in the region throughout the year, loving it hot and loving it cold, loving it in the long autumnal pause and in the breathless eruption of spring, really mean it when they say that they could not do without its extremes and extravagances. The round of the seasons is unquestionably dramatic, and though there is something distinctly rigorous about the setting-up exercises to which the climate subjects us, few would be willing to give up the full treatment.

3

WAVES OF INVASION

IN THOSE RUDDY DAYS when men and women of great vigor and resource were bustling about, creating in the wilderness a home for part of the human family, many curious little dramas occurred in the towns of the frontier. There was, for example, a revealing incident in St. Paul when an elegant young lady newly arrived from the East went to call on an acquaintance whose family had been among the early settlers. As the caller approached the large and imposing house she shuddered daintily at the sight of an old Indian woman whom she must pass on her way to the front door. The squaw, looking old and totally indifferent to all that went on about her, occupied a strategic position on the front porch, from which only the patient hand of time seemed to have power to remove her.

The sight, plaguing though it was to a fastidious newcomer, was not particularly surprising. Already the young lady from the East had learned that this was the way in which the Indians who lived near by supplied themselves with food. They would simply take up a position in a promising locality and, without begging, without assuming even a look of urgency, superbly wait for their needs to be supplied by the members of the household.

Still, the young lady could not resist mentioning the little circumstance when at last she had been received by her young hostess inside the house.

"My dear," she murmured sympathetically, "doesn't it frighten you to come home and find that horrid old Indian woman sitting on your front porch?"

The daughter of the pioneers glanced out of the window to make sure that she knew to whom reference was made. Then as she began pouring out the tea, she answered quite casually: "No, it doesn't frighten me in the least, because, you see, she's my grandmother."

Our region has been extremely informal, by tradition and by taste, in its belief that people must learn to live together as best they can. On the frontier the state of society was completely fluid, and rigidities of class distinction, imported by the immigrants from Europe, were likely to be scrapped in the first long hard winter. A Hungarian nobleman settled in what is now Wisconsin and, though his tastes in music and literature continued to be fastidious and cultivated, his way of life was otherwise indistinguishable from that of his least-instructed neighbors. A buoyant young Irishman who had had an excellent education in a Jesuit college was soon, when he arrived in Minnesota, in demand as a public speaker. But that did not deter him from working during the daylight hours as a laborer. "America was promises," but in the frontier world when those promises were not instantly fulfilled in any glittering way, adaptations and adjustments were made and no one's pride was the worse for it. Certain harsh necessities had a way of whittling the great down to the size of their humbler brothers.

Feelings of racial superiority do not flourish in so robust an atmosphere. Belonging to the hothouse, they have tended to wither in the climate of Wisconsin and Minnesota.

One bit of knowledge about the region in which the rest of the country feels most snugly secure is the belief that it is the place where all those Scandinavians live. So deeply ingrained in the American consciousness is this item of information that a man from Minnesota feels as though he were disloyally repudiating his heritage when he is forced to admit that he has no Scandinavian background. An actor who went out from St. Paul to make a career in New York found himself typed in all the production offices and agencies as an interpreter of Swedish and Norwegian roles. Once or twice he felt obliged to disclaim any special aptitude and to confess that his ancestry was wholly German. But this proved to be a futile gesture toward candor and integrity.

"But I don't understand," an agent would murmur in gentle perplexity; "the card says that you are from Minnesota." In the end the actor had to give up and accept the birthright that had been thrust upon him.

It is quite true, of course, that these states owe a great deal to their Scandinavians. Wisconsin once had the largest Norwegian population in the country, and Minnesota has it now. The firm yet lilting modulations of Swedish and Norwegian speech are familiar everywhere in the region. So, too, are the surnames. You find them thick in the ballot lists. In Minnesota they are attached to far the greater number of governors, legislators, and judges. The Scandinavians have brought to the region their staunch love of independence, their easy and casual adaptability, their taste for "the middle way."

But it is greatly to oversimplify the story of our development to suggest that it is exclusively the record of the Scandinavian migration. It was less than a hundred years ago that the Swedes and Norwegians began to find their way to a region in America that reminded them of their homeland. But before that the pageant of wandering peoples had been going on for a very long time.

In the beginning (or at least as close to the beginning as the modest imagination dare plunge) there were the Indians, men and women chiefly of the Sioux and Algonquin families. They had fine tribal names, Winnebago and Dakota among the Sioux, Potawatomi, Chippewa, Ottawa, Sac, Fox, Menominee, Cree among the Algonquins. They were the descendants of tribes that some five hundred years ago built, probably as tombs for their leaders, the famous Indian mounds. These stand high on the bluffs commanding some of the finest views of the Mississippi. Clearly, the Indians appreciated their land and wished to give their great ones glimpses of the valley to carry with them into eternity.

These nations raged furiously together, the Sioux in their lithe and sinewy resolution, the Algonquin in their heavier and more stocky persistence. Though the Sioux are thought to have been the mightier warriors, their rivals finally prevailed. A backward glance at the history of the white man finds this alteration of Indian fortunes convenient, for the Chippewa and the Sacs got on comfortably with the French when these Europeans made their peaceful and jovial invasion.

Next in the pageant of people sweeping through the region came the French. They brought drama of a full and varied repertory. There were the priest explorers like Father Marquette, whose rhapsodic and intensely personal devotion to the Virgin made him long to lead all of the dear children of the wilderness into her arms; and like Father Hennepin, a very different sort of man, who understood the arts of advertising and of publicity long before they had been codified and sanctified in the decorative office suites of metropolitan skyscrapers. Preceding and following the priests came the trader explorers, Des Groseilliers, Radisson, Nicolet, Du Lhut—each with a firmness of character that fitted well into the rugged design of life in the wilderness though it did not always fit equally well into the latter-day biographer's design for a hero.

Radisson, for example, had the great virtue of adaptability. The more finicking ethical subtleties, however, had no part in his plan for a career. When as a boy he was kidnapped by Indians, he persuaded his captors to like him and ended by becoming an adopted member of the tribe. The same adaptability seemed less admirable when, as fur-trader, he gave his loyalty now to England and now to France, so that in the end neither trusted him. But as far as the story of the opening of the country is concerned, the great point about the French explorers was that they knew well how to get on with the people among whom they lived. The French were never ones to make a ritual of dressing for dinner in the wilderness so that the natives might be impressed and understand their place. Their cozy casualness made them good neighbors, but it did not make them good colonizers. Casual people tend to be absorbed and not to cling to a dominant position. However, the French made a home in the wilderness for those who were to come after. As the late Louise P. Kellogg, most important of recent authorities on the French in America, has written:

"None knew like the lighthearted French Canadian habitants how to endure courageously the dangers of the wilderness, how to breast and run the swift rapids of the northern streams, how to portage around the falls and obstructions, how to seek the distant hunting grounds of the Indians, how to barter with the red men for their valued pelts."

It is a spirited moment in the scenario of the wilderness invasion when the French traders come upon the scene. They are preceded by an off-stage chorus and then, there they are in their bateaux piled high with fox furs and otter skins, singing to make the work easier, singing to emphasize the rhythm of the paddles, singing to deepen their enchantment with the dark forest and the sky-tinted water, singing to waken remote memories of love and to quiet recent memories of fear.

It is perilously easy to sentimentalize the *voyageurs* and the *coureurs de bois* who went up and down the streams of Wisconsin and Minnesota acting as links between the Indian hunters and the traders with their headquarters in Canada. They were picturesque with their bright-colored shirts, their feathers in their caps, and their endless singing. They were gay with a capricious gaiety that wasn't quenched or even abashed by drunkenness, violence, murder. They added a fine moment to the wilderness story.

The souvenirs of the French invasion are by no means obliterated from the contemporary life of the region. Many beautiful names remind us of the spontaneous poetry of the first European dwellers in our country. *Lac Qui Parle* is surely one of the most charming inspirations ever given to a man who loved a lake. *Traverse des Sioux* is the setting of a famous treaty conference with the Indians. Wisconsin has a town, Somerset, in which much the greater number of the surnames of the residents are French in origin. In near-by Farmington one drops in for a glass of beer at "Eddie Montpetit's place." There have recently been alive in St. Paul old men who remembered a time when French was spoken on the streets more generally than English. Some erudite forebear gave to a city street in St. Paul the name Pascal, though it would be a mistake to expect to find it populated today by "thinking reeds" brooding over the *Pensées*.

The tides of invasion were responsive, of course, to the movements of world history. As England began to take domination of the New World away from France, a trickle of her people came

into the wilderness. Scholars who love to fill their nostrils with
the dusty scandals of old documents still have not made up their
minds about the true motives of the Earl of Selkirk. He pretended
to be acting as a philanthropist when he brought to the New
World the evicted tenants of Scottish and Irish properties, but
he may actually have been playing the game of the Hudson's Bay
Company, which wanted men to exploit the fur trade. It matters
less to the casual observer of the pageant why they came than
that they did come, bringing still another lively element into the
already vivid comedy of community life. The Scotch and the
Irish, with their pronounced tastes for whisky and theological
conversation, brightened the intellectual tone of the settlements
in northwestern Minnesota from which they began, presently, to
filter through the whole region.

In the Selkirk community the Scotch and Irish did not manage
immediately to dominate the life of the community. There were
still the French and Indians all about them, living together in
more or less permanent, more or less sanctified, domesticity. The
religious life of the community was still largely French and it is
in French that one reads of the difficulties that the missionary
priests had to solve. To their bishops, back in Canada, they put
such touching questions as: "Is it permissible to celebrate the
Mass while wearing moccasins?" and "Which woman may a man
keep who has several and wishes to be married to one?" To the
bishops also went such plaints as: "Baptisms are many, but confessions few."

The Irish continued to come in a steady, if thin, stream. The
well-born among them, tired of the obligation to keep up estates
which, year by year, buried them alive under ever heavier loads
of debt, came arm-in-arm with peasants running away from fam-
ine. Aristocrats lived in sod houses and swore that they did not
regret the change. When the son of such a man once asked what
life would have been like for him had the family remained in
Ireland, the father answered: "Oh, you would be able to drench
a horse, worm a dog, and ride to hounds, but you would know
nothing useful."

When Lord Selkirk's colony broke up, the Irish and Swiss
wandered away from Pembina to settle in various pockets of the

region. They traveled in the ox-drawn Red River carts, those curious symbols of the fact that the several racial groups already assembled had begun to collaborate in creating a native way of life. The French provided the original model of the ox-cart, copying it after the Normandy peasant's vehicle. But every other branch of the Pembina family made some contribution to its design and it represented, in the end, a sort of study in international co-operation.

In its final form the Red River cart consisted of a box with a pair of shafts mounted on an axle connecting two enormous wheels. These were broad at the rim so as not to cut perilously into the prairie sod. The whole thing was made of wood. It had, as a contemporary writer put it, "no iron about it so, if it breaks, the material to repair it is easily found." The axles were never greased and the cart made such a racket that it was said to offer an answer to the conundrum: "What makes more noise than a pig under a gate?"

Creaking thus noisily, the Swiss and Irish dispersed their groups over Minnesota and Wisconsin. Later they were joined by others of their kind who migrated north out of Illinois. Each took up the practice of the crafts that were traditional with the group. The Swiss went once more to watch-making and cheese-making, the Irish to their favorite occupation of dramatizing their humorous and wildly poetic temperaments. While the railroads were being built, the Irish worked cheerfully at back-breaking labor. Their songs, their fights, and their tall stories added great charm to the record of bringing transportation facilities to the region. Later their natural histrionic gifts and their skill at improvising wittily before audiences led them into the sympathetic atmosphere of the law courts. There they presided and argued and insulted one another happily. As the years increased, the type sobered, became erudite, became distinguished, all without sacrificing the love of impudence and wit. A brilliant heir to this tradition was the late Pierce Butler, who ended his days as a Justice of the United States Supreme Court.

And then came the Yankees. They followed the lumber trade and the fur trade, which they had already learned in New England, the young men seeking in a new region the opportunities that their fathers and grandfathers had begun to exhaust in the East. On the banks of one logging river, the St. Croix, they established at Marine a village of frame houses, frame churches, a stone jail which looks today like a bit of New England that a whimsical but well-ordered cyclone has transplanted whole. It would be a mistake to assume that these young men were dour and earnest. At Marine-on-the-St. Croix they had a race track and pretentious houses and all the gaudy attractions of a sophisticated way of life. There were scandals, too, upon which the summer dwellers still brood with a mixture of antiquarian and merely malicious satisfaction. For desire didn't flourish under the elms any more dramatically than under the pines, and it was an untrammeled existence that the loggers lived in the towns of early Wisconsin and Minnesota.

The fur-traders gave the region its first great names of permanent dwellers, its first conscientious designers of a solid society. Dousman of Wisconsin had the Christian name that such a builder deserved; Hercules, he was. And Henry Hastings Sibley of Minnesota was never far from the council table when the affairs of the state were being organized into a pattern.

American-born citizens came into the region also as executives. One of them was Alexander Ramsey, first territorial Governor of Minnesota, born in Pennsylvania of Scotch and German ancestry. With a decade of experience behind him as a member of the Congress, he brought his personal strength, resolution and imagination to the great engineering task of creating a commonwealth in the wilderness.

The next to arrive in the rapidly accelerating westward movement were the Germans. This group was finally to be the most influential of foreign-born citizens throughout Wisconsin and in certain communities of Minnesota, such as St. Paul and New Ulm. The Germans came seeking to escape regimentation, which has now put a whole people in a kind of communal straitjacket. In the sturdy minds of the men and women who came to the wilderness there was a healthy love of independence and a great distaste for the ancient quarrels of Europe.

Typical of the intellectuals among these exiles from Germany was Carl Schurz, who had a vivid and dramatic career of rebellion behind him when he came to America at the age of twenty-three. Schurz was only nineteen years old, a student at the University of Bonn, when he began declaring emphatically for the principles of liberty which he later espoused so eloquently in his adopted country. He combined active resistance to authority with verbal attacks, under the direction of his tutor in revolutionary tactics, Professor Johann Gottfried Kinkel. They were an energetic pair, sharing the work of editing the *Bonner Zeitung*, organizing coups against Prussian authority, once being ridden down by the Prussian cavalry for their impudence, and finally being forced to escape. Schurz made his way to Switzerland first, and from there organized a plot to free Kinkel from the prison fortress at Spandau. Unwelcome in Switzerland, the refugees made their way to England, where Schurz for a time was employed as a teacher and where he married a compatriot from Hamburg. But the revolutionary spirit in him became increasingly restless, inhibited by what Winston Churchill has proudly called "our British phlegm." He sailed in 1852 for America.

There were four years of transition during which he lived in Philadelphia, but it was when he came to Wisconsin that Schurz was fully reborn as an American. He loved the scene immediately and, what was more important, he found the ranks of the newly formed Republican Party ready to receive him as a leader. Living first at Watertown and later at Madison, he identified himself with both local and national affairs, and it was as a resident of Wisconsin that he went out to campaign with Lincoln in his famous contest against Douglas. Schurz's career as diplomatic representative of America to Spain, as a high-ranking Army officer in the Civil War, as a United States Senator representing Missouri, as Secretary of the Interior in the Cabinet of Rutherford B. Hayes, as editor of the influential *New York Post*—all this was built upon his successful initiation into the American way of life as an adopted son of Wisconsin.

As Secretary of the Interior, Schurz fought for conservation and established a merit system, forerunner of the idea of civil service. Both of these were to be made important issues in Wisconsin politics when Robert La Follette the elder, another angel with the flaming sword of reform in his hand, made his dramatic appearance.

Not all the Germans who came into the region were eloquent and active champions of liberty. Most of them were merely healthy, useful people who carried on in the New World the crafts and skills they had learned in the Old. The Germans provided a new variation on the theme of fur-trading. They began to make up the skins into garments, so that communities like St. Paul became centers of the retail market in coats. Actresses traveling across the continent would wait until they reached St. Paul to supply themselves with this item of their wardrobes.

The Germans also farmed and built up dairies and brewed the good beers of Milwaukee, Minneapolis, and St. Paul.

Carl Schurz translated the German spirit into something more brilliant than it showed itself to be in any other individual. But all of the German-Americans shared his distaste for the decadence of Europe and his desire to protect the principles of liberty in the new country. One must remember Schurz in order to understand the reluctance felt by the Germans of Wisconsin and Minnesota to see their adopted country becoming involved during the first World War in the old black quarrels of the Continent.

Then, at last, in the second half of the nineteenth century came the Scandinavians. "Tall, blond, and sturdy" goes the routine description of them offered by gentle lyric-writers who like to reduce the whole wild, disordered wonder of heritage to a neat pictorial symbol. So they appear in post-office murals, "tall, blond, and sturdy," though they actually showed no such robotlike conformity to a single unimaginative model. Forgotten are the "black Norwegians," who have given us some of our most creative citizens. Forgotten are the little plump Swedes like the late Magnus Johnson and the rather frail-looking, intellectual ones like John Lind, whose temperamental variety has done so much to enrich the interest of our social and political life.

The impulse to spread a formula smugly over complicated matters, with all kinds of loose ends left dangling, is characteristic of our thinking about racial groups. The Scandinavians, we say with the bland confidence of ignorance, are strong and silent.

They are inclined toward stolidity and for that reason make good farmers. They like the long hours and do not notice the monotony. Warming to our task of analysis, we say that it must be wonderful for them not to have a nerve in their bodies.

O. E. Rölvaag seems sometimes to have labored in vain. In *Giants in the Earth* he made an effort to show that the silence and the stolidity of the Scandinavians spring out of depths of feeling that cannot be expressed in the light fountain play of garrulity that passes for conversation and for thought with many of us. The dark drama of guilt that went on in the secret mind of Rölvaag's Beret; the sun-drenched, yet shadowed drama of compassion that ended for Per Hansa with the quiet nobility of his sacrificial death in a blizzard—these were more universally characteristic of the life of the Scandinavians making their way in America than any but the intuitive have seemed to know.

The Scandinavians came defiantly, leaving behind them the frustrated rage of the landowners and the priests. The departure of the emigrants robbed Norway and Sweden of cheap labor, and the ruling class responded by screaming in helpless protest. "Go, then," the priests said, "if you are so soft in spirit that you haven't the hardihood to accept the rough embrace of our northern mother. Go to your easy, self-indulgent lives in the new country, betrayers, slackers, weaklings." It is an ancient cry often repeated on the same futile, whining note. The memory of it must have made the first settlers smile with a kind of grim, tight-lipped irony as they hewed their way through a wilderness, built sod houses, turned the undisciplined soil, drilled wells into stubborn earth—all while the temperature sank to forty degrees below zero or rose to one hundred and ten degrees above. It was best for them to exercise their art of silence.

They met defiance in the New World, too. To the Yankees who had come out of Maine and Connecticut and New Hampshire, it seemed that, as the "old stock," they had established a sort of protectorate over the rapidly developing region. According to democratic principle they could not pretend to own it, but at least they could give themselves the perverse satisfaction of looking down their New England noses at the newcomers. The emotional climate into which the Scandinavians moved was as chilling as the physical climate. They were greeted with cold stares on the highways. At school a Yankee's little girl was not permitted to sit next to an immigrant's little girl.

But this hostility could not last. The Yankees and the Scandinavians farmed side by side, and both prospered. The barrier of language fell away as they began to speak each a little like the other. In many stretches of the region the Scandinavians seem to have inherited the earth, so persistently do their ancestral names appear on lists of leaders. They have inherited it, however, not through meekness but through a firm hold on their world, the pressure of which never has become oppressive or even noticeable. They have moved into places of prominence, not as former Scandinavians, but as Americans.

These are the chief racial sources of the vitality of the region. But other peoples have come to pour their strength into its bloodstream. There are the Finns, blond and solid-looking as though they had been packed into their skins under pressure, as explosives are packed away into the sleek covering of bullets. On the soil of the north country they work as loggers and continue their folkways, parboiling themselves in their steam-filled *saunas*.

There are the Czechs, so in love with song that an early teacher among them, Antonin Jurka, even set spelling and arithmetic to music.... And the Italians, whose universal gift of physical beauty fills the eye with charm quite as spontaneously when it is seen on the upper levee in St. Paul as it would in their native Abruzzi. The Italians, with a flourish of grace that is characteristic of them, add final "i's" to our names and find new and enchanting rhythms to vary the less liquid emphases of our speech. They came as laborers and have stayed on to feed us in hotels, restaurants, and tiny (legal) survivors of speakeasies. . . . And the Poles, who, because they were used to operating vast estates in the old country, found the big farms of the region to their liking. In many a room filled with banners, eloquence, and the hint of an imminent flood of tears the Poles have sighed and sung of freedom denied, freedom won, and freedom lost again. . . . And the Dutch, who have found the pastoral lands congenial to their needs. They have enriched the abundance of the region by their savory cheeses. . . . And the Mexicans, wearing a mellow look of patience that turns even their poverty into wistful charm. They were first shipped in by the carload from Texas to work in the sugar-beet industries. But they have not become well adjusted to the exacting climate, so they have tucked themselves away unobtrusively, keeping their discomfort tactfully out of sight.

Thirty racial groups have come to the region, all told—Austrians, Hungarians, Russians, Armenians, Roumanians, Ukrainians, Serbs, Croats, Greeks, even a few Chinese. In St. Paul a Festival of Nations is presented every season or two, and here all the elements in this pageant of people are gathered together for evenings of eating and singing and wondering at the multiplicity of skills and crafts. Bright in the embroideries of their native costumes, confident in the attraction of their foods, their dances, and their songs, men and women of many backgrounds move through a drama of mutual esteem that symbolizes the purpose and the hope of democracy.

The effort to provide in America a place where the huddled masses of the world may find room in which to give themselves a new opportunity has not been uninterruptedly benevolent. The men and women who arrived on the first wave of invasion sometimes have shaken the brine from their clothes and straightened themselves into attitudes of hauteur to receive the men and women riding the second wave. People of Anglo-Saxon stock have tended to glance discouragingly in the direction of people with strange European terminations to their names.

But in our corner of the world it has been less true than elsewhere. When the University of Wisconsin football team visits Minnesota for the annual "homecoming game" by which both rivals set such store, the young Americans in the Wisconsin line-up are likely to have such names as David Schreiner, Robert Hanslik, Lloyd Wasserbach, Leonard Calligaro, and Paul Hirsbrunner. Indeed, on a recent occasion those were their exact names. The boys on the Minnesota side in the same year included Roy Lilja, Vic Kublitski, Charles Dellago, Dick Luckemeyer, Joe Slovich, and Rudy Sikich—Americans all. No one thought the list in the least odd, or brooded about the absence of Joneses, Robertsons, Browns, Cartwrights, or Winthrops.

It cannot be claimed that the region has successfully assimilated all of its foreign-born peoples. There are among us Americans who have never learned to speak the English language. A Syrian woman may live through a half-century of uninterrupted silence because she and her Italian neighbor next door on the river flats have no tongue in common. In many a home there is tucked away in a corner of the kitchen a German grandmother who is cut off from human communication of any kind because the last member of the family who spoke her only language has died.

But our region at least has few prejudices, and it holds lightly any that it may happen to inherit. We have still to recover the beautiful and total absence of self-consciousness that abided in Pierre Bonga. He was a Negro, perhaps the first to come into the wilderness. Bonga was brought as a slave, but presently his master freed him. He married a Chippewa woman, became a prosperous trader and an honored citizen. In that period there existed just two kinds of people in the world, white men and Indians. If you were not an Indian, there was only one category in which you could place yourself. Yet it must have electrified those who were uninitiated into the customs of the country to hear Pierre Bonga, his black face shining with pride, announce: "Yes, sir, I was one of the first white men in this part of the country."

In our region we aspire toward the ideal of unity that Pierre Bonga so dramatically expressed.

4

FROM PRIMITIVISM TO
PRIMITIVISM

♆

BELIEVERS IN THE DOCTRINE of the perfectibility of man seem sometimes to suggest that, on the economic level, the steady and determined movement of the submerged classes should be toward the home with a three-car garage, one having a fine multiplicity of plumbing fixtures, radios, washing machines, and electrical gadgets.

Such theorists might be mildly aggrieved if they were asked to notice certain evidences of a lack of perfect docility on the part of people in Wisconsin and Minnesota. In many little pockets of these states there exist groups of people who stubbornly and contentedly refuse to evolve at all, preferring to conduct their lives in the old traditional ways quite without benefit of modern technology.

In our region we do not seem to move as one man onward and upward and into an ever more complicated and delicately organized pattern of existence. A few have reached the dizziest heights of magnificence in houses with self-operating elevators and walls hung with the more depressingly chic manifestations of the art of Rouault and Modigliani. But as the pageant of progress has moved forward, some have stayed behind, continuing to represent the previous phase of development. Behind the capitalist stands the enterprising small business man; behind him, the defender of the frontier; next in line, the trapper and trader; and at the end, the very nearly primitive man. Souvenirs of every way of life that we have ever had are left in this region. The variety of its contrasts

POST OFFICE, GENERAL STORE AND BAR AT PENASSE, MINNESOTA

Northernmost town in the United States

THE MISSISSIPPI RIVER AT LYNXVILLE, WISCONSIN

presents a kind of helter-skelter survey of the whole development
of social life in the United States.

The Indian is the most resolute of the opponents of change. A
thoroughgoing conservative, he likes things very much as they
were up to the middle of the seventeenth century and he sees no
reason for doing them differently. Today many of the Sioux and
Chippewa live on reservations, but not all. Some gather together
in settlements in the northern part of the region, and others put
up their shacks in isolated wilderness country. Yet wherever they
establish themselves they lead their traditional way of life, largely
untouched by three centuries of busy improvement, still enigmatic to the white newcomer, still indifferent to his affairs. Artists
are attracted to the alien and austere beauty of their best types and
want to paint them; the Indians submit indulgently, but with only
a transient display of vanity. Hunters who employ them as
guides often wish to make friends. But the bridges thrown across
psychological distances by the eager white men are seldom crossed
by the Indians, who appear to feel small curiosity about what is on
the other side.

A story is told of a young Indian boy whose dignity and whole-
someness delighted a vacation visitor to the north country. The
white man, being childless, but having an abstract taste for pater-
nity, decided in a night of inspiration to make the great gesture and
adopt the boy. Agleam with benignity, he announced to the
young guide next day: "I'm going to take you back with me to
Chicago. You're to be my son."

The Indian considered the suggestion coolly. What would he
do in Chicago, he wanted to know. Well, he would go to school
until he was old enough to enter the business. And after that what?
Well, he would work his way up through the various departments
of the factory. He would be a foreman, then a department head,
then general manager. The boy was beginning to look puzzled,
and the man who wished to be a foster-father felt his whole
scheme of life to be under critical examination. He wanted deeply
to justify it. "Finally," he went on in a great burst of generosity,
"when I die, you will inherit all that I have, my business, my
house, everything." The boy still looked aloof and unpersuaded.
"And then what?" he asked once more. "Why, then you'll be a

rich man. You can do what you like, you can retire and come up here and spend all your time fishing." The boy's eyes widened in complete despair at being asked to follow such whimsical nonsense. "But I can do that now," he said.

The white man's long way round to peace and contentment has no attraction for the Indian. Why leave home in search of serenity if one has it to begin with? Many an Indian woman has been persuaded to travel with white people who have come to care for her. One day, without warning, she ends the round of journeys to California, to Florida, to New York, to the Riviera, and retires to her tar-paper shack. Presently her daughter tries the outside world with the same generous and affectionate family. And eventually she, too, goes back.

On the reservations of Wisconsin and Minnesota the Indians seem to a casual observer to lead lives of insupportable dullness interrupted by occasional melodramas springing out of illegal indulgence in alcohol. But now as in the past their personal emotions are sealed away from us by the very dignity with which they choose to keep their private lives private. As James F. Williard and Colin B. Goodykoonz long ago observed of the white man's patronage: ". . . how could he realize that the Indian at home was a gossipy, talkative person fond of practical jokes, smart repartee, feasting and story-telling?"

We are still inclined glibly to dismiss the Indian as an intolerably untidy creature. But the more sympathetic Samuel Pond, writing in 1834 about the Dakotas and Sioux, reminded us that cleanliness is a matter of opportunity as much as of desire. ". . . In reading vivid accounts of the filthy and disgusting appearance of Indians," he observed, "I can hardly help wishing that the writers were compelled to take a nearer view of them and live with them as they do, through just one winter campaign. I should like to see which would come out the cleaner in the spring, the white man or the Indian."

Today there are Indians in the wilderness region who live with a decency and decorum that the French would call "correct," and there are also those who live in shacks with dirt floors and no windows in the midst of a distressing welter of mangy dogs and snuff-chewing children. In essential taste for cleanliness there is as wide a range in the Indian world as there is in the white.

Still, it is certain that they remain, and choose to remain, outside our culture, adopting only its less alluring ways. Sometimes the Indians put on full regalia to participate in the celebration of a great historical occasion, like the opening of the reconstructed fortress at Grand Portage. They look very noble indeed through the forenoon, but as the day grows warmer, the heavy costume becomes intolerable. The brave rubs impatiently at his perspiring forehead and, dislodging his headdress, dislodges also his fine black wig. Under it one sees that he has a crew haircut. Disillusioned but still curious, one studies the costume more closely and notices that it is completed by shoes of special modern construction intended to correct fallen arches.

For these dismal contributions to the culture of the Chippewa the white man is now sufficiently humble to recognize that he is responsible. He begins to appreciate native Indian arts, not patronizingly, but with full recognition of the fact that they are part of the heritage he must make his own if he is to close the hiatus between himself and the medieval past and to establish the continuity of American art.

Left quite to himself, the Indian preserves with a striking degree of efficiency and charm his traditional way of life. The father who makes a *tickanoggin* for his child and the mother who straps this early version of the rumble seat to her back collaborate upon a pictorially delightful dramatization of the sober responsibilities of parenthood.

The *tickanoggin* is made of a straight-grained cedar board hewn out to fit the conformation of the child. A thin strip of cedar, steamed and bent and put in place around the sides and at the foot, holds the baby in place. The accessories include deer-hide cushioning for the mobile bed and an elaborate lacing of deer-hide thongs to make the harness with which the mother secures the *tickanoggin* to her person.

And there is a family unit ready to face the daily emergencies of living! The wise and conscientious Indian mother of the twentieth century, like all her predecessors back through the ages, has had the forethought to fasten to each side of the cradle three small colored wheels made of twisted and dyed grass. These are to ward off the evil spirits of the air, a precaution the necessity of which all primitive mothers in all countries have understood. Watching such a madonna and child in the year of grace 1945, one seems to see the centuries melt away and all differences among peoples dissipated in the great unifying warmth of the idea of devotion.

Those forerunners of the westward movement, the *voyageurs* and *coureurs de bois*, have their counterparts among men who still live by hunting and trapping on the fringe of the wilderness. An amazing mixture of racial strains has been poured into the bloodstream of this modern *voyageur*—Indian, French, Scotch, Swedish, Finnish. But he emerges from the melting-pot very much the same sort of person that he was in the seventeenth century. He doesn't know any French today and his accent, like himself, is a blend of many influences. He doesn't go in for community singing in the way that the *voyageurs* so persistently did, offering a kind of preview to Hollywood's notion of history, which requires that it be set to music. Yet he is a picturesque fellow, very much in the way that his predecessor was picturesque. He has an innocent flair for costume. His shirt is bright, his fur cap jaunty. His hunting knife is an elaborate affair with a wicked curved blade thrust into an intricately ornamented deerskin sheath. And he lives exactly as his predecessor did. He matches his wits against the cunning of animals and is forever fascinated by the ways of these creatures, which are more his brothers than his enemies. He must hunt them, of course, but he likes them for their stoicism and resolution and feels a kind of fraternal pride in their fighting spirit.

This latter-day *coureur de bois* has an inexhaustible stock of stories of the woods which he likes to tell when he is comfortably settled, of an evening among his kind. His favorite yarn may be about the duel that he once saw between an otter and a beaver. He tells it with all the fervent building to a climax of a sports reporter describing the encounter of two spunky bantamweights.

The trapper came upon his beaver and otter fighting in the lake. The fresh competitiveness of spring was in them and they churned fiercely, registering the turmoil of their struggle on the surface of the water as they rose and sank and rose again. Finally they went down and were gone from sight for a much longer moment. Then the beaver floated up dead and after him the weakly swimming otter. But the surviving fighter had gone only seventy-five feet from the scene of the battle when mortality overtook him too. The trapper went out to retrieve the bodies, but the hides were useless. Both were full of tiny holes where the implacable fighters had nipped each other to death.

In the post-mortems of a day's hunting such a man likes to recall how once he sat silent on a lake shore near his cabin and watched otter diving for dinner, coming up to eat the catch and dive again in complete obliviousness of the onlooker. Then suddenly sensing the presence of a foreign thing, the leader, still frugally eating his fish, sniffed cautiously at the air, gave a special signal, and led his charges away.

He likes to tell about looking squarely into the faces of inquisitive old bucks whom he has attracted by snorting in a plausible imitation of the deer's own language; about tracking a bear that had picked up the trap in which he was caught and walked for miles still stubbornly trying to free himself; about the lore of beaver-trapping and how a man who knows his business will never take more than one beaver from a beaver house in a single season. After all, he means to live in this country and wants to keep its stock of animals high.

Occasionally he becomes discouraged, what with so many people crowding in on him that he sometimes catches distant glimpses of two or three of his neighbors all in one week. But his spirit is fundamentally as fraternal with other men as it is with bears and beavers. He has a trapping shack deep in the woods and anyone is welcome to use it, in case of need. As he tells his neighbors, he usually leaves "a little chuck" in a shallow pit under the trapdoor. A fellow hunter is welcome to avail himself of its communal advantages. He may take a can of beans, heat it over the air-tight stove, and then go to sleep on the pole bed spread with balsam boughs. He may use the fox stretchers and the mink stretchers too, if he has need of them.

After the *coureurs de bois* came the loggers. They have left not merely their kind but some actual survivors of the work. The loggers seldom found time to marry or the opportunity to establish anything even resembling a solid domestic relationship. In their seventies, and even eighties, they have gone back into the woods to live alone, eventually to die alone. They are usually of Norwegian ancestry, and therefore of a passionate, an almost ferocious cleanliness. There in the wilderness they live an endless idyll.

Like benevolent gods of the wood, these old men devote themselves to the care of their wild-life neighbors. Such an old logger will build a bird shelf outside his window and daily spread the table with suet. He himself presides at the feast, driving off the greedy birds and wooing the more reticent. The nuthatches and the chickadees are his special care, but he takes delight in the healthy appetite of the woodpeckers, too. Only the whisky-jacks (Canadian jays) really annoy him with their assertive impudence. In a season when natural foods are scarce, he nags the game wardens for hay with which to feed the deer, and if the hay fails to arrive he goes out and cuts cedar for them. He has his pets among the deer, identified for him by special physical characteristics, and they come back season after season.

After the loggers came the settlers. Their rush for land began in the middle decades of the last century, but it was still continuing in the first decades of the twentieth. When the lumber industry moved west, leaving its ghost towns behind, resolute men moved in to cut through the ruin of brush and stumps to find the soil and make it serve them. They stood in the midst of a scene that could not have charmed the eye. This was a used, a worked-out, a deserted world which it was their formidable task to reclaim. They had to blast out the old stumps with dynamite or drag out their stubborn roots with the crude mechanism of the stump puller, at which a straining horse and a cursing driver worked in angry collaboration. They had to cut the ragged young second growth of scrub and weed trees with scythe or brush hook. In the swamps near the land that they struggled many hours a day to clear stood the bare, blackened pillars of the tamarack, swept by forest fires. The settlers were neighbors to a ruin that was without dignity because the disaster of which it was a souvenir lacked the fascination of being a link with antiquity. The picture presented by the cut-over lands was like nothing nobler than an illustration of the bad news from yesterday's newspaper.

But the people who came to these lands persisted bravely in regarding them as havens of opportunity. Here at least was a land where there were fish in the streams and deer in the woods, where there was timber enough for fuel, for the rebuilding of the deserted logger's cabin, and for the fencing of the land. Straining with stumps and stones, living under the shadow of ruined trees, these newcomers counted themselves fortunate because they lived on a soil that turned fertile under the prompting of rain and the urging of their plows. They were the last survivors of the tradition of the pioneers, and in 1920 they were still moving into frontier country to hew for themselves a livable and prosperous life out of conditions that would have seemed utterly cheerless to any but men with a strain of indomitability strong in them. Gradually they pushed back the desolation left by the loggers. Large stretches of this land took on a prosperous look. A serene and smiling agricultural country grew up in the place where bleakness had stood before.

The swift-paced story of Wisconsin and Minnesota, which left in its dramatic flight unassimilated savages, trappers, hunters, and pioneers, produced also its own curious type of rebel against all the rules of every society. He was not a savage, or a trapper, or a pioneer settler. He defiantly refused to have himself forced into any category. His way of life partook a little of the nature of all of them. He was, and is, the irrepressible "jack-pine savage."

He gives a great deal of trouble and inconvenience to the orderly. When the government finds him living on submarginal land and tries to transplant him to a better place, he stubbornly refuses to go. When the depression overtakes him and narrows down still farther his little margin of security, he develops a guile that is trying in the extreme. The government supplies him with chickens and stock, which, being too lazy to feed and tend, he promptly kills and eats, making high carnival while the supplies last. When retribution threatens him and his mischief is about to be exposed to the relief investigator, he does not let his heart be troubled for long. He merely pulls himself together for one little show of energy and goes to the produce station, where he supplies himself with the carcasses of dead calves, cattle, and chickens that have died on the manager's hands. These become the properties of an affecting drama of misfortune. They are lined up in the appropriate places in barn and farmyard. When the relief investigator appears, the "jack-pine savage" assumes the role of Job. Tastefully perched on his dunghill, he describes how nature has betrayed and plagued him. Mischance has followed him through every enterprise of his life, dedicated to unremitting toil, and here in this stricken barnyard is the evidence of how his hopeful plans have been "hurled into emptiness." The relief investigator, his willingness to put off disbelief prodded on by a distaste for the smells of so many decaying animals, swallows the story whole and hurries to his office to make a sympathetic report. Presently more chickens and more cattle for more orgies are on their way.

The jack-pine savage is the inveterate and incurable non-giver-of-a-damn. He likes to hunt and fish, but only as pastimes. He likes sometimes to disappear from the village scene and live among the Indians. But their monotonous and reserved kind of life does not satisfy him permanently. What he wants chiefly to do is to prowl from adventure to adventure, making sure that he misses no aspect of the jauntier side of human life. He has no social sense; he is oppressed and prodded by no weight of personal dignity or individual responsibility. He is civilization's likable problem child, and his only importance lies in the fact that he contains within himself elements of all the ways of life that go to make up the varied pattern of primitive existence.

In the pageant of the building of this region there came after the pioneer settler the great anonymous mass of cautious workers who always follow the opening of a new country. Their descendants make up the great middle class of the region, the small business man and clerks and white-collar workers and members of the useful and decorative professions. The way of life of these patient imitators of each other has been described in so many novels that its neat, unsurprising pattern need not be described again. The middle-class design for living looks much the same wherever it shows itself. Suburbia speaks with a different accent in Memphis, Tennessee, from that used in St. Paul, Minnesota, but the sentiments expressed do not vary greatly. The voice of the essential suburbanite speaks about the handball courts at the club, and the price of whisky, and who is to be browbeaten into becoming president of the Parent-Teacher Association, and who has reported how many times to the blood bank, and how strong is the general disagreement with what the last speaker at the Foreign Policy meeting has to say about the flow of munitions to China, and whether or not Yehudi Menuhin should be boycotted for playing a Béla Bartók concerto, and the comparative merits of pheasant-shooting here and there, and whatever became of Greta Garbo, and how to grow ox-heart tomatoes, and the black-market sale of gasoline stamps, and how to discipline an adolescent son who towers four inches over one's head and shows a cheerful disposition to push the teeth down the throat of anyone who challenges his exclusive right to the possession of the family car.

Above the wide plateau on which the middle class comfortably stretches itself, there hang in the social life of Wisconsin and Minnesota certain great promontories to which the special few climb. They signalize their rise above the need of ordinary things by buying extraordinary ones. They may pay a fabulous price for the tiny Latin grammar for which Emily Brontë paid almost nothing at all or for the Poe manuscript that brought its author the price of a drink. They may hold their Utrillo paintings for a rise, or enter into a passionate and deeply sincere love affair with the Ming period of Chinese art. Since they live in a dairy country they are sometimes inspired to collect cattle instead of Oriental vases, and they establish model farms stocked with animals of fabulously long and impressive pedigree.

But this pattern is also familiar and departs hardly at all from that of other sheltered corners of America where what the late Stuart Pratt Sherman was once inspired to call "the soft-footed elegances" minister to comfort.

It is the great contrast between the least and the most elaborate ways of life that is interesting in the social design of the region and also the manner in which these strata lie conveniently exposed to view as though in a tremendous cliff, with primitivism lying solidly at the base and privilege crowning the crest.

There is, however, another interesting feature of the life, and it is one which would most greatly startle those who believe that the evolution of society is and should be toward a steadily more complicated way of living. In our region there is a thin but persistent trickle of citizens from all the various groups of its social life back into the wilderness, not for a mere vacation, not for an extended period of refreshment and healing, but for the remainder of their lives. Intellectuals, artists, and even those most rigidly conservative of human beings, the members of the respectable middle class find themselves surfeited with complications and sweep them all out in one gesture of renunciation, to return to the wilderness. A policewoman from St. Paul, exhausted by problems of juvenile delinquency, retreats as far as possible from the city streets and becomes the best hunter in her neighborhood. The son of a university president comes into possession of a northern resort and finds it the place where he has always longed to be. He takes his bride into this country as well, and within a year she has agreed to forget all about living at the mercy of gadgets. She has solved for herself the simple, fundamental problems of existence and does not hesitate to drive alone through a Minnesota blizzard behind a team of Malemute dogs in order to supply her household with food. A picture of how two young intellectuals have most comfortably returned to the wilderness may be found in the charming, dramatic, and utterly unstudied small book that William and Justine Kerfoot have written called *Moccasin Telegraph*.

The charge has been flung at the whole of American society that it has proceeded from primitivism to decadence without pausing to develop a culture in between. The sting of that epigram should not be neglected, for there is a truth in it that needs to be weighed. The swiftness of our development has tended to crowd the beginnings and to bring on a premature senility in the middle years.

But one of the many possible ways of looking at our history suggests an even more startling progress. It moves from primitivism back to primitivism, and in between there is a flash of very nearly everything of interest that has ever happened in human society.

5

THE FARMER IS A SCIENTIST

THERE ONCE WAS firmly entrenched in the native tradition of letters a belief that any novel of the soil, if it wished to be honest, must have a grim and frightening tone. The pattern, fixed and unalterable, reached a climax in the scene which toppled the desperately struggling family from the modest little plateau of hope to which its members had resolutely climbed, into a new chasm of despair. The crop had looked fair and full of promise. But just before it could be harvested, thereby ensuring a trousseau for the daughter, a liberal education for the son, as well as an assortment of major operations and new cream separators for mother, some great natural catastrophe would sweep the whole bright prospect away in one malign stroke. Drought or dust storm, plague of grasshoppers or blizzard—the approach of one of these disasters could be foretold readily by any practiced reader.

It was the appallingly monotonous predictability of the tradition that made most readers turn away from the novel of the soil. What remained in any urban mind as a result of the deposits of gloom left by these solemn studies was a sort of dam against the natural sympathies. Readers learned to dislike the land; they wanted nothing to do with the land, even vicariously; they were grimly of the opinion that people who were obliged to work the land anywhere were the damned, assigned to a long period of expiation of sins done, as the ghost of Hamlet's father puts it, in the "days of nature."

It is true that the history of our region shows a full record of natural catastrophes such as might well frighten those who are determined to escape all harsh experience. There have been blizzards so spectacular and disastrous that farm women, going dutifully to see to the stock in the barn, have become lost, smothered in a blanket of flakes, and frozen to death three feet from their own kitchen doors. There have been locust plagues of epical proportions. One woman pioneer has recorded how on a bright day she picked fresh tomatoes, peas, and onions from her garden, priding herself on their luscious fullness and solidity; then, rising from the noonday meal at which these goods of the earth had been eaten, she went with her husband to see what had suddenly darkened the sky. Under the strange noonday darkness she found her garden and all the fields beyond destroyed by grasshoppers down to the last green shoot. A telling item of the account described the pest as dining with a fervor that made the communal exercises of the swarm sound like a prairie fire.

Yet the fact that these isolated incidents are still recalled whenever a writer wishes to be at once intensely historical and immensely vivacious indicates in itself that this has been the exception and not the rule.

There have been great hardships in our region, not merely as a result of the violent whimsicality of nature but also because of the mistakes that man himself has made. Chief of these was the yielding to temptation that resulted in a tragic abuse of the soil. Wheat was the gold into which the early settler, playing the role of Midas, greedily attempted to turn all the natural richness of earth.

Agricultural history in the region really begins with the period of the Civil War. Before that time the soil was not so much cultivated as merely scratched to produce a bare living for the reckless ones who had come to live on the edge of the wilderness. But in the 1860's and 1870's the rolling prairie country began to gleam with grain. The Homestead Law of 1862 gave free land to settlers. The Chippewa Indians ceded the Red River Valley to the white man. Railroads were raying out over the land. The mills were eager for spring wheat. They could not get too much.

Wisconsin and Minnesota felt a special desire to feed the army that had gone out to fight the Civil War, for the two states had sent many of their own men. There was no isolationist sentiment in those days and many a farmer, before "the irrepressible conflict" came to a climax, had participated fervently and romantically in the activities of the Underground Railroad. The old river highways of the fur-traders had served as routes along which to help slaves escape into Canada.

With a tremendous impetus toward the production of big crops and with fewer workers to produce them, farmers eagerly accepted technological improvements which manufacturers of machinery began, at that psychological moment, to offer. In their new reapers and threshers they rode the land, feeling as never before like the monarchs of all they surveyed. Wheat, ever more and more of it, poured out of the earth. Statistics of the period show how it rolled up into a great golden tide, inundating the region and leaving only a third of its whole area for all other crops combined.

Thus, in the orderly and regimented way that sometimes seizes upon men's imaginations, the whole country went mad and devoted itself to the working out of a completely mistaken program. There was something highly dramatic about this colossal error. The spectacle of wheat-growing on this heroic scale, could it have been viewed with Olympian detachment, would have been superb. Even the glimpse that the merely normal eye sometimes got of it must have been tremendously dramatic. In the particularly fertile areas, there were bonanza farms of several thousand acres, and at plowing time as many as forty machines would move in a line across the fields. This anticipation of the mechanized army proved in the end, however, to be engaged upon a disastrous blitzkrieg against the soil. Repeated assaults upon its powers of recuperation finally exhausted it and revealed the mistake of concentrating upon a single crop.

"Earth never tires," Walt Whitman once sang. But this hopeful declaration of faith was made by a poet who did not have to subject his fundamentally sound intuitions to proof in every detail. As farmers found that the earth had tired of the monotonous routine of giving, over and over again, of the same resources and receiving no nourishment in return, their first impulse was to desert it. Some of them, inspired by the bitterness of ignorance, did act as though their legitimate hopes had been outrageously and whimsically betrayed. There was a movement across the land that directly paralleled that of the loggers. Irresponsible men forever show the same behavior pattern: take, exploit, exhaust, desert. The bonanza farmers swept westward from Wisconsin into Minnesota and then on into the Dakotas. They repeated their drama of recklessness on each new frontier until the last one had been passed.

But in the composition of human society there are always creative intelligences to take up the story where the destructive ones have broken off in exasperation. There are the patient doers who like to have a thread of continuity to their lives and who cannot forever be beginning again. These groups stayed on to repair the damage that bonanza wheat-growing had done.

Their experiments with diversification had begun early in the region's history. One of the land's intelligent collaborators had experimented with the cultivation of alfalfa until he had developed a type hardy enough to survive the severity of the winters in Wisconsin and Minnesota. Another introduced apples, so that the orchards of the region began to have great commercial importance. Presently a great many crops were being raised in rotation— oats, barley, rye, corn, potatoes. Each took and gave back to the soil, so that its resources were at last restored. Today no one crossing Wisconsin and Minnesota can miss the richness of its look. The black wealth of the earth, exposed in a newly turned furrow of a field near Spring Green, Wisconsin, or in the St. Croix Valley of Minnesota, must be evident to the least-experienced eye.

There was another change that gradually came about in the development of agriculture. Large sections of Wisconsin and Minnesota have been given over to dairy farming and they vie with one another in contests to determine which reaches the more impressive figure in the production of milk and butter. Indeed, their citizens are butter-and-egg men to the entire nation.

This came about through no plan. The first cows introduced into the region were driven in by drovers simply as work or meat animals. Meat packing is, of course, still of the greatest importance to the successors of those drovers. The very name of South St.

Paul has become a sort of summation of all its rugged interest and drama. (A loyal citizen of the community who once moved away from it and then returned offered an explanation of her distaste for the place to which she had briefly retired. "The air," she said meditatively, sniffing the beneficent breeze on her doorstep, "didn't seem to have no body to it.") But the typical glimpse of Wisconsin and Minnesota today is that of a rolling field in which tawny cows stand or lie in superb indolence, like so many beautifully cared-for odalisques in a pastoral harem.

As an inevitable result of their importance in the production of dairy products, Wisconsin and Minnesota are also the great cheese merchants to the country. These states have attracted to themselves immigrants with the right sort of background to develop this industry. As early as 1844 an imaginative blacksmith named Fridolin Streiff had conceived it to be his duty to lead a colony of Swiss men, women, and children to America. They very soon set about the practice of their native arts, with the final result that Wisconsin today makes seventy-three per cent of all the cheese of the Swiss type that is consumed in the United States. The Dutch found backgrounds in Wisconsin which were sympathetic to the kind of work they liked to do, and presently they were producing very creditable replicas of the corpulent balls of cheese, with a jaunty red exterior, for which the province of Edam on the Zuider Zee previously had had exclusive production rights. The dark recesses of limestone caves along the rivers of Minnesota shelter very large quantities of a kind of cheese to which the unpretentious description "blue" has been given. It is, of course, very much like that decadent aristocrat among cheeses, Roquefort.

Curiously, this phase of the industrial development of Wisconsin is several years older than its statehood. In 1844 a citizen bearing the sturdy American name of John J. Smith made attempts to market cheese outside the state. The swift rise of this enterprise was aided greatly by the intelligent sympathy of Governor William D. Hoard of Wisconsin, who managed, by persistent and imaginative campaigning, to get favorable freight rates. The appearance of refrigerator cars still further advanced the ability of the region to serve the country as its chief dairy farmer. Today the sale of milk and milk products from Wisconsin and Minnesota is a very significant item in the budget of each, running impressively into hundreds of millions of dollars.

A curious American passion that never disappears for long from our community life is the quest for the typical. Despite our history of pugnacious nonconformity, Americans enjoy the game of trying to track down the common denominator of thought. One organization, which seems determined to wipe out the last little trace of spontaneity in intimate human relations, has gone so far as to develop the distressing idea of each year naming a sort of all-American mother. But it would be extremely difficult to identify the typical farmer of our region. There is still so much room for the display of initiative, so much encouragement of creative enterprise, that no one way of life in the agricultural scene can be said to contain every typical element. The picture offered by Robert Frost of the New England farmer may be composed with an intuitive awareness of all the values, all the interests, all the hopes and limitations of the great majority of his neighbors. None of our regional poets could sum up so neatly all the attributes of our farmers.

At his best, the Wisconsin or Minnesota farmer is a man who has applied the findings of an exact science to the problems of his daily life. Perhaps he is a graduate of the University of one state or the other, a staunch believer in abstract knowledge who has studied problems of the chemistry of the soil, who understands the effects of a properly balanced diet on cattle, who permits himself to benefit by all recent laboratory discoveries about the treatment of pests or the prevention of disease in poultry. He is a completely modern man living in the present-day world and he is not afraid to learn from theorists. He makes as much use of the books in an agricultural library as a lawyer makes of the reference works on his shelf.

Or if this leader in his field happens not to be a graduate of one of the great universities, he is at least touched with the academic spirit. He reads the pamphlets that are issued by Agricultural Experiment Stations and absorbs the meaning of laboratory studies. He urges his sons and daughters to profit by the instruction made

OPEN PIT MINE AT HIBBING, MINNESOTA

HIBBING, MINNESOTA, WAS MOVED SO THAT ITS SITE COULD BE MINED (1919)

THE LARGEST IRON-LOADING DOCKS IN THE WORLD, SUPERIOR, WISCONSIN

THE GHOST TOWN OF TROMMALD ON THE CUYUNA RANGE

available to them through Agricultural Extension services and he himself explores, in the bulletins issued by the United States Department of Agriculture, such general problems as that of increasing the yield of his land. He is hospitable to the ideas of his Farm Bureau and of his county agent. He subscribes to and reads one or another of the important farm journals, of which the region has produced some of the most important.

It is not difficult for the enlightened farmer to see that it pays to subject his problems to theoretical analysis. For he lives much better and enjoys far greater success than the patient, unimaginative plodder who works from sunup to sundown without benefit of planning. A modern farmer may build up from nothing at all a business as solid and impressive as any created by a captain of industry. His dairy farm gleams from the roadside with unmistakable signs of immaculate efficiency. His cow barns are commodious and seem always to have been just freshly painted. Inside, the boudoir of each one of his cattle is as tidy as though it were designed for a fastidious and exacting tenant who couldn't be expected to stay unless she were ungrudgingly given the best. This sleek, well-washed creature is milked by machinery, tended by minor scientists as spotless and as disinfected as interns in a hospital, timed in all of her activities, turned out into the most carefully chosen of pastures. The atmosphere of such a dairy farm is that of a laboratory, with nothing about it of the huddled, hurried, inadequate, improvised feeling that every reader must have derived from the melancholy novel of the soil.

Again, the modern agriculturist may have borrowed from the business man some of his ideas about mass production. In the Red River Valley today farms as large as three thousand acres are devoted to the growing of potatoes. But this is different from the old days of bonanza farming. Operators on so large a scale do not make unregulated and irresponsible demands upon the soil. Their planting is a campaign, the steps of which have been planned in strict accordance with the requirements of scientific study.

This Red River farmer, becoming more conscious of the role that he plays as a capitalist, puts by his surpluses to use in expanding his property. He may buy two farms, five, eight, a dozen.

These are operated on a tenant system, but the details of the relationship between employer and employee are vastly different from those which the literature of the South has made familiar. The tenant farmer of Wisconsin or Minnesota is not the exploited creature who has sat for his portrait in so many novels, a man whose face is blurred with fatigue and despair and undernourishment, a physically maltreated creature who must pretend to uncomplaining docility as he receives scrip instead of money for his services, and who must spend that scrip at his employer's store where he is systematically overcharged and cheated.

Our tenant farmer is never used as an inferior to be exploited deliberately; if he is fortunate he may be accepted almost as a partner. His employer, acquainted with the abstractions of economics and knowing his way through the columns of a market page in the newspaper, often senses an agricultural trend. There may be a rising demand for flax or for corn. Traveling about from one to another of his farms, the owner tells his tenants to hold their crops for the rising market. Not only does he profit, but the tenant profits too.

Such self-made capitalists live well. The day is long since past when the farmer could be recognized instantly by his uniform, by a shuffling, abstracted gait as though he carried everywhere with him, even into the scenes of his private life, an insupportably heavy burden. You will find the prosperous young farmer standing at the bar of a summer resort near his home, wearing a well-tailored, well-pressed suit that makes him look like a brother to the young factory manager from Akron, Ohio, to whom he is talking. Anywhere in Wisconsin you are quite likely to find a farmer knocking off for a few hours to do a little landscape painting, a hobby in which the dean of the Agricultural College has encouraged him. In Minnesota, on "Symphony night," you may find the farmer and his wife driving thirty, forty, or fifty miles from his home to Minneapolis in order to hear Casadesus play a Beethoven concerto.

Next in the farmers' hierarchy is the ordinary good worker. His kind makes up the great body of the agricultural troops. He is a solid, conscientious fellow who has taken to farming partly because in his youth he had no positive inclination toward anything else, but partly because he loves the land. His affection is expressed in a quietly possessive impulse that makes him add more and more to his holdings. He does not feel quite respectable unless he has a hundred and sixty acres.

This farmer is essentially conservative in his politics and in his tastes. Throughout the successive generations his attitude toward holders of public office has been consistently experimental, but always within strict limits defined by caution. In both Wisconsin and Minnesota the farmer has voted for the representatives of a long series of mildly insurgent reform movements. But he has never allowed himself to be edged or prodded into anything like actual rebellion. When a party of his own creation threatens to get too much power or to establish itself too permanently in control, the farmer votes that party quietly out of office and waits for a new cause of irritation to lead him into another movement of equally discreet insurgency.

He goes to the Lutheran church, but is not fanatically religious. He drinks a few glasses of beer in town on Saturday night, but seldom too many. He has no more children than are to be found in the average American family of this period. Indeed, he is more conservative and cautious than his city brother, who occasionally takes it into his head that it is chic to have eight or nine children. The farmer of the moment seldom has more than three or four. His daughters train themselves as nurses or teachers and then marry, usually before the training has been completed. The father of boys has a mild, inarticulate desire to see the tradition of which he is a part continued by his family, but he makes no authoritarian effort to keep his sons on the land. If they wish to train themselves in radio or for professions, even if they wish merely to drift away to the city, he makes no vehement objection. He is as mild, half-hearted, half-intimidated a disciplinarian as is his city brother. But the system works out not badly. One of the farm boys usually marries early and is glad to have the prospect of inheriting the place.

It is no show institution on which this ordinary farmer lives, but his place is scrupulously clean. The barn is painted regularly; the machinery is kept under cover. The house is small and the family chooses to make it smaller still by living for the most part in the kitchen. The radio is there and so is a comfortable chair for the paterfamilias. (He has to fight for it, occasionally, but it can be recovered from the invader after a short stand.) The plumbing is very often, but not always, modern.

This farmer is not a scientist to quite the extent of his more prosperous brother. He must depend a great deal more upon himself, and it is easy to fall into the ways of improvisation. But he is influenced in all of his thinking by the idea that his prospects can be improved by study. The agencies of University Extension service and the Farm Bureau tend to tug him to an ever higher and higher level of effort.

Every farming community of the region includes in its cast of characters the man who seems forever to hang on the edge of disaster. Sickness, inefficiency, bad luck, a weight of debt, perhaps a combination of all of them, seem to defeat his conscientious efforts. His house needs painting, his barns sag, his farmyard is a pool of mire, his cattle look undernourished. Nature seems pitilessly to add further plagues. Erosion produces great crevasses in his fields and may even leave his house perched precariously on the edge of a cliff over a river.

He is patient under these trials, and with a kind of gentle dispiritedness tries to keep pace with the multiplicity of his tasks. But the evidence of his failure multiplies. His tractor stands out in all weather. The door of the outside privy falls from its hinges and is not replaced. The farmer sells a little of his land in an effort to put his affairs in order and to begin again. But it is his inevitable fate to lose his farm and become a tenant.

As a tenant he belongs to the one third who occupy farms in the region. His fate may be no better than it was before and he may stagger on in the same unhappy, bewitched state of helplessness to deal with his daily plight. But, again, it is possible that the benevolent influence of an employer with a talent for guidance may put him on a better path.

Glittering at the other end of this order of beings, but a little outside its interest in a catalogue of workers, is the gentleman farmer. He makes a superb game of living in an agricultural country, paying generously to have well-trained farm experts keep his toys in operation. His show place has exactly the sort of interest that is always attached to a superb, ornate, glittering imitation of the real thing.

In Wisconsin and Minnesota, the farmer has learned to recognize himself as a scientist. More and more he disciplines his mind and his program to the idea that the field is his laboratory.

A SAGA OF BREAD

IN THE YEAR 1680 Father Louis Hennepin, traveling in the northern part of the vast region known to the civilized world of his time as Louisiana, came upon a river that he called the Colbert and upon a waterfall in it to which he gave the name the Falls of St. Anthony of Padua, "in gratitude for favors God did me through the intercession of that great saint."

The name of the river has been changed to the Mississippi, but the Falls of St. Anthony is still known as Father Hennepin devoutly wished it to be known when he conducted a kind of baptismal service in the mist of its own swirling waters.

On that day Father Hennepin enacted the first incident of a saga that was to link two worlds closer and closer with each passing century. It is the saga of bread, or more accurately of flour. On the site of the Falls Father Hennepin stood dreaming of a great new empire that was to be dominated economically by La Salle and spiritually by the brothers of the Recollect Order. There was nothing naïve, impractical, or humble about Father Hennepin. He dreamed with a kind of restive fervor, his eyes rolling one moment toward heaven and the next, with shameless greed, toward earthly fame. Yet even he could not have foreseen the extent to which his Falls of St. Anthony of Padua would influence a broad, teeming, turbulent world. There was to be a great empire created just below those Falls, one which would help to nourish all the surrounding country as it grew out of its infancy into a hearty, hungry, demanding adolescence; which would later begin to feed the world; and which would finally assume the task of fighting starvation among the men, women, and children involved in two disastrous global wars.

From the moment that it first appeared on the maps of the known world, the Falls of St. Anthony was destined to play an international role. It began, appropriately, when a Belgian priest, exploring in the interest of Frenchmen living in Canada, named it for an Italian saint. Nowadays when Lend-Lease shipments of flour go out from the mills, destined for Russia, China, and Australia, the dramatic part that Father Hennepin hoped to see his waterfall play has been made rich beyond his most expansive dream. Indeed, if the drama were not now so grim, it might be said to be a success story written in the florid, self-congratulatory style of Father Hennepin himself.

One of the first scenes of his wanderings back and forth near the Falls had the note of anticipatory excitement that one likes to find in the great pageants of history. Father Hennepin reported that "While portaging our canoe at the Falls of St. Anthony of Padua, we caught sight of five or six of our Indians who had set out before us. One of them had climbed an oak across from the large waterfall and was weeping bitterly. He had a beaver robe dressed neatly, whitened inside, and decorated with porcupine quills and was offering it in sacrifice to this cataract, which is terrifying and admirable. I heard what he was saying while weeping bitterly: 'You, who are a great spirit, grant that our tribe pass by here tranquilly without mishap. Grant that we may kill many buffaloes, destroy our enemies and bring her captives, some of whom we will sacrifice to you. . . . The Foxes have killed our relatives. Grant that we may win revenge.' "

These pious, if slightly grim, petitions Father Hennepin says were on this occasion all granted. The Indians had a successful hunt, a triumphant revenge, and a very gratifying and entertaining scene of human sacrifice. The buffalo robe he adds, with fine European practicality, "was afterward useful to a Frenchman who took it on our return."

Father Hennepin, it should be pointed out, was never fanatically dedicated to the truth. He would have been quite capable of inventing such a useful little scene. But if the saga of the Falls did not begin in precisely that way, it should have, so neatly does it launch a story of struggle, rivalry, and sacrifice.

Today on the two sides of the river below the Falls rise the towers of the mills. They give the city of Minneapolis its distinguished profile outlined against the water. The later development of the community has made it spread wide and far. But still the towers of the milling district give it the familiar look that anyone belonging to the region recognizes as especially its own.

The tall cylinders of the elevators make the mills look a little like a gigantic organ, with the towers as the ornamental pipes. Traveling from top to bottom of a modern mill, watching the successive processes by which the wheat berry is turned into flour, one manages to feel like an intruder in the inner workings of an organ. The polished and immaculate wooden tubes that vein the rooms are actually part of a conveyor system inside of which the wheat is carried from treatment to treatment. But the stubborn imagination still insists that they might be the working pipe-flues of an organ. The lively agitations of the machines in which the product is sifted in the course of its evolution into flour serve an obvious function. But that does not quite keep the vagrant mind from imagining that these are the bellows of the organ.

Another thing that makes the mill seem to be dedicated to some special kind of harmony and purity rather than to any merely commercial purpose is its absolute cleanliness. Implicit in the contract between the miller and the unseen buyer of his product is the promise that the food will be kept from any kind of contamination. That promise is respected in the neat compactness of the machines which make sure that, as the wheat berry goes under the rolls to be pulverized, it is never exposed to the air; in the conveyor system which makes it possible for the product to be passed from one phase of treatment to another without being handled; in the fact that the flour is packaged, sewed into its bag, stamped, and sealed without receiving so much as a contaminating glance from the gross human world.

It has not infrequently happened that sensitive souls watching the mass commercial handling of foodstuffs have turned pale with dismay and decided, at least momentarily, to retire out of the modern world and live like the characters in an idyll by Edith Wharton on a diet of "pulse and wild simples." Disturbed and angry novelists like Upton Sinclair have written books to expose the mischief and cynicism of such institutions. But no doubts would afflict the most finicking visitor to a modern mill. There is a balletlike elegance and formality to the whole procedure. The motif of daintiness is carried out in the white costumes and caps of the workers, in the endless sweeping of the floor. Even the freight handlers, for once disciplined into decorum, pile the big sacks into cars fastidiously lined with paper. Archibald MacLeish, in the choreographic story that he once did for a ballet called *Union Pacific*, made an effort to reduce railroading to a formal rhythm. The ribald found it faintly ridiculous, insisting that, when the bawdiness of the tradition was removed, nothing very believable was left. But the milling industry would lend itself much more plausibly to the same sort of treatment. It could even be set to the music of Debussy if it were not for the fact that the dynamos that absorb the water power out of the Falls and the machines that do the grinding of the wheat make an almost Wagnerian amount of noise.

Tradition has always insisted sentimentally that the miller is a creature apart. In the time of man's innocency, when he worked alone and on a very small scale, he appeared in song as "the jolly miller," living a life of idyllic seclusion with only a beautiful daughter to keep him company.

Milling, in the great centers, has departed rather far from that picture postcard dream of beauty, and yet it has not greatly altered its essential ways for a very long time. As one of its spokesmen lately observed with an undertone of mild surprise: "Just two significant developments in the mechanical technique of flour milling in twenty centuries and neither in our time!"

These two mechanical improvements, which alone make the modern miller able to smile indulgently at the innocence of the Egyptians, are the use of grinding rollers instead of millstones, and the development of what is called "the middlings purifier." These changes make up what the industry, just a trifle magnificently, calls "the milling revolution."

The milling process consists in eliminating the undesirable elements of the wheat kernel and reducing what is left to the familiar snowy product that comes out of the sack in the kitchen. What must go are, first, the oily wheat germ and, second, the coat of bran. There remains the inner part of the kernel, the starch and gluten proteins.

It has never been easy to perform this act of separation. With the hard, red, spring wheat of the region it was, to begin with, particularly difficult. The bran coat persisted in pulverizing and mixing with the flour. But the milling revolution at last solved the problem.

The purifier was evolved first. Its job is to discourage the undesirable elements of the cracked wheat by a combination of processes that involve sifting and suction. Air currents are blown through a series of moving sieves. These reverse the classical method of separating saints and sinners. For here the desirable elements are drawn down into the protection of heaven while the dark and gritty particles are rejected into a sort of aerial purgatory.

There was a twofold need for improvement in the system of grinding. The old millstone merely crushed the wheat, mixing germ and bran coat inextricably with the flour proper. What was needed was a roller that would crack the kernel, permitting the purifier then to do its work.

The ancient mill wheels were also dangerous. Sixty years ago a bitter tragedy in a Minneapolis mill made history from which a significant improvement in technique dates.

The day shift had just left the mill and a few stragglers were still inside, as were also some early arrivals among the night shift. Suddenly an explosion shook the walls, blew the roof spectacularly into a street blocks away, and all in a few moments reduced the building to rubble. "Horror on Horrors" read the almost jubilantly hysterical headlines of the next day's paper. "The Most Terrible Calamity Which Has Ever Befallen Minneapolis. . . . The Whole City Shaken and Stunned. . . . The Sickening Details So Far As Ascertained. . . . Excitement and Consternation at St. Paul. . . . Two Steamers Sent to the Scene of Disaster."

What had happened, experts believe, was that some foreign matter, perhaps a nail dropped carelessly into a sack of wheat, had come in contact with the close-set wheels. A spark had been caused which, flying into the dust-filled air, had set off the explosion. But this was only the first of a series of explosions, which, as though in the contagion of hysteria, followed one after another until the whole mill had been brought down in ruins.

The grim finality of this act of God (as such happenings are not very respectfully called in legal circles) persuaded millers that they must find some way of protecting themselves against the whimsical working of natural law. So the picturesque mill wheel went into the discard to become a decoration for the private grounds of collectors with a historical turn of fancy. In its place came, first, the porcelain grinding roller and, finally, the corrugated iron roller, which does its job efficiently and safely. In the milling industry of Minneapolis they learned to measure time from "the year of the explosion." They do so still, quite without self-consciousness, just as farm folk in the homeliest kind of literature used to date events from "the year the white calf died."

The history of the development of milling draws into itself all the history of the whole region. In the frontier world, where the visionaries saw no limits to the spirit of enterprise, the same men were concerned in dealings over land, lumber, railroads, river facilities. They bought up the wilderness, cleared it of trees, disciplined it into becoming agricultural country, grew wheat. At the same time they built railroads to haul the wheat, and developed waterways to supplement the service of the railroads.

And that is not all that such strenuous men undertook to do. They were the political and social leaders whose right to take the initiative rested, quite solidly, on their willingness to do so. They raised the armies that went to the Civil War, and went themselves. They represented their communities in Washington. They improvised techniques for the care and nourishment of infant universities. They occupied statehouses as governors.

There were two such men in the milling industry of Wisconsin and Minnesota, men with fine rolling names that have resounded through the whole story of the region—Cadwallader Colden Washburn and John Sargent Pillsbury. They established themselves, one on the west side of the river, the other on the east.

Major General Washburn, back from the Civil War, regarded the whole region as his territory. He lived in a fine house at La Crosse, which admiring contemporaries described as having a circular stairway covered with gilt, and window casements and doors of solid oak reaching from floor to ceiling. He had another house in Madison, where the lakes and the rolling country poetically summed up for him the charm of the region. From these places of retirement he went out to deal, very firmly, with the world. It is not necessary to do more than look at photographs of his impressive face, which seems to have been carved with great precision and strength out of the rocks of his native Maine, to know that he was quite capable of meeting any emergency.

It was Washburn's mill in which the explosion occurred. The first thing that he did upon hearing the news was to attend a meeting of the board of regents of the University of Wisconsin and talk calmly and at length about matters having nothing to do with his private affairs. Only when these considerations had been dealt with resolutely did he travel to Minneapolis and walk to the ruins of his mill. Standing in his shirt sleeves, he directed the work of finding the foundation and of preparing to rebuild.

Cadwallader Washburn was never primarily or exclusively a miller, and he never acquired what is represented by tradition as the mood of jollity. He was indeed an austere and reticent man who frightened his associates and filled them with an almost superstitious awe. Perhaps he brought out of his native state something of that severity of moral outlook which Kenneth Roberts has told us characterizes all men of Maine. It was, Mr. Roberts suggests with apparent seriousness, because they could not tolerate the rudeness, the grossness, the injustices of the other colonies that the original settlers of Maine retired to its undefiled atmosphere.

But it is well for our region that it had a man like General Washburn to help create its society. He was undistracted by family concerns because his wife had lost her mind and was held, a comfortable distance away in New England, under what one biographer has elegantly called "solicitous restraint." General Washburn appears to have had no hobby except that of finding more work to do. He represented Wisconsin in Congress, where he sat with two brothers representing other states. They made a dramatic and personable trio of noble Romans, sternly seeking out the line of duty with the clear-sightedness of conscript fathers who held their children's advantage above their own. More than once Cadwallader Washburn voted against the interest of his own large holdings in land, lumber, and water power. As Governor of Wisconsin he often expressed theoretical opinions of government that would profoundly shock contemporary defenders of the rights of business. Washburn believed, for example, that railroads should be the property of the Federal government, and that they should be operated as a public service for the benefit of all the people.

In those same years after the Civil War the other great name of the milling center on the Mississippi was being written large across the history of the region. John Sargent Pillsbury had come from New Hampshire in 1855 to share in the opportunities of the new country. He traded in hardware, became a member of the council of the village of St. Anthony (later to be absorbed into Minneapolis), survived the great personal disaster of a fire that wiped out his capital, and then began again with a still broader view of the future. He, too, began to deal in land and lumber, and finally, in association with a nephew, to engage in milling.

It was, indeed, his young relative, Charles A. Pillsbury, who actively operated the mill, while John Sargent's mind remained free for a dazzling display of creative energy. In 1875 he became Governor of Minnesota, to be re-elected in 1877 and 1879. During that time he dealt with a variety of hazards, physical, ethical, and intellectual, that threatened the well-being of his people. The parable quality of each of these incidents leaves the Governor who mastered the crises in the relation to his state of a minor prophet. There was first the great grasshopper plague, complete with incidents like that of the farmer who tried to be forehanded by spreading hay over his truck garden, only to find that the swarm of insects had eaten hay and all. The Governor, gentle and paternalistic in everything that he did, visited the victims, fed them, and started them upon their careers as farmers once more. All this he managed with the efficiency of a successful executive, yet with the casualness of a friendly, helpful neighbor.

There was, second, an ethical crisis when Minnesota wished to repudiate the bonds issued for railroad expansion, the whole process of which had been interrupted during the panic of the early 1850's. The Governor, who had met and survived his own personal crisis of affairs in the burning of his hardware business, applied the same exacting ethics to the public problem and sternly refused to let the state act like a reckless and angry young man ready to say: "Nothing is lost save honor." The obligations were respected.

The third crisis was that of the University of Minnesota, which in its early years led the kind of precarious existence that the frail, precocious, intellectual youngest child of a large family leads among hearty and headlong brothers. In a world where everyone's impulse is to get on in a great hurry, the interests of abstract science, of philosophy, of scholarship in general are apt to seem not very urgent. It is certain that the university would have been elbowed about with vast indifference in the thumping impetuosity of pioneer life if the Governor of those years had not made it his favorite child. John Sargent Pillsbury is called in Minnesota "the father of the university."

So there they were, the embattled Governors, Washburn of Wisconsin and Pillsbury of Minnesota, one on one side of the river, one on the other, symbolic figures of the creative energy that was raising up a way of life out of the soil of what had recently been wilderness. Both made themselves rich out of the land, the lumber, the natural power of the region; yet both were strongly paternalistic in their attitude toward the interests of the people. Pillsbury, out of his ability to identify himself with the plight of the average man, and Washburn, out of a very different quality, an aloof austerity, had evolved the same philosophy. Each was genuinely concerned with the task of creating in this new world just, honest, and equitable institutions. What the Governor of Wisconsin said in effect to the Governor of Minnesota was; "Out of so rich a world which we have helped to shape it is right that we should take something for ourselves; but the real wealth must remain with the people."

The tendency of the milling industry began very early in its history to be one of drawing together into combines. Besides the large mills on the banks of the Mississippi at Minneapolis, there were many others scattered throughout Wisconsin and Minnesota. They made marriages of convenience from time to time, and presently many of them were absorbed into one or the other of the great Minneapolis institutions.

Then the same process began to operate on the national and even the international scale. The Pillsbury mills joined a syndicate controlled in Great Britain, though men of the family name continue the management in Minneapolis. Strengthened by the new energies brought by the Crosby family, also out of Maine, the Washburn mill extended its paternal influence east, south, and west. Many mills were absorbed into its system, but no international combine could wear down its own independence of will. Bright and civilized young men were sent out all over the world to look for export markets, and they found them in plenty. In 1928 the Washburn-Crosby Company changed its name to General Mills in deference to the fact that incorporated with the mother properties were other important ones at Buffalo, Chicago, Kansas City, and many other cities. These communities also had their pride and did not wish to live under the shadow of a married name. Indeed, today more flour is produced for General Mills at Buffalo than at Minneapolis. But its home, its headquarters, its strategic base for industrial campaigns which are distinctly and glitteringly global is still at the Falls of St. Anthony.

The Minneapolis miller, busy today in the task of feeding the United Nations, looks toward the future in eager anticipation of still greater challenges to follow. He foresees, after the coming of peace, a prosperous period for the United States, during which our production of food must be kept high, "not only to assist in feeding the undernourished peoples of the world, but also for negotiating purposes with foreign nations." He thinks that we must not withdraw into ourselves once more but be ready to exercise leadership in the world. "We must provide for greater trade between nations and we must remember that international trade is not carried over any one-way road. . . . The days of old empires have come and gone, and economic leadership is now the order of the day."

With the prospect before him of having much to do and the whole world in which to do it, the miller feels himself to be in harmony with what he hopes will be the mood of the future. It has not always been so with him. There was an unhappy moment of antagonism when he felt angrily that the hands of all the theorists were against him. These men rebuked him for bleaching his flour to give it a soft and silken attractiveness. Values in the wheat germ were lost, said the analysts, when those black and gritty particles were so carefully removed. Whole-wheat flour was more healthful. Vitamins were wantonly killed, and all in the name of purity! So one side of the argument sternly ran. "Faddists!" the spokesmen of the milling industry retorted in a frenzy of indignation. The hysterical prophets of the Department of Agriculture needed to have their beards pulled for giving the people such notions!

But now the differences have been adjusted. The word "bleached" must appear on the flour package so that the world may know precisely what it is buying. But the customer may now have his flour in any state that he desires, the completely unravished, the "purified," the "reinforced," which means "with vitamins added." Requirements of Lend-Lease shipments vary and these are followed with scrupulous respect for both law and logic. "Medical men indorse our product and the government is our best salesman," wrote a spokesman of the Minneapolis milling center. All unconsciously he fell into the Biblical rhythm suggesting that the millennium has come and that the unexhausted lion may now lie down with the once fretful but now properly lamblike lamb.

It is a rich and varied drama that Father Hennepin started on the day when he saw the Indian weeping and propitiating and praying with bloodthirsty zeal. The priest explorer established the first link between the Falls of St. Anthony in the wilderness and the great outside world. The product of the mills has gone over the entire globe. There is a traditional story that is frequently retold among those who love the lighter forms of irony. A traveler in the darkest corner of darkest Africa comes upon a fearsome savage dressed in a curious garment. Looking more closely the traveler sees that it is made of flour sacking, and that across the sturdy Negro's chest is spread the slogan of one of the great milling companies of Minneapolis.

Sometimes the setting of the story is China; sometimes it is the farthest reaches of Siberia. But whether the chest that the flour sack covers be black or yellow, it is good to reflect that its former contents has filled a needy stomach. Minneapolis has traveled far and not in vain.

The milling industry has produced its own culture, one which has very greatly enriched the region. The young men who went out over the world looking for export markets for flour were missionaries of a kind. Like wise missionaries the world over, they came back home re-educated by the experiences they had had in distant places, inspired by the beautiful things that they had seen. They were moved by the breadth of the world, the depth of its philosophies, and the color and harmony of its arts. They went out to sell flour, and many of them brought back ideas, beliefs, mellowness. One member of the milling community on the Mississippi has become America's most sensitive and understanding collector of Chinese brasses and jades, one of our best interpreters of the whole artistic impulse of a distant and alien culture.

Flashing across the night sky above the Falls of St. Anthony, the embattled governors still send challenging messages to each other. "Pillsbury's Best," one of them declares in all the lurid beauty of an electric sign. To which the other retorts: "Gold Medal Flour—Eventually, Why Not Now?" It is the modern method of propitiating those forces of fortune to which Father Hennepin's weeping Indian offered the buffalo robe.

7

RED GIANT IN THE EARTH

IN TIME OF WAR the importance of steel is thunderously evident. Tanks crashing to the attack in Europe, guns resounding in the South Pacific, testify eloquently to the grim significance of the role played in a moment of crisis by this most vital of raw materials. "Stalin," "man of steel," one of the United Nations leaders has chosen to call himself. Men of steel most of the occupants of the globe have been forced to become.

The iron ore from which steel is fabricated lies in deposits widespread around the world. Approximately one third of the earth's entire supply is mined in the United States; and of that third, eighty per cent is concentrated in the Lake Superior region.

Around the two fingers of the lake that point westward through Wisconsin and Minnesota are the ranges in which the ore is buried. the Vermilion, the Missabe, and the Cuyuna in Minnesota; the Gogebic, cutting across Wisconsin into Michigan, and the Menominee, which edges just over the Michigan border into Wisconsin.

Out of the open pits of the great mines of the Missabe range, out of the shafts from the underground operations of the Vermilion and the Gogebic, the ore flows uphill in a stream that is now twice as great as it has been in any year except 1917, when another war emergency stepped up production tremendously. Loaded directly from the pits onto the stocky-looking railroad cars (ones of the ordinary size and shape could not bear the weight of iron ore), this raw material from which the weapons of war are made is rushed to the towns of the inland ocean. There the red stream pours itself once more onto the dock boats to be carried east to the blast furnaces.

The whole operation is fantastically fast in times of emergency. The largest engines with a maximum amount of power are operated day and night to move the ore to its destination, so that no longer need the world whip itself with the rebuke of offering "too little and too late." The stream of iron ore plunges with the ordered haste of expert planning. Dock boats at Duluth, brought into place at the striking of the hour, have been filled to capacity before the half hour has arrived.

The wealth of these deposits is the result of a succession of tremendous natural dramas covering hundreds of millions of years of geological history. In that unimaginable twilight of the planet before man had brought his vanity and his need to be the measure of importance of all earthly things, great surging movements went patiently on and on in the unconscious heart of creation. First a shallow sea flowed over a region which included what is now Wisconsin and Minnesota. The water contained iron, carried away from the granite rocks of near-by land, and deposited it on the sea floor through the agency of bacterial life. With the inexhaustible patience of timelessness, this sediment hardened into iron-bearing rock. If man had appeared in that period of time, imperiously to demand the treasure, it would have done him little good because the proportion of iron to rock was so small that even his greedy ingenuity would have been discouraged.

But other superb, blind forces were at work, the end of whose labor was to be the production of the iron ranges. The waters fell back and the yawning and stretching of a planet that seemed slowly to be coming awake folded the ore-bearing rock back into mountain chains as high as the Rockies of today. Later these mountains were ironed down by the streams that carried most of their substance away and left a rolling plain.

Still the pattern of land and water, heat and cold, had taken on no final design, and the blind urgencies of nature produced great new changes. Seas once more flowed slowly over the region, depositing sandstone and limestone on the leveled mountains. The waters came and the waters crept away once more. Though they left traces of their visit, erosion presently exposed the iron-bearing rock. Then, for a long, patient moment of pre-glacial time, water worked its way down through the layers of various materials, dissolving away everything that yielded, packing down the hard rock into concentrated form.

The imagination of man, mixing poetry with a slightly paranoid belief in his importance within the universal scheme, persists in seeing a divine purpose in all these gigantic shifts and alterations. For the end of it was that iron, in great quantity, lay below the surface of the earth no deeper than the roots of trees can reach. But there was still the glacier to be dealt with. It moved superbly over the region, carrying away much of the ore, hiding another part under its carelessly strewn drift.

The impetuosity, however, left enough of the original treasure to see America through the whole period of mechanization under the Industrial Revolution, and through two wars besides. Each of these needs has seemed, as the world faced its pressing urgency, to be inescapably crucial, and the withdrawal of ore has been correspondingly reckless. Estimates of how long the ore of the region will last under normal conditions vary all the way from twenty years to nearly half a century. Hundreds of millions of years were required to concentrate the iron ore in the ranges of the Lake states; just one hundred years in the time of man will see it exhausted. We are, as all our friendly critics from Lord Bryce to Lin Yutang have pointed out, an impatient people.

The history of the search for iron ore indicates that impatience is often teamed, at the start of an enterprise, with inertia. Then urgency kicks over the traces and with fire in its nostrils races headlong away.

The Indians knew of the existence of iron ore in Wisconsin and Minnesota. As early as 1730 they had pointed out to explorers the curious interest of the ranges. The greatest of these they called the Missabe, which meant "giant" or "giant in the earth." (Missabe is the spelling generally in use today, though scholars and purists prefer "Mesabi.")

In their comparatively uncomplicated civilization the Indians had found no use for iron. Explorers like La Vérendrye and Dr. John McLoughlin were preoccupied with the potentialities of the fur trade and they mentioned, in their journals, the existence of iron merely as a matter of curiosity. There was nothing that they felt obliged to do about it.

Governor Ramsey was the first man to realize that society was ignoring a great advantage in its failure to recover the mineral wealth of the region. In 1854 he persuaded the Chippewa nation to cede lands where ore was thought to lie buried. But still interest lagged.

It was not until after the Civil War that the first tentative efforts were made to wrestle with the red giant in the earth. In the first months of peace large numbers of the imaginative and excitable stamped into the north country, as they were later to stamp into the Far West, looking for gold. The Lake Vermilion country of the Arrowhead region was a tangle of forests, thickets, and swamps, but these men made their way stubbornly through, loaded with heavy equipment, only to find that what had caught the eyes of their misguided informants was a compound of iron and sulphur called pyrites by scientists and "fool's gold" by those who have been bitterly disappointed by its pale yellow brass color.

Later explorers were more experienced and practical. Wisconsin, always a half step ahead of Minnesota in all historic developments, witnessed the first organized efforts at getting out the ore. Operations were begun at the Menominee in 1872 and at the Gogebic in 1873. By 1884 activities at the Gogebic were creditably strenuous.

During the same period Minnesota was beginning to organize its search for the red giant that lay sleeping under a thin blanket of earth. Three men—a prospector, a pioneer promotor, and an Eastern capitalist (the inevitable triumvirate)—were involved in the opening up of the Vermilion mine. George R. Stuntz, a surveyor by profession, was the perfect wilderness man. He loved discovery for its own dramatic sake. He loved the jungles and swamps of the wilderness. When the thermometer rose above zero, Stuntz felt that the atmosphere was getting intolerably stuffy.

George C. Stone was a man who loved his community and wanted to see it move from strength to strength. When Stuntz came stamping out of the woods with the report that there was a great quantity of iron in the Vermilion Range, Stone enlisted the financial support of a Pennsylvania millionaire. The family name of this financier was the entirely suitable one of Tower. His mother had had the presence of mind and the prophetic vision to have him baptized Charlemagne. So altogether perfect he was for this role that he might have been created by Henry James. With superb aloofness he directed the enterprise of opening the Vermilion mine from his office in Philadelphia while Stuntz trudged up and down the north country acquiring land—17,000 acres of it, for which he paid a frugal $40,000. Presently a railroad was constructed between the mine and the nearest access to Lake Superior at Two Harbors and by 1884 full operations were in progress.

The great Charlemagne left his surname behind in Minnesota attached to a mining town, while he swept away to a career in diplomacy, with appointments to Austria-Hungary, Russia, and Germany. He wrote a two-volume history of Lafayette's share in the American Revolution and glittered briefly in the eye of history while the two local Georges, Stuntz and Stone, retired into obscurity.

And still the great giant of the Missabe lay hidden. The story of its final uncovering follows what is, apparently, the classic pattern of "possessors . . . dispossessed." The design is like that of the drama of Charlemagne Tower, but richer in detail, better supplied with striking incident.

The central actors were the members of the Merritt family. They were timber cruisers who took an occasional side-line glance at other possibilities of wealth. The father of this clan, Lewis Merritt, had gone out from Duluth looking for gold and come back with packet of red iron ore. The belief that there was a fortune in iron buried in the Missabe Range became one of the major tenets of the Merritt family's faith. Just as several generations of the same clan may spend their lives in a laboratory working on an experimental theory, so the Merritts of three generations kept on looking for iron. In all kinds of weather they roamed the region, getting lost and finding themselves again, persisting with that mythical kind of dedication which is associated in literature with names like Lancelot and Galahad and with quests like that of the Holy Grail.

They drew another man into their search, Captain J. A. Nichols, and he at last made a discovery that justified the almost religious faith of twenty years. On November 16, 1890 he hurried down from the Missabe country to Leonidas Merritt's office in Duluth and ceremoniously closed the door. There was always a thin vapor of literary fervor hanging over the Merritt enterprises (Leonidas himself wrote verse in imitation of Longfellow), so probably Captain Nichols whispered the one word: "Eureka." He favored secrecy about the discovery, but, after so many years of searching, Leonidas wanted the world to know that there was iron in the Missabe just as his father had said.

The world did not hesitate to act upon the news. Almost immediately there was a great roar echoing through the region, the stamping, cursing, and elbowing of resolute men who wanted iron. They uprooted the trees, blasted out the stumps, began tearing at the surface of the soil to find the best means of getting at this wealth. Cornishman Captain John Gill came and German Frank Hibbing, and Mike Godfrey and Ezra Rust. There was something prodigious about all of them and about their audacity. They risked their lives daily and hourly, improvising ways of clearing this land over which a net of careless growth had become tightly woven.

After the leaders, the workers came—Cornishmen at first, trained by tradition in all the ways of mining; then the Finns and the Norwegians and the Swedes; finally the Austrians and Slovenes and Italians. They made up a vehement, noisy world of men without women. Fighters gouged and bit and pomeled each other into unconsciousness. Men fought duels with pistols in the street as an escape from excruciating boredom. The level of civic pride may be measured by the fact that newspapers proclaimed the triumph when, on a holiday, two hundred men milled through the saloons and houses of prostitution, all gloriously drunk, and yet not one arrest had to be made. The evangelists would occasionally take to the platform to get their little share of the wages of sin, but, as the great ladies of the brothels triumphantly pointed out, the efforts of the preachers had the invariable result of producing a bonanza for professional entertainers of the appetites.

No matter what may be said to make this seem like a time when demigods strode the earth, gleefully inviting the free expression of manly tasts, the mining towns were tragic places. Hunger and danger and boredom and desperation were all about. The primitive methods of mining sent the rate of accidental deaths soaring. The almost incredibly high rate of suicide testified to the fact that the burden of life lay heavy on the hearts of these isolated men.

While the mines of the Missabe Range were being opened up, nine in all, and while the towns were unfolding their luxuriant patterns of violence, economic progress was working out its own classic design in the typical example of the Merritt enterprise.

Leonidas, his brothers, and their sons had established themselves at a center which they named Mountain Iron. This was one of the places where the ore lay no deeper than the tree roots, and the Merritts proposed to get it out by digging from the surface. This was not an innovation, yet it lacked the approval of traditionalists, who have their own strong sense of what is owed to the dignity of mining work. The Merritts had difficulty in getting financiers to back their projects or workers to perform the labor which they contemptuously called "ditch-digging." Yet they struggled along, making their personal sacrifices and wooing help wherever they could find it until, in 1892, they had actually constructed a railroad line to the lake and begun to haul ore. Prospects began to look up and there was a golden moment when they could have sold out their leases and their docks and their railroad to the great Charlemagne Tower for $8,000,000.

But Leonidas did not sell, perhaps because to a man of talent the doing of a job is more important than any reward he may ever get.

In those early years of the nineties other men of the Charlemagne Tower type began to interest themselves in the development of the wealth of the range country. One of them was Henry W. Oliver, who came, like the God out of the machine in Greek drama, at precisely the right moment. Oliver had traveled to Minneapolis as a Pennsylvania delegate to the Republican national convention. When that business was concluded he had time to listen to the stories of iron ore. He liked what he heard and hurried to see this rich north country. In the company of hundreds of other men bound on the same mission he sought out a corner of a crowded Duluth hotel. It is said that he spent the night sleeping on a billiard table, a detail that did not dampen his eagerness, no matter what it may have done to his dignity as another Henry James financier.

The next day he bought a horse and rode it the whole distance of seventy-five miles to the Merritt camp. That day's activity ended in his taking a lease on a mine; but it was the beginning of the history of an enterprise that today bears his name.

Back in Pittsburgh, Oliver consulted with Henry Clay Frick of the Carnegie empire about his findings. At one of their interviews Frick was recovering in bed from the wounds inflicted by the ambitious anarchist and would-be assassin Alexander Berkman. (The unrealistic character of Berkman's vague desire to alter society was once charmingly demonstrated when, after a lecture in Minneapolis, he wired from Kansas City to his hostess asking that she send him a forgotten toothbrush. It would never occur to a conscious believer in a world without order that a new toothbrush could be had for less than the price of a telegram.) Frick, defying orders from the Laird of Pittsburgh, then traveling in his native Scotland, supplied funds from Carnegie Steel's resources to develop the Oliver property. So presently, all unwilling, Carnegie came to have a controlling interest in the Missabe mine.

While Carnegie was assuming leadership in one section of the range, Rockefeller was in the process of taking over another. In 1893 the Merritts were desperately in need of cash. They issued $1,600,000 worth of bonds, and one fourth of these made their way into the Rockefeller safe. At the precise moment when it could hurt the Merritt interests most, panic swept the country. In order to continue, Leonidas required cash, and the Rockefeller empire supplied it in return for an interest in a newly formed company.

Panic is a grim comedian. Its rowdy humor pulls chairs out from under men who have thought themselves securely situated. It trips up the too visionary expansionist and leaves him flat on his startled face. It juggles interests with furious, blind, and indescribable legerdemain.

In 1894 Rockefeller was in possession of the Merritt interests. Despite the fact that there were lawsuits and counter-lawsuits and accusations and eloquent utterances about conflicting rights, the end of the story was the same. The Merritts received as a settlement enough to pay a part of their debts, and the Rockefeller interests had the mine.

By the turn of the century Charlemagne Tower was in possession of the Vermilion district, Rockefeller of a part of the Missabe, and Carnegie of the rest. The Oliver Mining Company had acquired controlling interest in the mines of Gogebic Range as well. In 1901 these various groups merged with many of the other great steel interests to form the United States Steel Company, which today controls four fifths of the ore in the region. United States Steel owns the mines, the railroads, the docks, the steamship lines.

Nature's canyons, like the one which is rather unimaginatively called Grand, are admired for the superb, theatrical wastefulness of their yawning spaces, their lavish colors, their intimidating depths. They seem like settings for *The Twilight of the Gods*, but with the gods already gone and the scene of their last disaster left beautiful and barren.

An open-pit iron mine is like a man-made canyon, smaller than a great natural phenomenon, of course, but having the same kind of lurid color scheme, the same design and shape. It looks almost as though the hot interior of the earth had just begun to cool into various shades of yellow, brown, ocher, orange, and purple-black. The sight is the more impressive when one realizes that man has created the whole scene. A wilderness of trees, shrubs, grasses, and swamps has been ripped away to get this glimpse into the heart of nature's hidden creative processes. Man has felled the trees and dragged them away, blasted out the stumps, drained the marshes, dug under the surface, and penetrated to this secret wealth.

The Hull-Rust-Mahoning open-pit mine at Hibbing is the largest in the world. It stretches three miles long, nearly a mile across, and is, at its greatest depth, three hundred and fifty feet below the surface of the soil. It is like a canyon also in that its sides are cut back into terraces. The miners call them "benches" and they are "worked back" in tiers to get at the ore.

Infinitely slow and tedious the work was in the days when the sharp-tongued "Cousin Jacks" referred to it as "ditch-digging," but open-pit mining today is organized and mechanized and designed for speed. It works with the briskness of a panzer division. Even the names of the pieces of equipment show how completely the whole operation has been dramatized as an attack. The "wrecker," the "bulldozer," the "crusher" are isolated parts of the machinery with which the modern miner does his job. The dip of the shovel is a "bite." Everything about the poetry and folklore of the open pit suggests that the miner intends to be exactly as hard as the material with which he works, and just as active as it is passive.

The descent into this Avernus is made in a most unclassical manner, of which Dante would probably not have approved. It is managed in a Chevrolet, specially rebuilt to take punishment. The highways leading down are excellent because they are made of the materials of the pit, and iron is most satisfactory as pavement. But there are other stretches where the superintendent's car must bounce over ragged and uneven ground. The orange highways wind round and round the benches, while the canyon flashes the strident challenge of its bold color scheme in the eyes. Painters have been attracted again and again by the intense drama of the scene, and always they get their color tones so high that miners wince at what they regard as a betrayal of realism. Yet when the wife of a mining man painted the scene in pigments made from the actual materials of the pit, the colors seemed dull and quite unworthy of this garish splendor. The rash intemperance of the artist is, after all, more in sympathy with nature's own imagination.

Three primary processes are involved in open-pit mining: "stripping," the removal of the overburden; drilling and blasting to free the ore; and removal of the ore to the railroad cars which stand ready to haul it away for shipment. Each of these is accomplished with the aid of the biggest, neatest, best co-ordinated machines that the ingenuity of man has yet been able to devise. Diesel-electric locomotives operating huge shovels scoop up the sand, gravel, clay, and paint-rock and deposit this "overburden" in trucks to be hauled to the dumping ground. Mountains of such waste dot the landscape of the iron region.

The drilling is done with a six-inch auger, and the blasting follows, a little at a time. "We don't shoot heavily," the superintendent says. Despite the co-operation of nature in getting the ore concentrated, it is not even now stored away in neat packages. Its veins wander whimsically through the earth.

"We have to chase it where it goes," the superintendent murmurs patiently as though he were speaking of the pursuit of a burrowing animal.

The shovels that pick up the ore are giants, too. The biggest of them is a 300-ton affair with an eight-yard bucket that can take sixteen tons of ore at a bite.

"But you can't just put the shovel in," the superintendent comments. He is obviously afraid that the layman will think this merely a game played in a gigantic sandbox. "No sir! It means planning. Every morning of the year the heads of various departments have an 'ore meeting.'"

This thin shrewd man, who looks like a self-contained Yankee from Vermont, and whose speech has a Coolidge twang, fixes his visitor with an almost severe glance.

"The meeting is at eleven o'clock," he adds as though to dispel any possible doubt as to its regularity and solemnity. "You interrupted it when you came."

Then he goes on about the shovel.

"It has a boom ninety feet long," he announces with evident pride, "and dipper sticks of sixty feet."

The shovel makes an impressive sight as it revolves, biting at the ore seams with the spectacular efficiency of a trained dinosaur.

Standing at the bottom of the pit, one looks up as though from the inside of a hollow inverted mountain. Ten tiers of benches are evident in some places. The geological basis of the color scheme is not difficult to discern, for one sees the purple-black veins of the ore alternating with the ocher shades of the rock strata. The earth colors in their irregular striped design rise up to a flash of green at the rim of the pit. In contrast to the ocher shades of the mine, green seems curiously bright, almost as spectacular as red does in a normally green landscape. And overhead the blue of the sky adds a pale reminder of the familiar world.

At the bottom of the pit, too, one sees something of the complexity of the job which the superintendent has tried to under-score. In the center of the canyon is a "mountain horse," a huge pile of material that must be mined around because the whimsi-cality of the ore seam has taken it elsewhere and this huge block contains no iron at all. In other places the deposits are in spots so irregular that no tracks can be made to reach them. Here what is called in the lively slang of the pit a "scramming operation" is required to carry the ore away to a place where it can be handled. Comic little jeeps called "dumpsters," capable of being operated from either front or back, nose into such difficult places and carry the ore to the cars. In certain corners of the pit which cannot be reached by anything on wheels, the ore is carried out by huge conveyor belts.

Back on the ground level, with hands, face, and shoes smeared with the orange dust of the pit, one glances back, trying to grasp the immensity of the project in terms of statistics. Sixty miles of highway in the canyon! Many times as many miles of cable lying in intestine-like profusion over the ground, carrying power to the shovels! Two and a half times as many tons of material re-moved to get at the ore as was handled in digging the Panama Canal! Here on top, a stretch of track that is the most used in all the world!

Hercules in a "bulldozer" is doing a tremendous job!

For the classicist who clings to a strong, almost mystical con-viction that only underground operations are creditable, there are ample satisfactions in the range country. Underground mines are in operation on the Gogebic Range in Wisconsin and the Ver-milion, Missabe, and Cuyuna Ranges in Minnesota. Two hun-dred to two hundred and fifty feet below the surface of the earth, Americans out of Finland, Scandinavia, and central Europe drill at the rock to recover its treasures.

An underground pit is far from being an unpleasant place. Sug-gesting Alice's wonderland of improbabilities, it suggests also the familiar efficiency of a subway. The unearthly earthiness of the damp smell may stir fanciful notions, but the disciplined efficiency of the electrically controlled ore cars speeding over the tracks helps to restore the mind to order. This, in summer, is a cool, well-ventilated place. Indeed, winter and summer it maintains the same temperature, so that an underground mine may claim some of the advantages of a tourist resort.

A visitor wears miner's clothes, overalls, and a thick helmet to protect his head against the possible accident of falling rock. Into the brim he inserts a neat and jaunty lamp that generates its own gas by the dripping of water on crushed carbide. The gas expelled through a needle-point burner is ignited by a flint lighter, attached to the inside of the reflector.

Every task that man has created for himself has its special poetry. That of underground mining is rich in images and in the racy slang of action. The tunnels through which the miners make their way are "drifts." Despite the hardness of some aspects of this earth mother, the walls of the tunnels are called "breasts." The process of mining underground is to get to the "extremity" of a drift and then "retreat." Involved in the various operations are "scrapers," "slushers," "crimpers," "jackhammers." The timbers that support the walls of the tunnels while the ore is drilled from their sides are "snaked in." If an underground miner were told that his daily speech was that of poetry, he would probably look unbelieving if not resentful. But he speaks it just as surely as the surprised and pleased *bourgeois gentilhomme* spoke prose.

This type of mining is a little like building a house underground. The drifts are the hallways which ray out through the section of the mine that the engineer has made his home. Each of these hallways ends in what is called a "room." Here the actual work of recovering the ore is carried on.

Miners who, in the vigorous and positive slang of the industry, are called "producers" stand on platforms built up against the walls of the "room." They hold their jackhammers in their hands, boring holes into which dynamite blasts will later be introduced to bring off, a layer at a time, the ore-bearing rock. Modern mining has invented a system called "dry drilling" designed to eliminate the dust hazard. For the sake of efficiency both sides of the "room" are worked simultaneously.

The loosened ore is collected in the "rooms" by "scrapers," tough-looking little cars drawn by electrically operated "tuggers." It is then transferred to the cars which carry it down the drift to be dumped into other containers and hoisted to the surface. These chains of cars swinging over the rails in the mine's eerie blue light dramatize the whole operation and give the scene a permanent place in one's private gallery of pictures devoted to the theme: Men at Work.

There is a fine look of audacity to the act of drilling into and blasting out the very wall of the cave that is your shelter. But the drama is all in the forethought of the engineer who has designed the campaign. Actual danger of the kind about which romantic films are woven may be said scarcely to exist.

When all the ore has been removed from a "room," the whole is blasted down. The new extremity of the drift becomes the "room" to be worked. This, too, has a romantic sound and suggests the mad act of Samson in bringing down the temple about his shoulders. But in an underground mine it is a discreet and orderly affair. The sides of the drift, staunchly supported by timbers of Norway pine out of the region's own forests, resist any but the planned collapse.

Thus the miners "retreat" through the drifts. The careful crisscross design with which the whole section has been laid out ensures the removal of all the ore from each "room" in turn. When the shrewdly laid-out mazes of this underground house have been completely worked, the engineer can cross a part of the mine off his map of operations and know that its value has been efficiently exhausted. The job is finished.

An underground mine, for all its ordered efficiency, is a little like the fanciful wonderlands that are contrived by the operators of fairs to tease the imagination of children. There are similarities to mythical monsters in all the objects of use and to all the techniques for safeguarding health. The ventilator, through the fabric of which fresh air is pumped into the mine, crawls along the top of the drift like a great earthworm. Mushrooms thrust out their always fantastic growth along the walls. There is a constant ringing of bells, warning signals of the various operations of the cars. The little niches, set back in the walls as safety zones, are marked by blue lights. The imagination moving through such a world could easily persuade itself that it discerned in the dim blue distance a White Rabbit, in dress gloves, scurrying anxiously to an appointment with the Duchess.

The war has stimulated many lively dramas in the engineering imagination. At Mountain Iron, where Leonidas Merritt first discovered ore in the Missabe Range, operations were discontinued in 1908. With other richer resources more easily available, it seemed unprofitable to work this area. Gradually the pit filled with water and where there had been a hole in the ground, there was presently another lake added to Minnesota's ten thousand. The war emergency made it necessary, however, to reopen the mine. So the lake was pumped away, 2,525,000 gallons of it. It took from June to the end of winter to divert the waters safely and finally. But there at last was the pit, and now it is once more complete with its maze of railroad track. Approximately 3,000,000 gross tons of ore were recovered from it in the first year of its rebirth.

Perhaps it was the experience at Mountain Iron that has stirred wild surmises in other minds. Mining imagination apparently can dive as well as dig, for a group of men have begun to brood about the ore that may lie under the beds of natural lakes. As these lines are written, the State Executive Council has granted permits to prospect for iron under six northern lakes, the waters of which will have to be pumped away exactly as were those at Mountain Iron. If instead of 10,000 lakes, Minnesota should presently have only 9,994, there will be little regret should the result be the discovery of new sources of high-grade ore.

The threatened exhaustion of iron resources has been made more serious still by the exigency of the war program. Removal from the Lake Superior region has been at the rate of nearly 14,000,000 tons of ore in a single month. Still the danger is not immediate. Standards of what constitutes ore profitable for shipments have gradually been dropped from sixty-five per cent of iron to only a little more than fifty per cent. Methods have been developed for improving the quality of the ore found on the outskirts of the really good concentrations by washing out, screening out, or driving out by the application of heat the unwanted materials. Miners have a word for it. They call it "beneficiating" the ore. Originally it was their very own, but now it has crept into the dictionary, while the sterner academicians were not looking. No doubt it is destined for a wider usefulness, so that in the end

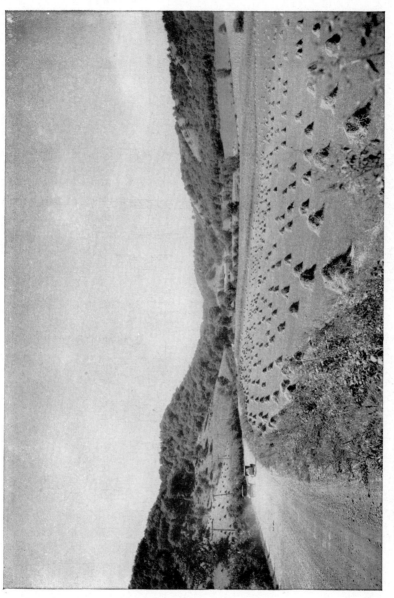

HIGHWAY THROUGH THE FIELDS NEAR RED WING, MINNESOTA

GRAIN ELEVATOR AT SUPERIOR, WISCONSIN

we shall hear Broadway play doctors speak of "beneficiating" inferior plays.

Laboratories maintained by the mines have developed brilliant precision methods for testing the quality of each carload of ore brought up out of pit or underground drift. An army of technicians (many of them girls, in these war years) goes through the small miracle of its alchemy briskly, so that by the time the ore has reached the docks the analysis of its grade is ready to travel with it to the blast furnaces.

Theoretical experimentation in methods of making low-grade ores, which exist in great quantity, profitable for handling has been conducted by the United States Bureau of Mines and at the universities. As the need for a technique becomes greater, technical experts of the mines' own organizations will no doubt add their experience to that of the academic explorers. All the exploits of the mining engineers in finding ways of doing things that looked impossible argue eloquently that this problem, too, can be solved.

Highly dramatic is the crusher at Mountain Iron which takes great chunks of ore into its amazing jaws and, with a great heroic throwing off of blue sparks, grinds them into fragments, which are tossed onto a conveyor belt and carried to cars on the tracks near by. "It could grind up the First National Bank Building in St. Paul," gleefully boasts the guide, "or even an isolationist's head."

Dramatic in a very different way was the exploit undertaken twenty years ago at Hibbing of moving a whole town that was found to be in the way of mining operations. "We have to follow the ore wherever it goes," the miner says, and when it was discovered that the wanderings led directly under the residence section of the old town, there was no decision possible except to institute a sort of super-moving-day on which the houses moved too.

The mining company bought a section that covered forty acres and put on wheels everything stout enough to stand transportation. Moving-day, in fact, took three years. It was a better-looking town that resulted. There had been no planning in the early days when the sudden need of shelter made any crazy structure seem sufficient. The houses seemed to have lunged into place and, in the midst of a great, wide-stretching landscape, they leaned together like bewildered and untrusting pioneers.

The cities of the mining district do not look like that today. There is a fine amplitude to the imagination that has created them. The mines, owned outside the states in which they lie, pay handsome taxes into the public treasury, and with these funds the cities have built fabulous school buildings. One of them serves as a civic recreation center as well as a high school. It has committee rooms in which labor organizations may meet, the floors of which are so deeply carpeted that, as one fanciful observer has put it, the unwary are in danger of breaking their angles simply in walking across it. The auditorium is fitted with pneumatic seats. Classrooms are equipped with automatic light-control systems, so that as dusk begins to fall, early of a winter afternoon, artificial light comes on without anyone's being distracted from his algebra or his Chaucer. There was a positively heroic moment in the recent past when a gigantic range high school boasted a corps of thirty-five janitors. After the morning invasion of the "forever panting and forever young" had occurred, leaving behind a trail of muddy tracks, this army of sanitation swept through the halls, making them immaculate once more in three or four minutes.

These northern communities like to assign themselves titles of nobility like "queen city of the range." They justify their claims to specialness by paving their wide streets handsomely and lighting them with lavish pride. The glittering little towns have parks and monuments in which much larger places might take satisfaction.

The range cities show a curious combination of opposites. The thoroughfares are as broad as those of Paris, but the buildings are the low ones that you would expect to find on Main Street. There is an air of urban swagger to the white leather, chromium-trimmed smartness of a public bar; but just around the corner are the approaches to the mining district, lying under a blanket of orange silt and looking much as they must have looked in the days before the range towns put on their grandeur.

These contrasts can be found, too, in the lives of the people. The Finn who works with his jackhammer in the mine speaks with an almost unintelligible accent. But he has sent his five children to college and launched his sons in the learned professions.

Little is left today of the old fever and frenzy of life in the early days of mining history. The citizens marry and vote and attend church just as do the citizens of communities that have no lurid past behind them. The statistics having to do with drunkenness and suicide are no longer swollen with the poison of loneliness and tragedy. The glittering, polished splendor of the city probably would abash anyone out of the impulse even to stage a scene. To engage in a street brawl against that background of splendor would be unthinkable.

The range towns are hard-working communities whose men devote their lives to heavy manual labor. They get into their over-alls early in the morning and put in a full day. But they wear their look of specialness with a kind of winking pride. It is as though they topped off their costumes of overalls with high hats and strode off to the mines carrying gold-headed canes.

In wartime three shifts a day go down into the pits to get out the ore. It is no dull routine that drives these men on in this exact-ing program. The miners know precisely why it is necessary to get a great deal of iron and to get it quickly. When their own work is over for the day, many of these men go to the broadcasting sta-tions to give messages in Finnish, in Slovenian, in Croatian to the people of their native countries, urging them to understand and to further the purposes of the United Nations. The government sponsors these short-wave broadcasts and it has found in the cities of the range some of its most eloquent spokesmen. These men have known what it is like to be regimented and driven, and also what it is like to be free. They speak with the conviction of Ameri-cans who have learned the lesson of democracy at first hand.

8

"TIMBER IS A CROP"

᪥

ONE WAY to tell the story of the forest in Wisconsin and Minnesota would be in the manner of the films. The scenario would call for a series of montage shots, one dissolving swiftly into another to compress a century's crowded, turbulent history into a few suggestive flashes. The whole kaleidoscopic survey would be accomplished to the accompaniment of a rich and varied symphonic score; something out of a symphony of Beethoven first, to suggest the noble serenity of nature before the invasion of man; a snatch of a portentous-sounding *Prélude* of Chopin to announce the approach of strange, destructive forces; finally a crashing passage out of the *Götterdämmerung* of Wagner as the drama reaches its climax in a mixture of grandeur and disaster.

There would be first, as the screen began its revelations, a glimpse of the forest primeval that once covered two thirds of the land of the region. The camera's eye would sweep up the streams, along the high banks densely wooded with oak and birch, sugar maple and elm. It would search into the wilderness of the north, finding out the stands of timber where mottled trunks of red pine and the deeply grooved bark of the white pine trees crowd together in groves of Gothic peace and seclusion. The northern lakes with their growth of jack pine clinging acrobatically to the faces of cliffs would come into the range of the camera's eye and also the tangled pattern of poplar, balsam, spruce, tamarack, and hemlock.

The forest would be glimpsed in the full dark splendor of summer and under the snows of winter, through the round of the seasons which American poets from Longfellow to Joyce Kilmer have described with inexhaustible fervor. The burden of softly persistent snow on the evergreen branch . . . the nest of robins in the crook of the oak tree's arm . . . the surge of autumnal color across the hillside rising high above a river. And the forest, in these glimpses bearing witness to the dignity of the natural life, would be seen as the haven of deer and bear, porcupine and beaver.

Then these idyllic shots would fade into others showing the first covetous glances of man. The camera discovers a first saw-mill being set up on the Devil River in Wisconsin. (The year is 1809.) Presently fur-traders all over the region are imitating the experiment. One (whose name in the records is Dan Whitney) steps from his canoe on the Wisconsin River and studies the forest with a concentrated and calculating gaze. Some friendly Win-nebago Indians come drifting by. He hails them, makes an agree-ment for the use of their lands, sets up a sawmill.

Dissolve to a scene of righteous indignation. The trader should have made his agreement with the Indians through the agents of the government. He is out of order in this wilderness world, which the soldiers mean to keep patrolled in accordance with the few rules set down neatly in their books. The musical score of this imaginary film takes on for a moment a thin pedantic note as the soldiers from the nearest fort move down on the trader's mill, to carry away his illegal shingles and destroy what they can-not transport.

But almost immediately the harsh and correct little theme of retribution is drowned out in a great laughing motif of discovery. On the screen the glimpse of soldiers in the wilderness, keeping the little rules in order, dissolves into a view of lumbermen mov-ing in resolutely from all sides. They stride into this new country with the great muscular movements of the inevitable, brushing aside almost without seeing them the now puny figures of the legal authorities who try to hold them back, discipline and regi-ment them. The lumbermen have taken possession.

Dissolve into a symbolic image of hands gripping the ax handle, swinging, letting the sharp edge bite deep into the bark of the tree. The single pair of hands multiplies into many, multiplies into innumerable duplications. Numbers of men, all with the same hearty and unruly impulse to get the timber, are in control of the wilderness. With bland and friendly cynicism they support each other in the theory that energy and endurance are now the only rules of this region. Each man buys a small tract for logging and when he has exhausted its resources begins to log the adjoining tracts on every side—those that still belong to the government, but which the government is too inept, too passive, too amenable to bribery to protect.

Now the camera's eye picks up the figures of the independent loggers, following them through their full routine. All winter long, choppers and sawyers work in the woods. The "fallers" make their V-shaped undercut to ensure the descent of the tree in the prearranged direction. When "she's notched," the crosscut saw eats with hearty appetite, yet with a kind of elegance and grace, through the trunk of the tree. The "bucker" saws the tree into log lengths. "Swampers" slash their way through the wilderness growth, creating rough roads over which the plodding oxen can make their way to the logs. Loaded onto skids behind crotches that hold the logs high enough so that the front end does not dig into the ground, the logs are dragged to the skidway. There they are scaled and prepared for loading. Three loaders work at the skidway, one on either side of the decked logs that are being rolled onto sleighs. Another logger on top operates with his cant hook. Road monkeys put sand on the hills and on the ice so that the movement of the teams can be controlled. Big loads have as many as thirty-three logs. Down to the rollways on the riverbank the sleighs move behind the heavy, swinging bodies of the oxen. In the spring the logs are made into rafts, three hundred feet wide. Equipped with sweep oars, they are floated down the rivers that flow into the Mississippi.

The drama of floating the logs down the river has its own climaxes: the log jams; the losses of life when it is necessary to run grave physical risks to keep the product moving; the games like birling, invented out of the very dangers of the trade, in which rivals dance as lightly as ballerinas, each trying to maintain his own footing while he strives to upset the equilibrium of his opponent and bring him to disaster in the water.

The camera takes a final glimpse of this strenuous world in which trees are falling on every side, each with a gigantic sigh, and at the vistas of desolation being opened up through the forest; then it dissolves into the image of a bearded little man with a shrewd, penetrating gaze who has a taste and aptitude for order and who has brought these assets into the lumbering realm. His name is Frederick Weyerhaeuser.

The camera sees him as a man of thirty-odd, wearing the look of authority that has come to him as a result of his many business successes in the roles of millowner and builder of farms. He climbs into a sleigh to drive deep through the Wisconsin wilderness to visit the timberlands he has bought on the Chippewa River. He travels many hundreds of miles through the pineries and logging camps and then goes home to read the Bible to his children, speaking in a strong German accent and counseling them to be good and simple men.

And now the camera must pick up that fabulous creature, the logger. Armed with his peavey and his enormous gift for quarrelsomeness, this worker comes stomping out of Maine, where he has previously been testing his strength against that of all nature. His ability to withstand cold, endure physical hardship, and drink whisky gave him his resolute character. Its outstanding mental traits are a curious aptitude for making tragedy seem trivial and to transmute trivial passion into something of monumental significance. Death in the woods under the impact of a falling tree is occasion for little comment and no grief. But a slight offered in the bunkhouse or at a bar results in a splendid battle, complete with knifing, kicking, and the gouging out of eyes. The circumstances of the loggers' lives made this reversal of the ordinary values inevitable. There could be no serious relationships for these men who lead a kind of monkish routine with all of the austerities and none of the spiritual comforts of a dedicated way of life. Only after the spring drive when they reached the river towns were the ameliorating influences even of the brothel available to them. In the woods they were obliged to live like boys and be satisfied with boys' entertainments. Since they could not nourish maturity on such limited emotional fare, they became a race of tense, frustrated, neurotic creatures whose behavior was a wild burlesque of boyishness.

Having no other outlet for the creative impulse which the average man expresses in family life, the logger, as the camera now picks up his story, becomes a folk poet. Out of his loneliness, out of his need to believe that physical prowess like his own is one of the attributes of godliness, he creates Paul Bunyan, the super-logger.

Nothing is impossible to Paul. Indeed, all of the features of the north country, which those who have nothing but book learning attribute to the action of the glacier, were actually his handiwork. Needing a reservoir from which to supply himself with good water, Paul Bunyan casually scooped out the bed of Lake Superior. Later, when he was working in distant parts of the forest, he sent his chore boy back to this reservoir. The chore boy appears to have been something of a demigod himself, for he carried mighty buckets on his yoke. These were so heavy that his footing was a little uncertain, and when he stumbled, water often splashed and filled the imprint of his footsteps. So we have the lakes of the border country as we know them today, running east and west across northern Minnesota.

The camera seeks out the figures of the old loggers sitting about the bunkhouse of an evening, each trying to top the story of the last resourceful liar. The bearded faces are earnest and almost severe in the concentrated effort of creation. Each day a new legend is added to the unrecorded wealth of stories about Paul Bunyan's exploits and those of his Great Blue Ox.

The best stories of his prowess, having a Rabelaisian tone, have passed merely by word of mouth, like the raciest verses of the soldier song *Mademoiselle from Armenteers*. But the significant service that Paul Bunyan rendered was not that of scooping out Lake Superior. The work of embellishing his fame offered an outlet for the imaginative processes of hundreds of isolated men. He probably kept the whole race of loggers from going simultaneously mad from boredom.

Dissolve from this fanciful interlude into a glimpse of the organizing genius of the region as it brings order into the chaos of a rapidly growing industry. When the independent lumbermen first began putting their logs into the river, each had his own distinguishing mark cut into the surface. At the mill it was necessary for him to recover his own particular logs and shepherd them through the whole routine of sawing. Frederick Weyerhaeuser suggested a simplification of the process. He organized the Mississippi Logging Company and, through its co-operative effort, a lumberman was able to take out of the water, not the identical logs he had put in, but ones of equivalent grade and value. A second and more important step in organization came after a lively feud with the men of the Chippewa River. The latter undertook to play the role of the tyrants of the region because they were the most active operators. In the spring when the stream was solid with logs, the mills on the Chippewa would hold up the drive while the owners picked out their property. The product that was headed toward the Mississippi would be held up and the work of the mills there was seriously handicapped. Again it was Frederick Weyerhaeuser who organized the Chippewa Logging Company, a gigantic pool that bought all of the logs of the region and distributed them to the mills of both the Chippewa and the Mississippi Rivers. It was in this form that the logging empire survived through the years of its great prosperity, on into the first decades of the present century.

Now the scenario approaches a high point of gusto. Its tempo quickens. The camera eye picks up scenes of lively and contrasted interest. The lumber of Wisconsin and Minnesota builds the barns of the incoming settlers. It builds the cities of the whole Middle Western region: St. Louis, Omaha, Kansas City, Des Moines, Minneapolis, and St. Paul. The Weyerhaeusers move from Wisconsin to Minnesota and build themselves great palaces in St. Paul, not of lumber, oddly enough, but of stone and brick. Other great lumber families establish themselves in Minneapolis—the De Laittres, the Boveys, the Shevlins, the Brooks. Elbert L. Carpenter, having helped to create a fortune out of the wilderness, becomes the chief sponsor of the Minneapolis Symphony Orchestra; Thomas B. Walker, after years of executive attention to log drives, turns to collecting Titians and Tintorettos. The music of the ax biting into the bark of the red pine has been transmuted into a symphony by Brahms, and the colors of the Minnesota forest have been exchanged for those of a Venetian sunset in oil.

Then, swinging away from these scenes of polite urban triumph, the camera picks grim glimpses of the forest fires.

Many times in the last years of the nineteenth century and in the early years of the present one fires have swept across Wisconsin and Minnesota like undeclared wars of nature against mankind. In the midst of the mingled hiss and roar of flames, great stretches of forest have been destroyed. Into this horrible symphony of sound are blended the shrieks of human victims caught before they could escape on foot, by team or train, and turned all in an instant into human torches.

For these disasters nature and man share responsibility. The careless cutting that has left a wasteland behind it, with a haze of dead and dying branches woven over the scene, has invited trouble. Then the sun, concentrating with unconscious but unremitting energy on the slash, has started spontaneous blazes. The greedy red tongues have, in many major disasters, at Peshtigo in Wisconsin and at Hinckley in Minnesota, licked their way through as many as 1,280,000 acres, taking towns and bridges, destroying everything inflammable. With what seems like horrible malignity, the flames have leaped ahead of trains on which the residents of the logging towns have sought escape, melting the paint on the inside of the cars and finally gobbling the metal itself.

After this climax the scenario of the lumber story comes to a pause. The tempo of the score slackens to indicate the slowing down of events themselves. Between the years 1915 and 1920 the lumbering industry in the region slumped first to a half, then to a third, finally to a fifth of what it had been in its peak year. The camera eye picks up glimpses of the mills closing one by one. It swings to a view of machinery being packed up and moved to the west coast. The roistering men move across Minnesota and on out to the place where the trees still stand tall and challenging. The shadow of Paul Bunyan lies for a moment across all of Wisconsin and Minnesota, raising his hand in a gesture of farewell before he lays an arm around the shoulders of the Blue Ox and strides away. On the west coast, they are now sure that Paul Bunyan never really came into his lordly own until he reached there.

Having achieved this anticlimax in the course of its story, the scenario might be expected to call for one last look at the wasted forests, the acres of stumps, and the ghost towns and then by way of finale to dissolve into nothing but tears.

The story of the logging industry is rather often told in exactly that way. The final fade-out comes with the suggestion that the rape of the forests has left nothing that is useful or beautiful. It is a closed incident of history, crowned with irony. When the Conservation Department wished to erect an impressive building on the Minnesota State Fair Grounds, it was necessary to import logs all the way from the state of Washington.

But reality is seldom as melodramatic or as final as that. There is perhaps a certain satisfaction to be gained by declaiming: "All is over." But the average industry, like the average man, finds the prostrate position one that it is impossible to maintain for a very long time. After the passing of its great days the lumber industry pulled itself together and began to make estimates of its remaining resources.

Wood is still the great essential raw material, the universal substitute for which no substitute has yet been found. In the midst of the war's effort to prop up a sagging civilization and to keep it from collapsing about our ears, forest products are more than ever necessary. The strange poetic insight of science has discovered the most amazingly diverse potentialities in wood. Having given man a roof over his head and heat for his hearth, this most adaptable of plant products stands ready to transform itself into clothing for man's body and even into food for his stomach. One chemical miracle topping another, timber becomes pulpwood, pulpwood becomes cellulose, cellulose becomes cellophane, rayon, wood cotton, and wood wool. Lignin, for long a waste byproduct in chemical utilization, lately has shown that it, too, has its points of usefulness as a basis for the production of plastic materials. Wood distillation produces methyl alcohol, acetic acid, charcoal. Nor has the last magic word been spoken. The beautiful and reliable abracadabra of the laboratory is able, by wood hydrolysis, to produce ethyl alcohol, yeast, lactic acid, crystalline glucose, and xylose valuable for the production of fodder and human food.

Both potentially and actually the forest lands of Wisconsin and Minnesota are still of enormous importance. Those who devote their talents to long sessions of keening over the fatal recklessness of the dead past serve the heat of drama better than they do the reality of cold statistical fact. Nearly one half of the total land area of Wisconsin and more than a third of the land area of Minnesota are covered today with a timber crop. It is true, of course, that the wealth of this raw material is only a small fraction of what it was a century ago. But the riches of wood are understood so much better than they were in the days of the rampaging pioneers that this crop is worth more in the market of our time than the original crop was in the market of its period. The world has passed from a pine economy into an economy that has taught itself to utilize fully the resources of those humble plants which the early loggers scorned as "weed trees." As society gobbled up the original forests, its metabolism seemed to function in a way that was gross and wasteful. Having made a science of diet, society today has trained its digestive processes to work much more meticulously. It obtains more nourishment from a less richly laden board. In fact, society now thoughtfully masticates the resources, board and all.

Highly dramatic was an episode of a quarter of a century ago that indicates how the sons of the pioneers have transformed the energy of their forebears into a more sober and reliable asset to the community. In 1918 one more forest fire brushed its malign brilliance across a still profitable center of the lumber industry. The town of Cloquet lived by the work that the Weyerhaeuser sawmill created for its men to do. A considerable wealth of timber remained in that region, and it was being utilized in the old traditional way. All at once that wealth disappeared in flame, and Cloquet, frightened, burned out, suffering from physical injury and tragedy, faced the further threat of becoming another ghost town, its occupation gone.

In the really rugged days of the frontier it was always the impulse and usually the practice of the pioneer, when he faced such a calamity, to shrug his shoulders and move on. But the new generation was of a very different temper. It felt an immediate and inescapable sense of responsibility toward the community. And not responsibility merely; the sons of the pioneers felt also a close identification with the place. Their own *amour propre* was involved in the fate of their towns. The love-the-land-and-leave-it technique was no longer acceptable to the social morality of the day.

So it happened that Rudolph Weyerhaeuser, and other men like him in other places, set about finding a substitute for the industry that was swept away by fire. With the help of their scientific experts they discovered a new occupation in harvesting the weed trees and transforming them into pulpwood, into insulating materials, into products of great and immediate commercial usefulness. Instead of being forced to draw a rusty veil of ruin over its history and disappear from the map, Cloquet became a busier, brighter, better-scrubbed-looking town than it had ever been before.

The situation of the forest lands of Wisconsin and Minnesota is one that the informed and realistic critic of social life regards with optimism. No longer would a man of furious and unappeasable appetite be tempted to rub his hands with anticipatory glee in facing the prospect of getting out these resources. The "come and get it" psychology that Edna Ferber dramatized in her novel of the lumber industry in Wisconsin will lure the greedy into other games of exploitation. But sober men know that the forests of the region still contain wealth which society must have, and they are going steadily and conscientiously about the business of getting out the timber.

The look of the forest lands is very different in different corners of Wisconsin and Minnesota. In some parts of the wilderness world which were inaccessible to the pioneers in their great hurry to cut and be gone there are small stands of virgin pine, dark and lovely souvenirs of the primeval world. The condition of second-growth timber on the cut-over lands shows patches of great vitality where there are excellent stands of pine, spruce, and hardwood; larger stretches given over to the low, twisted growths of jack pine and scrub oak; smaller areas where nature is just beginning once more to cover herself decently. In the Superior National

Forest and in many a privately owned tract reforestation projects have been begun. Great stretches of land are devoted to the careful nurturing of tiny green shoots. The delicacy of their infant coloring suggests that these are gigantic truck farms rather than the patient beginnings of a forest for the use of the generation after next. But out of a sense of social responsibility that is widespread and thoroughly vigorous a beginning has been made.

What is necessary now is to urge upon a whole people the realization that timber is a crop. In the consciousness of disciplined social planners today, the forest exists, not to give a minor versifier an excuse for writing a bad poem, but rather to be of use. It must be cut in such a way that more is left for tomorrow than is taken out to serve the needs of today. In the midst of the present war, which makes heavy demands to satisfy a thousand needs, experts are more than ever conscious of the necessity of keeping ultimate goals in view. A civilization worthy to shelter the perpetual peace which Mortimer Adler promises us for the world of five hundred years from now must not be shabbily bereft of trees. Consequently society must hold back the hand which would seize the three- or four-foot jack pine even though its infant growth can be made immediately useful. Systems of selective cutting, such as the canny Finns and Swedes have long required workers in their forests to follow, must become our own rule. Nor is the modern man willing to see the beauty of forest land destroyed by indiscriminate slashing. The whole program must conform to reasonable regulation governing the rights of the future.

What is encouraging is the fact that everyone nowadays subscribes to these general views. One discerns in all the talk and all the writing of professional lumbermen a wistful undercurrent of propitiation. If the pioneers were arrogant, their sons are not. To be sure, the younger men enter slightly aggrieved defenses of their forebears in the industry. They like to remind a new generation that its ancestors acted under a strong compulsion to get a whole new world and a whole new commercial plant created in the wilderness. But in every word that they write or speak one senses the polite discreet affirmation that they are different from the old boys. Ours, they admit, is a new world, one which is preoccupied with long-range rather than with short-range problems in creating a habitable civilization. So they have become leading exponents of the theory that timber is a crop.

The economic importance of wood industries in Wisconsin and Minnesota is great. Even in a survey that is more concerned with describing attitudes than with cataloguing facts it is impossible to avoid statistics altogether. (Such facts and figures strike the average mind about as cheeringly as hailstones strike the head, but no one should expect to lead a wholly sheltered life!) In recent years Wisconsin and Minnesota have paid annually to some 70,000 workers in the lumber industry $100,000,000 in salaries and wages. Wheels have turned in thousands of plants to manufacture products worth $300,000,000. Nearly twenty-two per cent of the entire population of Wisconsin has, in normal periods, been engaged in various occupations having to do with harvesting the lumber crop.

Wisconsin makes from its forests agricultural implements, boxes, butchers' blocks, railroad cars, conduits, wood pipes, chicken houses, fixtures, flooring, furniture, handles, musical instruments, scientific instruments, ladders, machinery, matches, refrigerators, sash doors, millwork, ships and boats, signs and scenery, sporting goods, tanks, toys, trunks, vehicles, Venetian blinds, woodwear, and novelties. Minnesota makes most of these things and, having a few ideas of its own, adds to the list laundry appliances, tobacco pipes, playground equipment, printing materials, and radio cabinets.

The activities of workers in the lumber industries touch our lives at so many points that a man cannot strike a match to light up his pipe and read the evening paper without owing a threefold debt to their energy. It can hardly be said, therefore, that the story of lumbering is one to be told in either the aggrieved undertone of lament or the piercing scream of righteous indignation.

Workers in the woods today are modern men living in the modern world. They no longer constitute a kind of rough priesthood dwelling apart from women and worshipping their own forest gods with ironic reverence. In a dwindling world the dimensions of the wilderness also have shrunk so that a man can escape from isolation in better time than the giant strides of Paul Bunyan could manage. The lumberjack of our time, when he becomes fed up with monastic seclusion, takes the aquaplane to town and is in the midst of his family circle or the urban world of entertainment within twenty minutes. In the present-day version of the lumber camp the worker lives, not soft, but very well. The "wanagan," a sort of floating dormitory and dining-room of a crew at work in the woods, is likely to present souvenirs of luxury such as are to be found in few de luxe hotels. Science has discovered the close connection between a well-balanced diet and the ability to produce work, and superintendents of logging operations, bowing to the authority of science, feed the men who wield axes in a way to make the mouths of sybarites water. Though point-rationing has made steaks valuable above rubies, they are always available to lumberjacks. In a time when ordinary civilians are being invited to tighten their belts and to ask for few luxuries, the woodsmen sit down to four Gargantuan meals each day. These workers who were once society's hardest-driven children have become the pets of a sensible civilization.

Wisconsin and Minnesota have come fully awake to their responsibility for the preservation of the forest and to the wealth that the timber crop still represents. If in the early days of our history there was a reckless indulgence of waste, and if wisdom has come tardily, at least recognition of past mistakes has sharpened "the edge of husbandry."

HUNGRY GULLS IN THE WAKE PICK UP SCRAPS

FISHING THROUGH THE ICE

DE-NETTING THE CATCH ABOARD A FISHING TUG

9

FISHERMAN'S LUCK

THE MACKENZIE FAMILY lives at Grand Marais on the shore of Lake Superior. The men are in partnership, and they fish for a living. The group is made up of Alec, the elder of two brothers; Jack, the younger; and Alec's son, Malcolm. They are all big men with huge red hands. They wear red-and-black-checkered shirts, khaki trousers tucked into high rubber boots, and, of course, the shapeless fedoras that complete the costumes of fishermen everywhere, in every right-thinking society.

Alec MacKenzie is a handsome man in his late fifties. When, with his brother and his son, he poses for his picture at the end of a day's fishing, he offers the routine warning that this will "surer'n hell break the camera." But the pleasantry is intended merely to keep the conversation going. After many years of shaving the weatherbeaten convolutions of his face at somewhat irregular intervals, Alec has almost certainly forgotten to notice what his features have become. The casual observer is able to see that beneath the leathery toughness of his skin Alec still possesses the firm, finely carved skeletal structure of a good Scotch face. The expression which, along with the stubble of beard, masks the aristocratic severity of outline is at once thoughtful, humorous, and reticent. Alec, one is sure, knows many jokes, of which the deeper ones he keeps to himself.

Malcolm is just such a muscular young man as Hollywood would look for if it wanted to do a picture having as its background the deep-sea fishing industry of Lake Superior. But Hollywood wouldn't find a man quite like Malcolm. The gift of casualness and candor that makes the youngest of the MacKenzies so immediately likable is seldom given to the nervous, hopeful, propitiatory young actor. Malcolm possesses real dignity because there is no one in the world whom he needs to propitiate.

Jack isn't handsome. He would have to be the character man in the imaginary film about fishing on Lake Superior . . . Spencer Tracy, without a comic accent.

The family sets out from Grand Marais just after sunrise in the sturdy boat that they built themselves. It is called the *Nee Gee*, a Chippewa (the MacKenzies pronounce it "Chippeway") word meaning "friend." The name fits well, for the wide contours of the thirty-five-foot vessel take the choppy waves of the great lake as comfortably as the broadening stern of a middle-aged housewife takes the movement of her rocking-chair.

Thirty-five feet is the maximum length permitted by law for commercial fishing boats on Superior. The MacKenzie family operates on as large a scale as any group on the lake. They are the best of their kind and somehow one knows they know it in those secret places of the mind where a decent man files his self-esteem.

The marine motor starts its loud, garrulous monologue and the *Nee Gee* puts off from the dock into the pearl-gray morning across the slate-gray sea. The neat-looking little town of Grand Marais recedes, the saw-tooth hills that rise behind it shrink until all the scene disappears into the line of the horizon, and the *Nee Gee* is surrounded by the illimitable look of the water under the immensity of the pale blue sky.

The sea-gulls follow, swinging beautifully about and about. The lovely scavengers are drawn by the expectation of plenty-to-come when the nets are drawn up and the fish too small to keep are thrown back into the water. Then they will dive en masse, and the winner of the race will scoop the fish into its big beak and take the meal at a gulp.

But there is nothing for them now, and the birds, who should be experienced enough to know that it is too soon, none the less seem displeased. They swoop near, making their raucous cries of protest petulantly audible above the noise of the motor. They rise from the water, fly strenuously, coast, brake themselves with their strong wings, dive, settle, and rise again, all in some pointless response to an urging of nature that has no way of adjusting itself to the stereotyped pattern of man's planning.

The gray-blue birds in this gray-blue world are like animated bits of water and sky. They break up the monotony of its design without changing its essential featurelessness.

The net toward which the *Nee Gee* is making its way is eighteen to twenty miles off mainland, lying north by south on the floor of the lake, four hundred feet below the surface. Sunk into place by lead weights and kept upright by plastic floats, it stretches like a tennis net some four miles long through the fish's submarine world. It is called a gill net because the gills of the trout or siscowet become entangled in its four-inch mesh and no struggle can be artful enough to free a fish once he is caught.

It takes two hours for the *Nee Gee* to reach the fishing ground, but the MacKenzie family, with the aid of the compass, has reduced this immensity of water to something as intimately familiar as the kitchen at home. The boat travels directly to the floating buoy to which the lines of the net are attached; the motor stops; the anchor is dropped; and the important operations of the day's work begin.

The MacKenzies have worked together so long that they move through the three separate phases of the job of pulling in the catch with the precisely timed harmony of men in a symphony orchestra. When they work together, one has the curious impression of listening to a composition the sound of which is too high for the ear to hear. It is, perhaps, impossible to communicate the persistence of this notion unless you can imagine seeing an orchestra through the window of a soundproof room.

The closeness of the co-operation leads to another curious impression. The work of landing the catch is hard, and the MacKenzies have evidently found it relaxing to change tasks from time to time. As they work on through the long hours, one has still the fanciful idea of looking at an orchestra. Occasionally without a word spoken or a sign made, the violinist will put down his instrument and take up that of the tuba-player; the tuba-player will silently slip over into the cello section; the cellist will take up the violin; and the composition goes on uninterrupted.

Standing beside the hatch of the boat ("window" would be the landlubber's word for it) is a mechanism called the Crosley Lifter. It consists of a motor-driven winch to which the lines of the net are attached for raising. From this revolving machine a metal trough extends out over the side of the boat. Down through the center of the boat another trough of wood stretches its six-foot length.

The three operations are these:

Jack stands at the hatch, guiding the net into the metal trough and gaffing the larger fish as their weight drags at the mesh. To "gaff" is simply to use a barbed spear to land the trout.

Malcolm stands at the wooden trough, disengaging the net from the winch and pushing it along where he can handle the fish conveniently and disentangle the gills. This is a delicate and intricate job involving a violinist's deftness of fingering, particularly when four or five fish lie in the trough at once. Some of them are still alive, flapping wildly in one last instinctive effort to escape. Malcolm picks up a stick with a nail driven through the end. He stuns the fish with a tap on the head and ends its flapping with a blow of the nail through the body.

Alec sits at the end of the trough, drawing the net toward him, freeing it of tangles, and dropping it neatly into the boxes that will hold it until the lines are put out again.

The fish begin to slide into the trough—the trout with their delicately beautiful patterns of green; the fat siscowet, full of meat and oil, looking colorless and plebeian by comparison. There is, of course, a great class distinction in the market. The trout will bring some thirty-three cents a pound, the siscowet only eighteen. Both vary in size from a few pounds to as much as twenty-five pounds. They pour into the trough at the irregular intervals of chance, several at a time, so that Malcolm's fingers do a cadenza dancing from one to another. Then for a stretch of several feet nothing at all, or only small ones which Malcolm tosses back onto the lifter for Jack to toss at his convenience through the hatch. Whenever Jack lifts his arm for one of these tosses, the gulls come swooping, crying, diving, fighting for possession of the prize.

After an hour it is Malcolm at the hatch with the gaff in hand, Alec at the trough disentangling the gills of the trout, Jack folding the nets in the heavy boxes. Sixteen of these are filled, in the end, with the net trailing across the deck from box to box.

It has been a reasonably good catch today, and the MacKenzies are satisfied, though if they were not you would never know it from their poised and reserved faces. Some seven hundred pounds of fish have been tossed into the wooden boxes under the trough. When they have been cleaned they will still weigh six hundred pounds and will bring perhaps $150 in the market. It is a good year for the commercial fisherman. Rationing of meat in wartime has sent the price of fish soaring, and the fishermen are strongly enough organized to make sure that they get their share of the gain.

Not a bad day's work!—though it is only half done. The Mac-Kenzies stretch and rub their big red hands. One knows now why they are red. The water of Superior never gets above forty degrees, or forty-five at the most, even in summer. The ropes of the net are icy to the touch on this July day, and the fish are icy, too.

The break comes for lunch at last. It is already past one o'clock. The visiting fishermen have brought a bottle of bourbon on board and it is passed around from hand to hand. This, for the MacKenzies, is an unusual but pleasant indulgence. Jack takes the bottle and tosses back his head with relish. The city men are laughing over their favorite jokes. The only trouble with a fishing trip, they say, is that there is always some fool who wants to fish. Another says: "I have a principle; I never drink until five o'clock. But, after all, it's five o'clock in Burma—or somewhere." And he tosses back his head. Alec takes the bottle with a smile seeming to creep slowly through all the convolutions of his leathery face. He doesn't have to wait until it's five o'clock in Burma, because he seldom drinks at any time, and this is done just for conviviality. It is Malcolm's turn, but he declines with his slightly aloof, yet genial smile. There's beer, if you prefer it, one of the city men says. They have tied several bottles to a rope that trails through the icy water and the beer has been nicely chilled. Malcolm decides that he will have a bottle of beer. His father looks at him with good-natured raillery. "It's good your wife can't see you with that bottle in your hands." But even with his father Malcolm is a little secretive and very much his own man. He smiles, finishes off the beer, and almost immediately opens a pint of milk.

The break has been short, but already the day is half gone and there is much more to do before the twelve-hour routine will have been completed. First the nets must be put out again. Alec takes the wheel; Malcolm stands high on the seat at the wide rear hatch, while Jack stands feeding the net to him out of the boxes. It must be released a little at a time so that the weights will fall at regular intervals and the net stand as neatly as it should on the floor of the lake.

Malcolm tosses out the net with the fluent motion of complete control. There is grace in the swing of his arms, just as there may be grace in the movements of a blacksmith swinging his hammer on the anvil or in the movements of an athlete throwing the discus. One thinks of the pages of *Death in the Afternoon* in which Ernest Hemingway analyzes the patterns of bull-fighting as though they were traditional ballet maneuvers, and one realizes that every physical skill has its prescribed rules, its unalterable code of procedure, out of which a perfection of movement may be produced.

Standing there, quite unconscious of the fact that he is doing anything worthy of admiration, Malcolm would make a fine model for a sculptor.

Laying the net takes two hours. One after another the sixteen heavy boxes are pulled up by the landlubbers. "How ever do these fellows get on without us?" they exclaim in the pride of having worked up an honest sweat. There are some humorous, abusive interchanges between the MacKenzies and the city men. "Jack, you're getting pretty haughty with the help," one of the landlubbers says. "You can't do this to me. I'm quitting you flat—at the end of the day."

Malcolm has no time to enter into these pleasantries. He is doing a tough job. When the net, now and again, threatens to become entangled, he must grasp it in his bare hands and hold it firm while his father reverses the motor and gives him time to release the snarl.

At last it is all out. The boxes are stowed away in corners of the deck. Malcolm takes the wheel. His father becomes host to the landlubbers and during this first moment of leisure answers landlubberly questions. Jack still has an important job to do. The fish must be cleaned for market before the *Nee Gee* puts in at the dock.

He pulls a big tin can into the center of the deck and over it lays a board with a square hole in the center. This serves him as a table for cleaning the fish. Through the hole into the can go the head and the entrails.

Jack sharpens his long knife and throws a fat siscowet onto the table. Here again is a flashingly brilliant technique. Any operation that is performed as well as possible is fine to watch. Surgeons in executive session are likely to grow lyrical over the charms of the tumor neatly exposed, deftly extricated. The layman winces, thinking of the flesh that lies so sweetly on his own bones. But when the patient is a fish and the surgeon a man as sure of himself as Jack, the sensitive think shame to themselves and acquire robustness.

There is nothing ragged about Jack's attack. One slash and the trout's head has been cut halfway through, the entrails have been removed, and the body has been left looking as cool and inviting as it will look in the butcher's refrigerator. The plebeian siscowet loses its head entirely. "One, two, one, two, and through and through the vorpal blade went snicker-snack." There is nothing distasteful in the operation at all. Even sportsmen will sometimes say that they like to catch fish, but that they draw the line at cleaning them. They need a postgraduate course with Jack on Lake Superior.

There is one last scene to be enacted. The entrails must be disposed of. There is no difficulty, for the garbage-disposal crew, sensing that the time has come, has gathered in formidable numbers. To please the landlubbers, who must, of course, have pictures (this is the inevitable amateur touch of all their kind), heads and livers are at first tossed overboard in handfuls. The gulls swoop down with a great crying and flourishing of wings. They descend to their banquet like creatures involved in some small purgatorial drama. Then the whole supply of entrails is dumped over and the *Nee Gee* leaves the gulls behind to their orgy.

The drama of fishing in the Great Lakes varies rather widely from state to state because of the curious dissimilarity of laws governing the commercial operations. In Wisconsin, for example, the pound net is legal; in Minnesota it is regarded as highly mischievous. The pound net is one in which the fish are persuaded to trap themselves in a net enclosure from which they cannot find the way out. In some regions it has been legal to use nets with mesh so fine that immature fish have been caught and by this kind of overfishing the waters have been robbed of their abundance.

Experts believe that what is needed to advance commercial fishing is a uniformity of state laws, which will do more than artificial propagation to make the enterprise a profitable one.

But men like the MacKenzies of Grand Marais have already done much on their own behalf. During the depression they organized a co-operative trucking system which took their catch to market quickly and safeguarded it against spoiling. Today more thousands of men and more thousands of boats are engaged in commercial fishing than in any recent years. The MacKenzies of Grand Marais have justified their faith in their occupation by pulling in catches which, at their best, have brought as much as $400 for a day's work.

In the world of fishermen conditions have not changed greatly from pre-Christian times when men put down their nets and pulled them up, without the aid of machinery to be sure, yet with precisely the same essential results. But if they live outside the world of dramatic change, they have found a setting that confirms them, if the MacKenzies of Grand Marais may be taken as typical, in their self-sufficiency, their human dignity, and their knowledge that many of the things for which men strive so mightily are necessary neither to comfort nor to self-esteem. The fisherman's luck lies not merely in the catch that he pulls in from his nets, but also in the quiet satisfaction that he derives from functioning so efficiently, so directly, and so simply.

HEARING FROM THE PEOPLE

ONCE AT A PUBLIC MEETING in Minneapolis the late James Manahan, then a member of the House of Representatives at Washington, rose to speak, following addresses by a bishop and a newspaper editor. He smiled at his audience with the genial Irish candor that had made even the most rigid of men forgive him for being a reformer and began: "Tonight you have heard from the pulpit and you have heard from the press. Now I think it appropriate that you should hear from the people."

Manahan had a mind as brilliant as his red hair, and there was nothing either naïve or humble about this suggestion that he spoke for the common man. It was an idea that he and the men like him have been determined to keep before the public of their region. Quietly but resolutely these men have said: "Let there never be an assemblage so austere, so erudite, so intimidating that the people cannot penetrate into it and make their voices heard. Let there never be a ring of influence so stoutly forged that the people cannot break it if they begin to believe that it shackles their interests and their growth."

The Jim Manahans, the George Loftuses, the Robert La Follettes, the Floyd Olsons, the Magnus Johnsons have clung tenaciously to this faith in the right of the common man to be heard. The tradition has had some results which, not infrequently, have made the East shudder at the rudeness of Wisconsin and Minnesota. When Magnus Johnson rose from his milk stool to go straight into the Senate as representative of Minnesota, there was a great arching of eyebrows among the hostesses of Washington. Our capital, despite its strenuous busyness and its glitter of worldliness, remains in many ways a huge village, and snobbery is its great parochial pastime. The man who looks with the blank misgiving of panic at the doily that he finds on the dessert plate after the finger bowl has been removed is likely to be regarded as an interloper. Though there may be many cogent reasons why the people at home have sent him to safeguard their interests, his ineptitude with teacups is regarded as sufficient reason for ostracism, if not for unseating. The professional politician, the career man of Congress, is likely to forget that what Wisconsin or Minnesota wants, and what it has a perfect right to have, is a representative whose best suit smells of the dairy.

It is just as well for their sensibilities that the glossier legislators never knew the whole truth about Magnus Johnson's rugged manners. When he had just been elected to the Senate, reporters from all over the state crowded into his farmhouse to interview him. They arrived just at dinnertime and the Senator-elect invited them to sit down with him. In the kitchen Mrs. Johnson stood over the stove preparing the meal, and after she had served the others she moved tentatively toward the crowded table with her own plate in her hands. Magnus Johnson saw that among so many hungry men a crisis of hospitality might occur if there were no one to keep an eye on empty plates. He waved his wife away, murmuring: "No, Mamma, you eat later." The episode shocked even the normally unfinicking reporters so that they all recorded it in their stories. In many a Minnesota drawing-room elderly ladies murmured unhappily: "And Mrs. Johnson a direct descendant of General Israel Putnam, too!"

But it all made nonsense to the men and women of Minnesota. Magnus Johnson was an effective and useful man who had helped to organize co-operative dairies. He knew what he was about, and his constituents knew that they could trust him.

The thing that has always baffled the East about Wisconsin and Minnesota is that its people seem never to follow a formula in dealing with political problems or in choosing political leaders. Just before Magnus Johnson entered the Senate, Minnesota had been represented by a man as completely unlike him as a man could be. Frank Billings Kellogg was a man of the great world who had belonged to a distinguished legal firm before he entered the Senate, and who after he left it proceeded through a brilliant succession of assignments as Ambassador to the Court of St. James's, as Secretary of State, as judge of the Permanent Court of International Justice and winner of the Nobel Prize for service to peace. No embodiment of the idea of conscript father could have been more satisfactory even to the most exacting writer of fiction than this urbane, cultivated, widely experienced man. But between the image of Senator Kellogg and that of Senator Johnson what a giddy and, from the standpoint of Washington, what a hilarious contrast!

The incongruity between the ideas of leadership as represented by these two men must be related to the rugged appetite for contrast that has always existed in our region. The people do not feel bound by the rigidities of tradition which make men of other communities declare, with a zealot's fervor, that this is a year in which they could elect a yellow dog if he were to run as a Republican, or that they would vote for the devil himself if he filed as a Democrat.

This is not a mere idle boast tossed off by a sort of a nonconformist Pharisee, dwelling fatuously on the thought that he is not as other men. The political history of Wisconsin and Minnesota has been that of persistent, though never violent or sanguinary, revolt against fixed formulas. We have had Republicans who have done themselves calmly over into Democrats without experiencing any pangs of spiritual doubt. We have had Democrats who have joined one fusion group after another without feeling that they had sinned against the Holy Ghost. When there has seemed to be no other cure for the ills of the moment, there has always been the remedy of the third party. The winds of the third-party movement seem always to rise in the Mississippi Valley and usually they do not blow very far beyond it.

Indeed, it might be said that the development of a technique of mild rebellion is the contribution of our region to the history of political thought in America.

The third-party movements have been rather like foundling

children, picked up and deserted again by their sponsors without much ceremony. But each one in turn has exercised an enormous educative influence. Whenever the urban groups have managed to unite in the best interests of the railroads and the elevators and have felt that they had the political machinery well under control, those mild but persistent rebels, the farmers, have broken out of the mold. If neither old-line party seemed quite to represent them, they could always start a third.

This comedy of the elusive electorate has gone on almost since the beginning of the history of Wisconsin and Minnesota as states, and it persists today. The farmers of the region made their first resolute stand when, after the Civil War, they were required to retrench to the extent of accepting fifty cents a bushel for their wheat while the mere dealers in grain were permitted to expand to the point of selling it for eighty-five cents a bushel. Farmers accused the railroads of having extremely whimsical ideas about freight rates, nice and small for the big shippers, awesomely big for the small shippers. Favored towns were charged less for carrying freight a certain distance than Cinderella communities were charged for carrying it the same distance. The great elevators were regarded as tyrants, too, grading wheat down when it was brought in by the farmer, and grading it up again sharply when the dealer sold it. As one of the wits has said, the grain-elevator operators seemed to understand the art of growing grade-A wheat on the tops of their mahogany desks.

The farmer smarted under other injustices. As a capitalist he was obliged to borrow money at high interest rates to buy new machinery and keep up his plant. But when it came his turn to make a profit in a good season, the bottom always seemed to drop out of the market. The farmer was, in fact, the little brother of the capitalists. He was pushed about quite unceremoniously in that family of rugged boys.

Out of these conditions sprang the "agrarian crusade," which has had its excursions and alarums down into the very heart of our own time. It was the agrarian crusade that made the La Follettes of Wisconsin act in a way that no orderly Republican of Maine or Vermont could understand.

It was the agrarian movement that sent Magnus Johnson to

Washington; that organized the co-operatives; that launched the Farmer-Labor Party.

It is the agrarian crusade that cuts through all other affiliations, loyalties, and prejudices to give to politics in Wisconsin and Minnesota its unexpected turns, its vivid dramatic tournaments, its knights in overalls. Politics in our region has always been like a great fair, complete with impressive exhibits, merry-go-rounds, serious discussions, hot-dog stands, intelligent planning, freak shows, noise, dust, cries, and cheers.

Many brilliant men have plunged through this dusty arena. The minds of some have been distinguished; the minds of others merely glittering and full of ingenuity.

Ignatius Donnelly of Minnesota had what was surely a brilliant and facile mind. He was a plump and earnest fellow, full of eloquence, beer, conviviality, idealism, and passion for reform. But he must not be belittled. Indeed, if his life is to be measured by its strenuosity, variability, and noticeability, it was a huge success. He was elected Lieutenant Governor of Minnesota when he was twenty-eight years old. He served several terms in Congress, and lived out his life in what amounted to permanent tenure of a seat in the legislature. He wrote books which went through many editions, and when one of them appeared under what was obviously a pseudonym, the literary folk of the time buzzed with speculation as to whether the work was actually that of Mark Twain or Robert Ingersoll. The intellectuals of his time praised his novel *Cæsar's Column*. He was the author of many different kinds of books, including an awesome if perverse and bemused work of scholarship called *The Great Cryptogram*, in which he proved to his own satisfaction that Bacon wrote the plays attributed to Shakespeare.

Besides all this he practiced law, had grandiloquent ideas as a real-estate operator about making his town of Nininger blossom like a rose, married twice, and reared a family. All of his projects brought him attention, but they did not always bring him praise. His love of reform met often with rebuffs. Yet he stands well in the foreground of the tradition of providing a platform for the people, and all that he did was honorably done.

He was an interested observer of the very first scene of the agrarian crusade. Its chief actor was Oliver H. Kelley, a Minnesota pioneer, who organized the Patrons of Husbandry, or, as the movement came less grandly to be called, the National Grange. The purpose of the societies fathered by Kelley was chiefly educational. They were secret, and in their executive sessions they planned campaigns that looked toward the reform of freight rates and fares. At the height of the history of the Grange there were branches in twenty thousand towns of the nation.

Donnelly plunged into the midst of the movement, functioning as the most eloquent and voluble of its sponsors and the most persistent of its candidates. He survived many changes of formal organization within the crusade, as the Grange evolved into the Anti-Monopoly Party, the Anti-Monopoly Party merged in a moment of lassitude with the Greenbackers, the Greenbackers joined the Farmers' Alliance, and the Farmers' Alliance organized its own party, the People's or Populist Party.

It had been Ignatius Donnelly's idea from the first that an educational society was largely useless unless it sought political influence. As he tartly expressed it, a reform movement that possesses everything but political power is as foolish as a gun that can do everything but shoot.

Through one unsuccessful campaign after another he hurled his huge bulk tirelessly, never even remotely approaching the presidency, which he sought as a Populist candidate. Donnelly was accused by his loyal followers of digging graves for reform movements with his tongue. But he served a useful purpose as a leader of the elusive electorate that declined to be corralled into orthodox patterns. The votes of the rebels had a nuisance value which Republicans like Knute Nelson recognized. As Governor, Nelson took up the cause of reform. When the railroad men tried to prevent the farmers from building elevators on their lines, Governor Nelson said: "It is not for the railroad companies to say who ought, or ought not, to have a warehouse and side track facilities. . . . All discrimination should be eliminated." The people had been heard, partly because Donnelly had so long and so patiently coached their protests.

Even today Donnelly's books do not seem like literary oddities, fit only to be explored as museum pieces of baroque prose, like the fantastic novels of another politician, Disraeli. Donnelly's books are full of the fervor and pugnacity of a man of conviction. *Cæsar's Column* dramatized the essence of Donnelly's political philosophy, warning of the critical need to protect democracy against monopoly and special interest. *Dr. Huguet*, another highly imaginative blending of fantasy and propaganda, confronts a reader with the tragic and revealing miracle of a sensitive and cultivated man's mind being forced into the brutalized and suffering body of a Negro. Though racial equality is the theme of *Dr. Huguet*, the book rhymes on other preoccupations of Donnelly's political life. "The curse of our land is party slavery," he wrote. "God have mercy on the man who permits another to do his thinking." Donnelly's epitaph must be: "He helped the people to be heard."

Similar in temperament was Wisconsin's Robert Marion La Follette, who for nearly half a century kept politicians in a state of ruffled apprehension by his refusal to stay pigeonholed. At the time of the elder La Follette's death editorial opinion in Republican papers permitted itself a last sigh of irritation and relief. The Senator had been a man of courage, integrity, perseverance, and vitality. But he was not orthodox. Heterodoxy in the mouth of so obviously honest a man is disturbing to those who pride themselves on their political "regularity." It is difficult to brush off the heresy without seeming to reject the honesty.

The temperament of the elder La Follette baffled many of his contemporaries, but in retrospect it seems to have been quite simple. In his own state he undertook to provide the means by which government could hear from the people.

There was great need for someone to perform precisely that service when in 1880 La Follette first began running for office. Wisconsin was smugly and discreetly stowed away in the pocket of boss rule. The political machines named their candidates without any upstart nonsense from the people; there were at the time no primary elections. United States senators were named by the legislature, so that the element of popular choice was reduced to a comfortable minimum which could be controlled by the judicious use of bribery and patronage.

Into this curiously undemocratic arena strode a small, slight, but very resolute young man. The political lions were cheerfully confident of their ability to make a martyr of him in record time. But forty-five years later the lions had all been killed, tamed, or driven back into the jungle and Robert M. La Follette had tidied up the arena into a livable and secure place for the people.

Like all the progressives of this type, he was earnest and eloquent. He was also an actor *manqué*. The first noticeable thing that La Follette did in his life was to represent the University of Wisconsin in an interstate oratorical contest held at Iowa City, where he won the chief prize with an original essay on the character of Iago. There was something prophetic about that early triumph, for he was to spend his life identifying Iagos, unmasking their treacheries, and denouncing them with spirit and conviction.

Early pictures show him as the perfect type of young idealist. The deep-set eyes looked out challengingly upon a world whose deepest mischief the young La Follette seemed determined to penetrate. The well-shaped head was crowned with an abundance of hair, excellent for tossing in crises of eloquence. The well-chiseled features declared the resolution of a man who would make no compromise with his principles. In legislation, La Follette once wrote, no bread is often better than half a loaf. He justified the belief by clinging fanatically to the abstract ideal, suffering whatever was necessary in the way of humiliation and hunger until he could get the whole loaf.

The men who had claimed for themselves the privilege of running Wisconsin did not in the least want this upstart about. "Don't you know," one of them said to him at the beginning of his career, "that no congressman has been nominated for fifteen years who hasn't had our support? Why haven't you consulted me?" La Follette replied that he had been out in the country consulting the people and that he was planning to consult a great many more.

He did it in a very direct and simple manner. Driving in a buggy from farm to farm, he talked things over with the men whom he wished to represent. Despite the bosses, these men began to elect him to office—District Attorney of Dane County first, then Congressman when he had just turned twenty-nine, then Governor at thirty-five, and finally United States Senator.

There were a great many things that he meant to do for Wisconsin when he managed to get into office. He wanted to give

1

2

3

4

THEY LIT THE FIRES OF REFORM

1. *Victor Berger*   2. *Floyd B. Olson*
3. *Ignatius Donnelly*   4. *Robert M. La Follette, Sr.*

more authority to the voice of the people by putting through primary-election laws. He wanted to force the railroads to pay a more just proportion of the expense of government; he wanted to put an end to discrimination in rates and the objectionable system of rebates. He meant to correct abuses like that of allowing men with expansive ideas to farm out public funds to favored banks. He was deeply conscious of the debasing effect on public life of the spoils system of patronage, and he hoped to supplant it with a solid civil-service administration. In the early years of the century he advocated ideas, then new in America, about adjusting the burden of taxation by passing inheritance and graduated income-tax laws. All of these things he accomplished.

He accomplished them in the midst of an atmosphere of hostility and contempt. The cynical men who waited with cool, appraising gaze for every man in public to name the price at which he would begin to bargain were first incredulous and then outraged when Robert La Follette stared coolly back at them, denying that he had any price at all. Throughout his life such men alternately threatened and cajoled, trying to make it clear to this political changeling that if he would only be "regular" he would "be taken care of."

When La Follette rejected all their overtures, his rivals for power tried to ridicule his movement out of existence. They called themselves the "stalwarts" and La Follette's adherents "the half-breeds." In a world that remembered the Indian struggles clearly, the term "half-breed" was the most contemptuous in all the vocabulary of abuse. But its contempt was deeply tinged with fear.

La Follette himself continued to be maddeningly incorruptible. There was nothing that he wanted except what he could get as the honest gift of the people, the right to continue to speak their collective mind and to cling doggedly to their rights. He chose to make himself simply the spokesman of the good sense of the average man. His assignment was to keep the people's house in order.

Often when he stood up before the great national audience, La Follette seemed like an unfamiliar figure. He did not live in the easy, gracious climate of concession. He did not wear the affable smile of the adaptable leader. La Follette had chosen a different role. He continued to be an actor as his career unfolded. His small, slender body, frequently shaken by illness, managed despite these trials to take on a look of heavy compactness. The gestures with which he emphasized his points in a political discussion were aggressive and vehement. They suggested the arena and he came inevitably to be known as "Fighting Bob." The mane on his leonine head turned gray, but he still tossed it with the old defiance. His deep-set eyes darted electrical sparks of indignation. His powerful arms threatened; his mobile mouth wooed with eloquence. He was, until the end of his life, in pursuit of Iago, and the chase seemed to him at the end just as exciting, just as hot, just as important as it had in the beginning.

Several times he offered himself as a candidate for the presidency, and each time he found the same kind of loyal but far from sufficient support that Ignatius Donnelly had had from the progressives. In 1912 when Theodore Roosevelt was angrily looking for an occupant of the White House who would satisfy him better than his own choice, William Howard Taft, La Follette persuaded himself to believe that he had the support of the old leader. But Roosevelt's insurgency proved to be of a more cautious, or perhaps of a more opportunistic, kind than that of La Follette. In a flurry of repudiation Roosevelt disclaimed any commitment to La Follette and became himself a candidate for the Republican nomination. When he failed to win it away from Taft, he ran as an independent candidate, thereby providing La Follette with a pattern for defiance which he used in the presidential campaign of 1924.

In that year the object of the rebels' resentment was placidly inactive Calvin Coolidge. Having failed to capture the Republican nomination away from him, La Follette accepted the endorsement of a third-party movement. On the Fourth of July, at Cleveland, he spoke his own ringing Declaration of Independence.

But his chance of election was so slight that no one outside of his own group of followers took his campaign seriously. The orthodox press declared dismissively that La Follette "represented nothing but protest." In 1924 optimistic expansionists and speculators saw the shining sky as the limit and few of them had the slightest hint of how soon it was to fall about their ears. To protest against the status quo was the unforgivable sin. It was "un-American" not to admit that Coolidge was leading our society straight into the millennium.

But La Follette, whose belief had ever been that "the supreme issue involving all others is the encroachment of the powerful few upon the rights of the many," saw much about which protest should be made. He saw it in the strange, petulant passivity with which Coolidge allowed his image to become the mask of Yankee simplicity behind which the powerful few operated to their own advantage. He saw it in the fact that the Democratic Party nominated for the presidency James W. Davis, who, despite his record as a vigorous liberal, was thought to have an unbreakable commitment to the world of privilege. Once more, at a moment when leadership seemed to have forgotten the length and breadth and variety of the American land, La Follette tried to become the voice of the people.

He did become the voice of an amazingly large number of Americans. Though he received only 34 electoral votes out of the total of 552, the popular vote more accurately revealed how great a hold he had upon the imagination of the people. Running as a third-party candidate, lacking the benefits of prestige, tradition, or political organization, La Follette was able, none the less, to attract 4,686,681 votes as against 15,748,356 for Coolidge and 8,617,454 for Davis.

It is interesting to speculate as to what his chances of election might have been had he not, only a few years before, adopted an unpopular pattern of thought about the European war. As a member of the Senate he had opposed our entry into the struggle with characteristic stubborn resolution. Because his constituents were chiefly German in ancestry, he was accused of following an obvious line of prejudice. To believe that of him, however, was to credit him with a kind of modesty that he never possessed. As he himself once wrote of another issue, "I estimated my own worth to the Progressive cause too highly to consent to being used . . . for a time, and then, to serve some ulterior purpose, conveniently broken and cast on the political scrap heap, my ability to serve the Progressive cause seriously damaged."

When La Follette opposed intervention in the World War it was on the same theory that had been the basis of all his thinking.

He wanted the people to be heard from, and the struggle of 1914–18, he considered, was not their war. Having taken his stand, he held to it with an almost furious consistency. La Follette became the highly theatrical figure in the center of the scene when a spectacular filibuster against Wilson's armed ship bill was staged. He voted against the declaration of war and opposed the draft act. Wilson named him as one of his "twelve wilful men" who tried to obstruct destiny.

When the entry of America into the war had become a *fait accompli*, La Follette surrendered consistency to patriotism. He voted for the war appropriation bill and for others that implemented the decision actively to prosecute the struggle against Germany. Still, he had been faithful through all his strenuous campaigns to the one dominating principle of his philosophy. It was, he held, the right of the people to say what they wished to do with their lands, their resources, their lives, and their destinies.

The dramatic presidential campaign of 1924 left an imprint on the Progressive movement in America. Unhappily, it left also an indelible mark on La Follette himself. His never reliable heart was irreparably weakened by the strain, and within a year of the election he was dead.

There has never been any monotony to our region's orderly but persistent revolt against domination by special groups. All sorts of men have played in separate scenes, each contributing the flavor of his individuality. La Follette, armed with the splendid, glittering broadsword of his rhetoric, hacked his way theatrically toward reform. At almost the same time John Lind of Minnesota moved forward as soberly and as nearly silently as it is possible for a man in public life to move.

Lind was the first of the Swedish-born Americans to reach great prominence in the affairs of Minnesota. He looked very little like the popular caricature of the Scandinavian politician. His distinguished, sharply chiseled features gave him an air of aloofness, almost of austerity. Like Elinor Wylie's "eagle of the rock," he seemed to live apart and "stare into the sun."

He came into the political world, not with a Wagnerian roll of drums announcing the entrance of a hero, but almost by accident. He had meant to train himself to be a civil engineer, but a mishap with a gun robbed him of his left hand, and he was obliged to turn to a less strenuous way of life. He became first a schoolteacher and later a lawyer.

Yet despite his lack of gusto and of conspicuous aggressiveness, Lind had precisely the same set of principles as the more vehement progressives. He wanted tax reforms and control of the railroads. He wanted to give voice and strength to the people's will. He was indifferent to party regularity, and though he appeared in public life first as a Republican, he rebelled against its discipline. He was elected Governor of Minnesota as the fusion candidate of the People's Party, the Democrats, and the insurgent Republicans. His favorite theme was a homely variation upon that of La Follette. "The people have used me pretty well on the whole," he said toward the end of his career. "They trusted me and I trusted them."

He was a good man at observing silently, as Woodrow Wilson discovered when in 1914 he sent Lind to do his "watchful waiting" on the Mexican border.

Lind's program as Governor was handicapped by the legislature, which intended firmly to scuttle all of his reforms. There remained at the turn of the century a great deal of work still to be done of the kind that La Follette had been doing in Wisconsin. The task fell into the hands of two witty, tireless Irishmen who gave the defenders of special privilege no rest. These men were George Sperry Loftus and James Manahan, both in part products of the Wisconsin philosophy. Loftus had been born in Wisconsin and was an intimate of La Follette. Manahan had attended the University of Wisconsin, where La Follette had many advisers and adherents. The team of Loftus and Manahan therefore vigorously expounded the La Follette system.

It was their delight to make raids deep into the country of privilege. The enterprise began when Loftus, as a private man of affairs, found that his hay-and-grain firm was being ruined by the rate discrimination practiced by the railroads. His six feet two inches of firm, aggressive resolution revolted against this injustice, and his Irish wit told him precisely what to do. He inaugurated a one-man revolution against economic tyranny, shrewdly using democratic processes to screw his rebellion to the sticking-place.

Wherever he discovered high-handed action, he collared the offender and forced him into a well-lighted place where the acoustics were good, and there made him account for himself. He sued the railroads for discriminatory rates. He sued them for charging the same amount for an upper as for a lower berth. He hounded timid legislators into confessing their political allegiances and forced the do-nothing variety out of office. As an influential member of the Minnesota Progressive Republican League, he furthered a program, like that of La Follette in Wisconsin, which had broad social aims: housing improvement, conservation, tariff revision, legislation controlling child labor, civil-service reform, and enactment of income-tax and primary-election laws. He assumed the sales managership of a farmers' co-operative grain exchange at a moment when it was in the midst of a bitter fight for its existence.

His chief ally in all these activities was the lawyer Manahan, whose red hair always made his head seem to be enveloped in flames. Yet Manahan managed to combine coolness of judgment with fiery alertness of wit. Whether he made the courtroom or the legislative hall of Congress his center of activity, he had the same ruling interest, that of safeguarding the rights of the common man.

There was something attractively youthful about the co-operation of Loftus and Manahan. But they were no Robin Hood and Little John playing at a game of social justice. They were enormously in earnest and intended to improve the pattern of existence for their fellow men. Loftus had known grinding poverty in his youth; he had seen his early efforts as a small business man thwarted by combinations of influence which tended imperiously to sweep aside the interests of an independent operator. Yet he was not infected with personal bitterness. His temperament was radiant with vitality, curiosity, and humor.

Manahan had traveled a path much less carelessly strewn with obstacles and hazards. Though he was one of twelve children of an Irish immigrant father, he had managed to give himself the advantages of attendance at the University of Wisconsin and of graduation from the University of Minnesota law school. He had arrived at his philosophy, apparently, by the study of abstract values and by virtue of having put to himself many times the question:

"Why?" It was the probing, surgical insistence with which he dug with his "whys" into the minds of men whom he had on the witness stand that made him the terror of his enemies and the joy of his friends.

The devotion of these two men to each other was touching. Advocates of co-operation have seldom co-operated so perfectly, and muckrakers have almost never done their raking with such precise and accurate strokes, performed in unison. There was envy and intrigue within Loftus's own organization, but dissension never touched the relations of these two leaders. The personal quality of their integrated effort and the link of affection which it had through Loftus with the La Follette movement in Wisconsin gives to this phase of the region's political history a glow of idealism that it is still reassuring to study.

The "verray parfit gentil Knight" of the reform movement was, appropriately, the first native-born citizen of Minnesota to achieve great prominence. Appropriate also was the fact that on both sides his ancestry was Swedish. John A. Johnson was a genial, winning nature, a man with a homely readiness of wit and aptitude for gentle, undisturbing eloquence that give him the magic qualities of attraction which politicians group under the word "availability." What they mean is the ability to avail oneself of votes.

Johnson had this art to such an astonishing extent that in a period when Minnesota was being most staunchly Republican, he was elected over and over again as a Democrat to the governorship. If he had not died in his forties, he would have been in 1912 a very strong candidate for nomination to the presidency. He had been discovered, even before 1908, at a session of the Gridiron Club in Washington, D.C. His pretensions had previously been regarded with skepticism by national leaders who know that "favorite sons" are usually worthy of no more than the family indulgence they receive in their own states. The idea of sending to the White House a man from Minnesota, and one whose parents were foreign-born, must have made many a knowing eyebrow arch itself with amusement or with distaste.

But when the press and the official world of Washington had seen this tall, handsome man with a look of benignity about the eyes and of humor about the mobile mouth, when they had heard him parry the routine insults of the evening artfully, they changed their minds and gave him an ovation.

Charles H. Grasty, journalist and politician and picker of candidates, wrote of Johnson as he appeared on that occasion:

"Here is a Democrat without demagogy. A leader whose head is not in the clouds. A sober thinker with the saving grace of humor. A right doer whose temperature is perfectly normal. A man of action without strenuosity. A young man of seasoned judgment. A man of the people who looks well in evening clothes. The possessor of that greatest gift of the gods, sense—which means judgment and taste—but all the while a virile son of the West with every red corpuscle intact."

He had, in short, availability.

Even the tragic circumstances of his youth became a political advantage to him. Johnson's father had been the village ne'er-do-well in St. Peter, a blacksmith who lacked the austere virtues ascribed by Longfellow to the brotherhood of blacksmiths. The elder Johnson was a likable, story-telling tippler who neglected his family shamelessly. But his Rip Van Winkle temperament did not turn his wife into a Dame Van Winkle. Johnson's mother, the washerwoman of the community, created a kind of fiercely immaculate poverty as the environment for her children. Her effort deeply touched her son. He once said the proudest moment of his life had come when, as a boy, he began to earn enough so that he could go to his mother and tell her she need never take in laundry again.

John A. Johnson had the same war cries of reform as Ignatius Donnelly and John Lind. "The Independent voter," he said, "is the ideal citizen. The hope of the nation is in all the people aroused from the sleep of party bigotry, armed with the breastplate of conviction and the sword of Conscience. . . . I care not for the name of the party I choose, so long as it stands for the rights of the people."

As editor of a small-town paper in St. Peter, Johnson had made the discovery that the vagaries of the public mind must be dealt with gently for fear of losing the opportunity to deal with them at all. Unlike La Follette, who was austere and uncompromising where matters of reform were concerned, Johnson preferred, as he said, to make haste slowly, availing himself of the technique of compromise as he moved forward. His administration did accomplish much toward permanent control by the people of the resources of their state. He was instrumental in the passing of a new insurance code, the establishment of a state banking department, a new code of laws controlling timber sales from state-owned lands, a law facilitating municipal ownership of public utilities. He liked to call himself a conservative radical and sometimes the balance between the two hovered vaguely and enigmatically. Johnson's veto of a tonnage tax bill designed to reform taxation on iron ore in the northern part of the state was attributed to the belief that the bill was badly drawn. But if he was, on occasion, more liberal in rhetoric than in action, his whole record is that of a man who intended to serve the interests of the common man. As Lincoln Steffens, writing on one aspect of his struggle, pointed out, ". . . This Democratic governor of a Republican state has put through his Republican Legislature too many and too democratic laws to qualify as any railroad's man." Nor could he be accused, for all the affable patience of his methods, of being in anyone's pocket unless it was the commodious, carelessly filled pocket of the people. It was to his credit that he managed not to get lost in it.

Next in the pageant of reform came Charles A. Lindbergh, Sr. He had his own variation on the theme that all the others had sung. His ambition, as he said, was "to do some good for the people." Lindbergh provided a kind of link between the various scattered movements which had swept through Minnesota politics (sometimes vaguely and fitfully) and the one which was to come after, that of the Farmer-Labor Party. When he announced that he wished as a member of Congress "to equalize the advantages of individuals" and to urge society on toward the time when "those who furnish the energy of the world's progress will govern," he provided patterns of thought for many later leaders.

Lindbergh and Johnson revealed in their characters and in their lives the folly of trying to fix a uniform mask upon the face of a whole people. Though both men were of Swedish ancestry, Lindbergh was as austere as Johnson was genial. Lindbergh was as solemn and uncompromising as Johnson was witty and flexible. Lindbergh was as completely lacking in gifts of leadership on a personal or emotional basis as Johnson was gifted and rich in magnetism.

The personal history of Charles Lindbergh, Sr., is of importance for the comment that it offers on his unswerving devotion to a single set of ideas. He was born in Stockholm to a father who had been so active in public affairs that he was regarded by orthodox conservatives as a socialist agitator. When August Lindbergh resigned as a member of the Swedish *Riksdag* and came to America, he did not renounce his ambition to be a man of influence. The home that he established in Minnesota was known to immigrants as a sort of halfway house at which they could adjust themselves to new conditions and obtain information about the new country before they started out to create their own farm homes.

Charles Lindbergh, Sr., was only a year old when his parents brought him to America. Yet the frontier hardships never afflicted him or embittered his outlook upon the human experience. His father's house was a place of comfort and social opportunity. Lindbergh was educated in law at the University of Michigan, and when he returned to Little Falls, Minnesota, to practice law he had immediate success. He became a director of a local bank and a man of property.

It was not, therefore, as a willful Swedish immigrant on the outside of opportunity and looking in with bitter, envious awe that he developed his theoretical ideas about the danger of government by wealth. These ideas belonged to a tradition of reform with which Lindbergh allied himself for no other reason than that he thought it his duty to do so. When, ten years after his debut in public life, he voted against America's entry into the first World War, he was following the austere dictates of the same uncompromising conscience. It seemed to him to be a war in which the people had no stake. The integrity of his conviction cannot be questioned, but the people rejected his leadership and retired him from public life.

But not before he had made one last and tremendously dramatic appearance before the public of Minnesota. In 1918 he ran for governor as the candidate of the Nonpartisan League in one of the most violent and bitter campaigns the region has ever seen.

The Nonpartisan League was another manifestation of the impulse toward reform that had characterized the "agrarian crusade" through all its phases. Its objects were to establish state-owned terminal elevators, stockyards, packing houses, and cold-storage plants. The League wanted better inspection of grain dockage and grading; it wanted hail insurance and rural credit banks, run for the benefit of the farmer.

The leader in this new movement was a dramatic creature, Arthur Charles Townley, who had a lively career beginning as a schoolteacher, proceeding to farming on a huge scale with mechanized equipment and, following the classic pattern of the tragic novel of the soil, to bankruptcy "when the bottom fell out of the flax market." Determined to organize farmers in a revolt against conditions that made success almost unattainable, Townley set out, first in North Dakota, to bring together enough strength to control elections. His purpose was purely educational. He wished his League to choose candidates on a nonpartisan basis, offering support to any who, in turn, would support reform.

He set out to talk directly to the people, just as La Follette had done when he went from farm to farm in his buggy. Townley went in a battered old Ford. Presently he enlisted other workers, and ten similarly decrepit cars began wheezing up and down the highways. Finally this mechanized division of the agrarian army had increased to forty cars and there were 22,000 members in the League. It had happened so fast that when Townley wished to make arrangements for the distribution of his publication, the *Nonpartisan Leader*, the postmaster to whom he talked could not believe that his organization had so huge a membership. The postman had never heard of the Nonpartisan League. "What the hell of that?" Townley exclaimed. "I've been organizing farmers, not goddam postmasters."

All of the reformers of the region were drawn into the new movement: La Follette, Loftus, Lindbergh. With the zeal of religious cultists and the camaraderie of an intimate and cozy family group, the adherents met with wives, families, children at huge picnics. Sometimes the cavalcade of farmers in their cars would be twelve or even twenty miles long as they drove to their meeting-places.

But, as Ignatius Donnelly had learned earlier, an organization without direct political power is not an effective weapon. Presently workers of the urban communities formed a group called the Working People's Nonpartisan Political League, and leaders saw an opportunity to capitalize actively on all the enthusiasm that the reform movements had roused. The Nonpartisan League and the Working People's League merged into the Farmer-Labor Party, which in the election of 1918 offered a candidate for the first time. This was Charles Lindbergh, Sr., and before the ordeal of the campaign was over he had faced every humiliation that can be offered a man in public life. He had been abused as pro-German; he had been refused the use of public halls as though he were a criminal; his meetings had been broken up by professional rowdies, and Lindbergh himself had been pelted with rotten eggs.

As a political figure the elder Lindbergh did not survive this distasteful session with prejudice, and he disappeared from public life, to die six years later. But the Farmer-Labor Party had just begun. It succeeded in electing two of its candidates to the Senate, Dr. Henrik Shipstead in 1918 and Magnus Johnson in 1924. Then in 1930, when the conditions of farmers and laborers had once more become acutely hard, Floyd Olson emerged as a leader of the new party.

It was in Floyd Bjerstjerne Olson that the revolt of the people of Minnesota found its most cheerful embodiment. He brought about a workable, if not complete, reconciliation between the watchful, cautious, slow farmer and the noisier, more plunging city worker. Olson was a city man himself. He had been, from the early days of his childhood in Minneapolis, a resourceful and adaptable product of the pavements—paper boy, bootblack, freight handler. To the end of his days his wit and all his ways were urban. He loved night clubs and the slashing, spontaneous interchanges of the vaudeville tradition, practical jokes and gambling. The only thing about his personal habits that was in the least rustic was his love of a corncob pipe. But what might so easily have been a political asset to a man who had to appear often before rural audiences, Olson scrupulously hid. The corncob pipe was for his private enjoyment. Smoking it in public, he felt, might have been interpreted as a pose.

He was honest in his conviction that society must be remodeled after the design of what he called the co-operative common-wealth. Though his opponents drew their breath in pain to tell Minnesota that this was communism, it was actually nothing so very startling after all. Olson simply devised his own restatement of the familiar faith of the agrarian crusaders. He wanted a modi-fied economic order, achieved through democratic, parliamentary processes, looking toward government ownership of basic in-dustries and regulated by the theory of "production for use" rather than that of "production for profit."

Olson looked more like a vaudeville tap-dancer (of the vigorous George M. Cohan type) than he looked like a politician. But his urchin mischievousness of face and tongue could not mask his real shrewdness. He had begun his career as a reformer when, as County Attorney in Minneapolis, he had forced an investigation of graft and put four conniving aldermen snugly in jail. A re-former he meant to continue to be, no matter who put obstacles in his path. Sometimes the obstacles were put there by members of his own party, wishing out of sheer high spirits to trip him up. He moved always with a catlike wariness through a period of great unrest when there were many strikes in Minneapolis. His campaigns were so skillfully managed that when the strikes were over, the conservatives could not accuse him of favoritism and the strikers could not accuse him of sabotage.

Olson was unapologetic in his faith that points were won for insurgents by "boring from within." He was good-natured in his contempt for those stern sons and daughters of the voice of God whom he called "ritualists." As he once put it, "The trouble with the leftists is that they want to ride on a white horse with a pennant flying, hell bent for the barricades." He could bide his time more patiently and deal patiently with any issue, however maddening, that he was required to face. Once at a public meet-ing of women a righteous soul rose to demand that he answer to charges that had been made about a certain lack of circumspection in his private life. Olson seemed to consider the matter deeply as he walked down to the front of the platform. "Madam," he said, fixing the questioner with what might have been a rueful, almost filial glance, and which might on the other hand have been one of guileful impudence, "Madam, that is the cross I have to bear." Period. Next question. . . . He had many crosses to bear, and he carried them all with the same insouciance.

Having been defeated in his first attempt to win the governorship of the state of Minnesota, Olson came to understand better than most of his associates the dual nature of a reform party. It must attract adherents and win elections if it wishes to become effective; but it must also keep a clear view of its fundamental purposes and not become fascinated and satisfied with power. Olson was elected to the governorship in 1930 after he had insisted upon having the privilege of writing his own platform. He was re-elected in 1932 and 1934. His talent for staying in office began to infuriate those who had once had the art and lost it. They, of course, began to decry his machine, the graft and corruption, the extravagance of his party. But more sober men with an impartial view of the problems the Farmer-Labor Party faced were not inclined to be severe about Olson's handling of such matters as patronage. Knowing the superb dramas of influence that had been enacted in other chapters of American political life, these disinterested observers considered the affairs of the Farmer-Labor Party to be almost childlike in their innocence.

The objectives of reform were not mislaid after the Olson victories. The old causes for which all of the progressives had fought needed special attention under the tragic conditions of the depression. Olson's program included a mortgage moratorium bill that worked well without wrecking the financial structure of savings banks; a huge relief bill; another which spread funds available for educational facilities so that the poorest counties had opportunities equal to those of the richest ones; and the establishment of a Land Commission which looked toward rehabilitation of cut-over lands and made a start toward forest conservation.

Then, just as he was about to enter on the larger political scene, Olson died. He had intended to run for the Senate, even when he must have suspected that the cancer which was causing him acute and uninterrupted suffering would not permit him to survive long. But he regarded his private difficulties with characteristic jauntiness. It gave him special pleasure to flout his enemies who were speeding him unceremoniously on his way out of life.

Shortly after his last Farmer-Labor convention in St. Paul, Olson observed with urchin pride: "A lot of people thought I had bellowed my last bellow and had me already in the dust. I spoke for an hour and a half just to show these birds I could do it."

That last bellow was to outline the "co-operative commonwealth" and to suggest, frighteningly to some, that while the work of the Farmer-Labor Party in the past had been largely educational, it was now ready to put principles into active practice.

But despite his irrepressible impudence, this was the beginning of a swift end. Within a few weeks Olson was on his way to Rochester to die. He went by plane, and as he reached the city he was awakened to see the sunrise. "Isn't that the pay-off?" he murmured with one last flash of the gambler's enthusiasm.

There was a curious fatality about the timing of his death, it followed so exactly the pattern of another reformer's life and death. Like John A. Johnson, Olson died just when he seemed to be about to step before the national scene. And as at Johnson's funeral, the public grief that saluted Olson was something that could not be feigned or forced. Both Governors were men who had captured the imagination of all the people, not merely the ones who were their political followers, but also the ones who were their opponents. Even these found themselves charmed out of anger, if not out of opposition.

In 1938 a wave of conservative sentiment swept the region. Minnesota overwhelmingly voted to retire Floyd Olson's heir to leadership of the Farmer-Labor Party. The governorship went to Harold Stassen, a tall, stocky, red-haired young Republican, then in his early thirties. At the same time Wisconsin retired from the Governor's chair, also by an unmistakably emphatic majority, young Phillip La Follette, heir with his brother, the younger Robert M. La Follette, to their father's tradition of rebellion against party regularity.

Presently it became apparent that what had happened in Wisconsin and Minnesota was more significant than merely the loss by insurgent elements of single elections. An end, indeed, had come to another phase of the agrarian crusade, and the farmers were zigzagging back to belief in the two-party system. One by one Minnesota's political leaders returned to strategic bases in the Republican or Democratic parties. They acted like no prodigal sons, either. There was no humility or contrition about them, for they took home a welcome supply of bacon in the form of votes which hungry Republicans and Democrats were glad to see.

Finally, from the former Farmer-Labor leaders themselves came the suggestion that a convention be called at which the party should vote itself out of separate existence and merge with the Democratic Party. If the end of this movement is less dramatic than its beginning, at least the leaders knew how to bring down their curtain on the anticlimax with a certain amount of style.

History lately has repeated itself in reverse in Minnesota. First the Republicans and Democrats became insurgents and then the insurgents became Republicans and Democrats. But this variability of mood among the people should suggest to many that they may at any time change again.

History has seemed to repeat itself, with curious variations, also in the matter of the region's response to war's alarms. Even the same names recur in the story. In Minnesota a Charles Lindbergh preached against America's entry into the first World War; a Charles Lindbergh preached against our entry into the second. In Wisconsin a La Follette was opposed to our participation in the European struggle in 1917 and a La Follette made a similar crusade in the months just before Pearl Harbor.

But it would be a mistake to assume that there has been no change, during all that time, in the mood of Wisconsin and Minnesota with regard to international affairs. The younger Lindbergh in no way represented Minnesota. It is extremely different to discover from a study of his enigmatic personality and elusive philosophy what he did wish to represent. Certainly it was not the farmers of Minnesota, among whom he had not lived for a very long time and who knew him solely as a young flier who had had some fine triumphs and also some deeply tragic personal experiences.

When he was in the midst of his campaigns against our partici-

pation in European affairs, Lindbergh II made a speech at Minneapolis in which he referred to his father and his father's battle
of 1917. The implication of what he said was that, since he came
of a long line of seers, he must be believed when he spoke of the
invincibility of the Nazis. But many Minnesotans knew his father's
philosophy better than, at that moment, Lindbergh seemed to
know it. Certainly it was not for the people, the commonalty
of humankind the world over, that Lindbergh spoke when he suggested that America look the other way while the Jews, the
Czechs, the Poles, the Danes, the Norwegians, the French, the
Belgians, the Dutch, the English, the Russians were inundated by
"the wave of the future."

Phillip La Follette's philosophy is also elusive. Behaving with
bravery, if not with perfect moral consistency, the young La
Follette himself went to war in 1917 after his father had advised
his country against doing so. Again in 1942, after preaching earnestly against a program that would lead to war, Phillip La Follette went himself. His behavior must be said to show gallantry;
it may also be thought to demonstrate political resourcefulness.
For he is now in a convenient position to let a swinging door admit
him quickly to either of two shelters. If Wisconsin decides to give
itself to internationalism after the war, Phillip La Follette fought
the good fight; but should it return to isolationism, then he
preached the gospel in good season.

But the Lindberghs and the La Follettes should have read the
philosophy of their states more clearly. There is no isolationism
in Wisconsin and Minnesota except in isolated alcoves where the
unreconstructed rebels of our time have taken refuge. The German communities of the two states which in the first World War
were stubbornly unconvinced are not this time out of sympathy
with the nation's program. Their young men have gone with the
same resolute recognition of the necessity of rolling back the
Lindberghs' "wave of the future" that has characterized the conduct of young Americans everywhere else. The bond quotas and
Red Cross quotas have been oversubscribed; the blood-bank centers have no need to urge co-operation.

What is more significant still, the men whom these states elect
to office are those who have unequivocally committed themselves

to the idea that America must participate in world affairs, not merely now but in the postwar world as well. Senator Joseph Ball of Minnesota has done so again and again. So also has Harold Stassen, who, before he resigned from the governorship to become a lieutenant commander in the Navy, had outlined a program for international co-operation that includes establishment of an airways commission to control the world's great airports; establishment of an administrative body to control all ocean gateways; promulgation of a code of international justice, with a court to administer it; establishment of a commission to supervise world trade; and organization of an international police force to lend authority to a new world order.

One of the leaders of the agrarian crusade once spoke of the "little fires of reform" that he and others like him had started. It was significant that he stressed their littleness. Reformers of his type wanted no spectacular changes, no bloody revolution, complete with tyranny and terror. They wanted simply to make the processes of democracy serve the people.

The leaders have been of many different backgrounds and many different temperaments. The region's gallery of reformers has included a garrulous, witty Irishman who improvised endlessly out of the wealth of his creative imagination; a handsome and aggressive creature of French extraction who looked like an actor of the classic tradition, about to play Brutus; a Scandinavian who was by nature as austere and ascetic as an early Christian martyr; a Scandinavian who was as jaunty as a café-society playboy. They have been Populists, Nonpartisan Leaguers, Republicans, Democrats, Farmer-Laborites, big men and little men, hearty men and sad men, healthy ones and sick ones. But they all wanted "to do something for the people."

Now the little fires of reform seem to be merged in one very large fire, the one which Wisconsin and Minnesota, along with the rest of America, hope will burn away the Nazi heresies against the people and clear the ground for the building of a new international society.

11

COWS, COLLEGES, AND CONTENTMENT

⁊

A FAITHFUL BUT HUMORLESS CITIZEN of a Minnesota community was once inspired to suggest that it adopt as its slogan the boast that it was the home of "Cows, Colleges, and Contentment." That statement was unassailably accurate, at least on its first two counts. For the town lies in the very center of rich dairy country, and though its corporate limits are not broad, it has found room within them to tuck away, in appropriate academic seclusion, two important institutions of higher learning.

Our region has always been deeply and uninterruptedly devoted to the idea of education. Long before Wisconsin and Minnesota had even achieved statehood, residents of the wilderness territory were brooding about the establishment of universities. The first official documents of both call for the creation of centers of instruction. There has been from the beginning a close, intense, and almost connubial union between the legislative and educational services of the two states.

This is clearer, perhaps, in the history of the University of Wisconsin than in that of the University of Minnesota, though there, too, collaboration has been intimate and enthusiastic. The campus of the University of Wisconsin lies, in a neighborly readiness to serve, within walking distance of the statehouse in the pleasant town of Madison. "Fighting Bob" La Follette, himself a graduate of the university, used to find it convenient and helpful to take the members of the faculty into his confidence whenever he was planning any extension of his program of social reform. His old teachers and the new ones who were added after he had gone into public life made up a kind of informal cabinet. There was, one imagines, a great deal of strolling back and forth between campus and statehouse. The implications of that congeniality seem both pleasant and proper. If society is to be planned, surely the planning should be accomplished by a collaboration between those who have devoted their lives to the study of theory and those who must put theories into practice.

The "Wisconsin idea," as the program of reform has been called, germinated in the brains of the university's professors. But those men did not give themselves unreservedly to the support of all the La Follette attitudes. When "Fighting Bob" as Senator became one of Woodrow Wilson's "wilful men" who fought our entry into the first World War, the faculty of the university repudiated his policy. At the moment when Milwaukee was burning him in effigy, the university regretfully rejected the turn his thought had taken. This rupture in the marriage of minds has not been repaired, and today the La Follette Progressive movement takes a course that the faculty watches from afar.

Like Macbeth's castle, the campus of the University of Wisconsin has a pleasant seat, and the air off Lake Mendota "nimbly and sweetly recommends itself" to the senses in all seasons. College grounds need bodies of water to make their charm complete, and though lazy little rivers have the preference of tradition and literature, there is a kind of appropriateness that in lake country this campus should spread itself along a broader expanse of blue.

It cannot be said in all honesty that the buildings are beautiful. They are a kind of patchwork accumulation, lacking any kind of unifying influence to draw them together. But they crowd in pleasantly on one another and the whole stretch of the campus seems to run jauntily and tirelessly up the hill beside the lake. What a century can accomplish in the way of creating an effect of venerability, the years have done to the university. But the total effect is rather more that of being "forever panting and forever young," as a college should be.

New and old have been mixed on the campus with a bold hand. Representative of the new is the theater where Alfred Lunt, remembering his Wisconsin heritage, sometimes takes his wife,

Lynn Fontanne, to co-star with him in special performances. It is the very model of a modern auditorium, with everything indoors done for the comfort of eye, ear, and spine and with an exterior that greets the scene with a flowing graciousness of line. An enclosed arcade that arches around the entrance provides an ideal gallery for the hanging of picture exhibits. Beyond, out of doors, there is a stone-flagged terrace that gives Madison a momentary look of being Monte Carlo. Farther still, the blue of the lake blends itself discreetly into an altogether charming scene.

There are other monuments to modern taste in the midst of the cozy, haphazard character of this campus. If you search diligently enough through the corridors of the musty old law building you will find a way leading to a recently added annex. Up a flight of stairs in the least accessible corner of the building is the law library where one of John Steuart Curry's murals adorns the walls. It shows the monumental figures of Negro slaves, their arms lifted in frenzied exultation over their emancipation. The pictured clamor of thanksgiving seems to engulf and dwarf the room and to reverberate violently in the silence.

Dear to Wisconsin's tradition is the idea of maintaining a close, almost familial association with the whole community. Under the influence of Chris L. Christensen, who was for more than a decade dean of the Department of Agriculture, the university extended its influence far beyond what is usual, to encourage the creative life along all the little bypaths of the countryside. The Department of Agriculture has bought the paintings of Wisconsin primitives and exhibited them for the encouragement of others who wish to express their homely gifts as craftsmen.

The university is the patron of many another expression of the folk spirit in regional literature and regional drama. It wishes to occupy an important place in the social life of the whole community, not merely during the student years, but on into adult life.

Edwin R. Embree, president of the Julius Rosenwald Fund, once observed admiringly with what success the state universities play this role of Alma Mater to the entire community. Knowing, as he must, how sensitive and jealous of their prestige colleges are, he took his life resolutely into his hands by writing an article for the *Atlantic Monthly* of June 1935 in which he named the great educational institutions of America "in order of their eminence." His discussion offered a definitive comment on the findings of the Committee of American Education, which had brought all the colleges and universities into a kind of academic arena and there, in a sedate free-for-all, let them demonstrate the distinction of their various departments. The exacting requirements found the University of Wisconsin and the University of Minnesota not wanting in excellence. Indeed, they emerged among the top-ranking eleven.

Mr. Embree wrote: "The list closes with two of the most interesting of the Midwestern state universities, institutions which have combined the advancement of learning in its very highest branches with general educational service to the whole population. Wisconsin has the older history of scholarship and state-wide service, but, during recent years, Minnesota has been climbing rapidly while Wisconsin has lost some of the distinction she held during the great days of [President] Van Hise. Under intelligent leadership of presidents and deans infused equally with imagination and common sense, with political sagacity and downright courage, Minnesota offers today the very finest example of what a university may mean in influence upon a whole great state."

The University of Minnesota at Minneapolis is larger than the University of Wisconsin by several thousand in normal enrollment. (During the last prewar year there were some 17,000 students at Minnesota, 12,000 at Wisconsin.)

Not even one who loves it well could say without doing violence to his artistic conscience that the campus of the University of Minnesota is happily situated. It stands high on the east bank of the Mississippi River, and from the top floors of some of the new buildings there are handsome views of Minneapolis, including the austerely beautiful silhouette of the milling district across the water. But something of the traditional charm of academic seclusion is lost by the fact that the campus is cut into splinters by the two streetcar lines that link Minneapolis and St. Paul; that railroad freight cars serving the milling district puff sootily along an underpass just at the main gates; and that a wide thoroughfare open to trucks, sends its uninterrupted and sonorous rumble into the classrooms of Folwell Hall. On the islands isolated by these furious streams of traffic there are vistas of restful charm. Various student traditions are associated with "the knoll," which manages to look sylvan when it is spread with the green of spring, and with the riverbank where, also in spring, fraternity pins and tentative vows are exchanged. But it must be admitted that those who find in the University of Minnesota merely a great, impersonal, machinelike competence, rather than the soothing and protective tenderness that the sentimental look for in an Alma Mater, have its appearance to support their contention.

Architecturally the university campus may be said to have had two eras, the first characterized by a spirit of uncritical improvisation, the second by a spirit of somewhat stern efficiency in planning. The campus bisects itself once more between the two periods. The older half has something of the cozy, lived-in look of a living-room into which an amiable and perhaps not very affluent owner has put just any piece of furniture that happened to come into his possession. It is full of neo-Grecian temples, Romanesque wonders, and other architectural curiosities that defy classification. It is possible to say only that they are rather like volcanic eruptions frozen into stone.

In the course of the past quarter of a century the university has grown with the sturdy irrepressibility of its youth. Hemmed in by two cities, the institution had to expand as best it could, rather as a big boy does who has outgrown his only suit. The university's shoulders strain at the seams, and its heavy, bony wrists hang out of its coat-sleeves.

A great expansion program recently has given the university many new buildings for its scientific schools, for its library, for its auditorium, for its center of student activities. These red brick structures have a family resemblance of design and the face of each is a little severely set in the sober pattern of serviceability and durability. But following a design made by Cass Gilbert, the university has arranged the additions to the campus along a central mall which has impressiveness and charm as it looks toward the river and the skyline of the Minneapolis business district. The interior decoration of the new Coffmann Memorial Union is a masterpiece of taste. Indeed, it is so beautiful that upstate legislators from the agricultural districts have been known to cluck their tongues wonderingly over the luxury that it seems to represent. Actually, the effect of grace and ease has been achieved skillfully within the limits of simplicity and strict usefulness.

There is a certain amount of tongue-clucking also over the great *palazzos* of the fraternities and sororities that line University Avenue along the edge of the campus. But again the alarm about the invitation to the sybaritic life which these institutions seem to offer is exaggerated. The only objection to the fraternity system at a Middle-Western university is the one that may be leveled against it anywhere: that it tends to regiment the social life of its members in a narrow and parochial design. In and out of fraternities the pattern of student life at the University of Minnesota remains unpretentious. Though the parking problem on the campus grows more and more acute, this is not evidence of urban ostentation, but merely a reflection of the fact that distances are great in the sprawling region from which the university draws its students, and that jalopies are cheap.

Dress on the campus is modest. The baggy slacks (for both sexes), the leather jacket, the moccasinlike sandals worn in all seasons—these items make up the standard uniform in normal times. If individual case histories could be examined it might be found that this lack of ostentation is sometimes positively ostentatious. But a uniform has always the advantage of erasing distinctions, and the costume which has the blessing of fashion at Wisconsin or Minnesota definitely obliterates the line separating the boy who wears shabby trousers because it is being done from the boy who wears shabby trousers because they are the only trousers he owns.

Those who sometimes mourn over the fact that a minor local scandal, the details of which are no longer of interest, robbed the university of an opportunity to establish itself on the banks of beautiful and broad Lake Minnetonka, ignore a certain compensatory consideration. The position of the campus, huddled as it is between two cities, gives it a positive advantage that it would not have had in splendid isolation. It serves the whole community admirably where it is. In Minnesota all roads lead to the campus of the university, and its central position makes it available to many who might not have acquired the habit of using it so constantly had it been tucked away in some corner, nobly aloof.

In the little family feud which the Twin Cities have cultivated —in latter years only languidly—the university has come to act as arbiter. It offers itself as neutral ground upon which the warring Montagues of Minneapolis and Capulets of St. Paul can meet without risking conflict.

There was a time in the flamboyant past when both cities had symphony orchestras. St. Paul, in a moment of depression, allowed its own to be disbanded. For many years thereafter the Minneapolis Symphony Orchestra played a concert on Friday evening in Minneapolis and on Thursday or Saturday evening in St. Paul. Then another moment of stringency came and it seemed necessary to avoid the expense of giving two performances of the same program. Lips in St. Paul tightened in a spirit of noncooperation as patrons anticipated the suggestion that the setting for the one concert should be in a Minneapolis auditorium. The inspired solution was to remove the series of symphony concerts to the large Cyrus Northrop Memorial Auditorium on the campus, which is as close, in actual distance, to the residence district of St. Paul as it is to the residence district of Minneapolis. A psychological distance between St. Paul and the campus does not exist at all.

So the whole community has fallen into the habit of looking to the university for an important part of its intellectual nourishment. It drops in for lectures; it attends the experimental plays of the student theater; it is lured happily into taking refresher courses offered in a multitude of fields, from dentistry to psychiatry, at the Center for Continuation Study; it patronizes a series of artist recitals; it visits the art shows hung in the Little Gallery of Cyrus Northrop Auditorium.

The community, to a gratifying extent, has lost its mixture of awe and contempt for the academic mind. Indeed, some of its best friends are college professors. Town and gown meet without any nervous and guarded feeling that each must make allowance for the other. It would be difficult at a social gathering anywhere in the Twin Cities to identify by costume a business man, a lawyer, an artist, and a professor. The four stand near the fire, drinking highballs together and speaking an idiom that they all understand readily. The closeness of the university to the community it serves is in part responsible for a great and desirable change. Minneapolis and St. Paul want their ideas about public affairs to have the imprint of university thought. When the Foreign Policy Association of either city needs someone to debate with a visiting Chinaman, Argentine, or East Indian, they go hopefully and respectfully to their friends at the university.

This might have been a sterile union or a Victorian marriage "in name only" if old ideas of the impracticality of the academic mind still prevailed in Minnesota. In many groups, if not in all, those old ideas have long since been filed in the oubliette of outgrown prejudices. The university men have proved themselves to be useful in too many ways to be distrusted any longer. Experts have explored the problem of making profitable the recovery of Minnesota's great supply of low-grade iron ore. Men of the university have designed important plans for reforestation and for the efficient use of remaining timberland. The faculty of the agricultural campus has never considered its function to be limited by obligations toward students enrolled in prescribed courses of study. It has lived close to the agricultural community, known its leaders and many of its typical representatives, offered itself as a center for the exchange of ideas and the dissemination of the news about theories of scientific farming. The university does not merely keep its finger on the pulse of community life, in theoretical and detached interest; it holds the community firmly by the hand.

Once more on the lighter side, the community takes a highly vocal and unashamed delight in the distinguished record of its football team, the Golden Gophers. A proper home has been built for them in the huge stadium and the fully equipped athletic buildings near by. The actor Roman Bohnen offers the slightly rueful boast that he very nearly sacrificed his speaking voice, when he was "rooter king" at the university, for the cause of whipping up enthusiasm among "old grads" to get the stadium built. Fortunately, since he is one of the best character actors of the stage and screen, he did not manage to toss his profession away in that moment of youthful exuberance. The superb corner of the campus devoted to sport exists as a monument to the seriousness with which the community takes its college football.

Creation of the University of Minnesota has been the cooperative enterprise of so many men and women that their contributions could be listed only in a corpulent encyclopedic work. But the pageant of its presidents may be taken as symbolic of its growth. The first, William Watts Folwell, had the imagination to get it started and the patience to see it through its infancy. Dr. Folwell was the perfect example of the academician as pioneer. He seemed virtually indestructible, though he was small of stature and in no obvious way aggressive. He survived the Civil War, in which he had served as an officer; survived fifteen years as an educator; survived for a long period as president emeritus, during which he wrote the first important history of the state; survived on into his nineties, still alert, curious, genial, and full of hope for the university. Students used to delight in him when they called at his little brown house and received out of his little brown person a warmth of inextinguishable faith.

He was succeeded by Cyrus Northrop, who was an ideal executive and disciplinarian to preside over the university during its turbulent adolescence. He too was a genial spirit and there was something so pre-eminently fatherly about his white walrus mustache that he could speak any words out of it, however exacting or stern they might be, and give them the sound of benediction.

Dr. George Edgar Vincent was a man of a very different sort. Like Edward Arlington Robinson's Richard Cory, he "glittered when he walked" and more particularly when he talked. He had that special gift of wit, like Bernard Shaw's, which seems communicable and contagious. Sitting before him at convocation, students felt themselves lifted out of the rut of their sullen skepticism about the higher learning. They pleasantly imagined themselves to have become, by exposure to his brilliance, also intellectually dashing and deft. President Vincent created an atmosphere in which the concerns of the mind seemed both valuable and charming. Before he resigned to become head of the Rockefeller Foundation, he had given the university a brilliant faculty and a tremendous prestige.

His successor, Marion Leroy Burton, was a gifted man of affairs whom legislatures could understand and like. Under him the great and long-needed building program was begun. Lotus Delta Coffman, the fifth president, trained in the special field of education, devoted his administration,to consolidating the achievements of his two immediate predecessors and to creating a solid pattern within which the university could develop the standards established by President Vincent in the selection of its faculty and by President Burton in the creation of a physical plant.

Guy Stanton Ford, who since his retirement as sixth president of the university has become editor of the *American Historical Review* in Washington, D.C., is a man of George Edgar Vincent's type and stature, a brilliant liberal, a leader whose breadth of outlook has helped to widen the horizon of the whole academic world.

President Walter Coffey, now the head of the university, was previously dean of the Department of Agriculture. He is a vigorous executive whose faculty in all the many departments value his gifts of insight, understanding, and creative imagination.

Anxiety over the problem of academic freedom has furrowed the brow of all those who have shared in the growth of American educational institutions. An anecdote may serve to show with what zestful defiance the young university of the region has clung to the right to speak its mind.

The wife of one of the presidents of the University of Minnesota once wrote a play which a woman's club had agreed to perform. Before sending her manuscript to the play production committee, she submitted it for criticism to a member of the English department, a middle-aged eccentric who guarded his privacy and his æsthetic conscience with a fierceness that was more courageous than graceful. He returned the script with the succinct comment that it was the worst play he had ever read. The president's wife, greatly agitated, hurried to his house, not to reproach him, but to ask for help in putting her ideas into more respectable form. The maiden sisters of the professor met the president's wife at the door and, fearing their brother more than any other imaginable authority, barred her entrance. Their brother they said, was not at home. But while they talked he appeared in an upper hall. The president's wife, now completely reckless in her anxiety, leaped past the stern sisters and halfway up the stairs, calling: "Mr. Jones—Mr. Jones—I must see you." The professor paused and, glowering over the banister, pronounced the portentous words: "But, Mrs. X, I have said that I am not at home." The president's wife became, all in one breath, insistent, plaintive, and submissive. "I understand, quite. But, please, Mr. Jones, if you are not at home now, when will you be home?" There was an instant of silence, the portentousness of which only a Homer could have described adequately. Jove preparing to hurl a thunderbolt might have been of comparable awesomeness. "Mrs. X," Mr. Jones said, "I shall never be at home to the author of that play." So, it may be said, the academic world of the region has ever declined to be at home to those who would invade and corrupt freedom.

Sometimes the timorous have looked at the bigness of the University of Minnesota and objected that so huge an institution must be oblivious of, if not indifferent to, the welfare of the individual student. Such critics murmur plaintively about "factories of learning" and "education from the assembly line." Yet to a grateful multitude the University of Minnesota has seemed always to elude the discomforts of its bigness. There is, on the part of the faculty, a cheerful readiness to meet the student body in casual, informal ways, at student forums, in a hundred different student clubs, at teas and dancing parties. The small college sometimes imagines, just a little Pharisaically, that it has an exclusive monopoly on the virtue of friendliness. But the bigness of a college does not of itself impose upon faculty members attitudes of austerity and aloofness. At Minnesota the academic way of life manages to be casual enough so that professor and student may discuss plans for a thesis while they swim side by side in a lake near the campus or tramp over the country highways together. A prominent American leader once said that he would rather have sat on the end of a log if his favorite private counselor were on the other than to have attended the best university in the world. That states with dramatic extravagance the case for the private contact of minds as an educative force. There is no reason, however, why that kind of illumination cannot be given

to the student of a great university. Many a Minnesota undergraduate and his favorite teacher have sat on the ends of logs
through long, revealing private conferences. A great university
like Minnesota is all things to all students.

The luxuriant growth of educational institutions in Wisconsin
and Minnesota has produced schools of very nearly every sort
that the whole range of teaching inspiration can show. Mr.
Embree names as a very particular favorite among his personal
choices in small colleges Carleton, at Northfield, Minnesota. It
is a co-educational college which puts its emphasis upon giving
students a broad cultural appreciation of the possibilities of human experience. Its president, Dr. Donald J. Cowling, is a vigorous leader in the movement to prepare the mind of America for
active participation in world affairs when the war is over. He
interprets the essential obligation of a college to be that of equip-
ping young citizens to assume the responsibilities of living under
a democracy.

Established as a Congregational school in 1867, Carleton has
contributed some of the most notable of Minnesotans to public
life. Thorstein Veblen was one of its graduates, Frank B. Kellogg
another. Their very dissimilar attitudes and achievements perhaps
suggest the range of Carleton's ability to offer stimulation to the
receptive.

The college has a beautiful campus. Its handsome buildings,
many of them new, are grouped about a small private lake in a
stretch of rolling country. The situation combines the advantages
of rural retreat from the world with those of accessibility to intellectual stimulation. Carleton students frequently drive the short
distance to Minneapolis for symphony concerts, or to St. Paul for
Foreign Policy Association meetings. The college has its own
lively cultural program. It has had an energetic student theater,
where a start was once made toward the evolution of a kind of
regional drama when the undergraduates presented a dramatization of Rölvaag's *Giants in the Earth*. The author of the play,
Thomas Job, then a faculty member, has since moved on to Broadway with his psychological melodrama *Uncle Harry*, and to
Hollywood for a variety of film assignments.

Marquette University, at Milwaukee, is another institution

which gets along without the advantages of academic seclusion. It is neighborly with the business district of the city, and this juxtaposition to the crowded human scene is appropriate, as Marquette is concerned with training students chiefly as engineers, doctors, dentists, lawyers, journalists, and nurses.

The Jesuit order conducts the affairs of this Catholic university, and under the conditions that prevailed before the present war it had an enrollment of four or five thousand students.

Three other Catholic institutions of the region have earned places of distinction in the esteem of the academic world. They are St. John's Abbey, the College of St. Catherine for women, and St. Thomas Academy and Military College. St. John's at Collegeville, Minnesota, is nearly a century old, and is one of the largest Benedictine abbeys in the world. Its movement to revive the communal spirit of the early Roman Church has attracted wide attention. Something of the mood of another day is recaptured by its graceful exercise of the art and virtue of hospitality. Taking in wayfarers in the traditional way, it quite frequently receives distinguished scholars and philosophers who discuss great and deep matters with the genial and meditative fathers through long week-ends. St. Catherine's has created a handsome estate in a district of St. Paul which until recently had been countryside, and which has now become suburbia. Academic standards have placed the college among the best of institutions for women. St. Thomas Academy in St. Paul occupies another fine, parklike stretch of land under the towering trees of Summit Avenue just before that highway ends its career on the heights above the Mississippi River. St. Thomas's benefactors have given it some handsome modern buildings; but its real wealth lies in its association with notable names. The academy was the particular pride of one fine scholar, Archbishop Ireland, and for many years it was under the guidance of two other scholars of equal distinction. The late Monsignor Humphrey Moynihan was its president for a time, lending his beauty of spirit and his gifts as a man of learning, particularly as a Dante scholar, to the enrichment of its reputation. He was succeeded, after an interval, by his brother, the Very Reverend James Moynihan, who, until his recent retirement, maintained the same high standards.

Macalester College and Hamline University are two other institutions that have managed to create islands of academic contemplativeness in the very midst of the urban bustle of St. Paul. Streetcar lines, however, merely bound them on one side instead of bisecting their campuses, and each achieves an admirable air of poise in which to cultivate the minds of its four hundred or five hundred students.

Macalester, founded by the Presbyterian Church in 1885, once numbered Cass Gilbert among its students. Hamline University, created by the pioneers of the Methodist Episcopal Church, wears the venerability of its ninety years with an air of jauntiness, and is ever ready to receive new ideas. Under the direction of Dr. Charles Nelson Pace it has lately created a College of Liberal Arts, of which Thomas Beyer in literature, Lowell Bobleter in the graphic arts, and Ernst Křenek in music are the particular adornments. Křenek, a recently acquired American citizen born at the turn of the century in Vienna, is the distinguished composer whose opera *Johnny Spielt Auf* has been performed by all the important European opera companies and also at the Metropolitan in New York.

Among Scandinavian institutions the most important are Gustavus-Adolphus and St. Olaf. The first, founded by the Swedish Lutheran Church at St. Peter, occupies impressive high ground overlooking the Minnesota valley. Still better known is St. Olaf, famous for its *a cappella* choir, which, under the direction of Dr. F. Melius Christiansen, has sung in every quarter of the nation and earned enough money on its tours to give the campus a handsome new music building. The feature of the campus of St. Olaf, at Northfield, is the Vale of Norway, a deep winding ravine which early Minnesota pioneers of the church planted with Norway pines so that students might never forget the tradition of their ancestral land. At St. Olaf the late O. E. Rölvaag was a teacher, and his fine spirit warmed many student's minds.

The small colleges of Wisconsin have still longer memories. All of them are approaching their centennials. Beloit, at Beloit, was established by the Congregational Church in 1846; Lawrence, at Appleton, was created for the children of Methodist Episcopal

FRANK LLOYD WRIGHT AND FOUR OF HIS DISCIPLES
Taliesin, Spring Green, Wisconsin

THE CAPITOL (DESIGNED BY CASS GILBERT), ST. PAUL, MINNESOTA

frontiersmen in 1847; and Ripon, at Ripon, by the Congregationalists in 1850.

Especially interesting for its pioneering history is Milwaukee-Downer, a distinguished school for women. Its beginnings are to be found in the revolt of women against the neglect of their education. Two very vigorous-minded pioneers were its sponsors. One, almost inevitably, was a Beecher. A wit once said that the human race could be divided roughly into three groups, saints, sinners, and Beechers. The last division seems to derive its spirit from the first and its vitality from the second. With the utmost resolution all the members of the famous family undertook to reform something. Harriet Beecher, after she had become Mrs. Stowe, staked out the problem of slavery as her preserve, while sister Catherine, like many of the male Beechers, took on education.

Having lost her fiancé at sea, Catherine, all of her Beecher vitality marshaled, tried to sweep from the schoolmistresses' heads their stereotyped ideas. She managed a school at Hartford, Connecticut, and later, in order to be near her father, who headed Lane School at Cincinnati, took up teaching there. The later part of her life was devoted to the theoretical consideration of problems of education for women and she wrote, among other treatises (the titles of which all have a slightly menacing sound), one called *True Remedy of the Wrongs of Women.*

Mrs. William Parsons of Milwaukee, being similarly persuaded of the need for reform, invited Catherine Beecher to go there as adviser to those of sympathetic belief. It was out of the philosophy of Catherine Beecher and the executive ability of her ally that Milwaukee-Downer was created. It was a progressive school far in advance of its time, and though its sponsors indulged in certain fads of education and stirred up little skirmishes of questioning and doubt, their principles were sound and their practice intelligent. Frances Willard was one of Milwaukee-Downer's distinguished products. Lucia Russell Briggs, daughter of the late Le Baron Russell Briggs, most famous of Harvard's deans, is its present head.

To this list, I must add the name of Carroll College, of Waukesha, Wisconsin. There is a reason for giving it special attention in a postscript to these notes.

As I sat recently in the beautiful library at Carroll College, warmed and soothed by its wholly sympathetic modern atmosphere, I thought of a curious bit of the town's early history, or prehistory. The incident took place in the pioneering days when the community called itself Prairie Village.

Certain good women of the village banded themselves together in a little army which they called the Female Moral Society. They passed some formidable resolutions which read, in part, as follows:

> "*Whereas the sin of licentiousness has made fearful havoc of the world, corrupting the flesh, drowning souls in perdition, exposing us to the vengeance of a holy God whose law is trampled on almost universally not only by actual transgression but by tacit consent of the virtuous and by an almost perfect silence of those whom he has commanded to cry aloud and spare not . . .*
>
> "*Whereas, it is the duty of the virtuous to use every consistent moral means to save our country from utter destruction . . .*
>
> "*We do therefore form ourselves into a society for this object. . . .*
>
> "*Article III—This society shall consist of those ladies who cordially approve of its objects, sign its constitution and pledge themselves not to admit to their society any person of either sex known to be licentious. . . .*"

Sitting on the pleasant campus it occurred to me that Prairie Village created the college in order to cure itself of precisely this sort of bigoted complacency.

Large and small, the universities and colleges are performing their assignment well.

12

VOICES IN A QUIET ROOM

NOTHING DEFINES THE CHARACTER of a time or place quite so clearly as the quality of its abstract thinking. Out of the insight that his heritage gives him, out of the circumstances of his daily life, out of the temperament that his environment puts upon him, the intellectual creates ideas. But these ideas, once he has shaped them, become quite independent of him. The alchemy of the mind has disguised the thinker's little personal traits so that his ideas no longer describe him but rather the moral and intellectual climate of the world in which he lives.

I have taken a sampling of the minds of the men of Wisconsin and Minnesota in an effort to determine what features they have in common. My six creative thinkers are not at all like each other in superficial ways; they would not have agreed very well if they could have been brought together in one place (heaven forbid!). I chose them first because it seemed to me that each, beginning as a teacher in a classroom, lifting up his voice in the quiet obscurity of the academic world, had finally acquired unique authority in his own field, so that his voice reached out through all the world of thought.

Then, as I studied my six more closely, it seemed to me that I discerned two characteristics that they had shared: a realistic approach to their material and a self-reliant unwillingness to be imposed upon by the accepted beliefs of the immediate or distant past. Dissimilar in mood, they appeared to be alike in independence. Dissimilar in interests, as economists must be different from chemists, chemists from historians, historians from literary critics and scholars, still they are alike in boldness of insight and in common sense.

Here they pass in very brief review.

BITTER, SHACKLED EMANCIPATOR

Thorstein Veblen was the most disturbing analyst of the modern business system to appear in our time. During his life he never had a great following. Classical economists of his own day rejected his beliefs as those of a bitter crank. His books were never widely read. The greater part of his life was spent nursing grievances against his colleagues for coming to see the value of his work only when he himself had lost interest in personal recognition; against the colleges that denied him posts; against the whole reading public, which was generally unaware even of his existence.

Yet his influence has spread wide through the whole world of ideas and sunk deep into the mind of the student of economics. Many a man quotes tags like "conspicuous waste" without knowing who invented them. In his own field Veblen is regarded as an emancipator. He set imaginations free to explore previously accepted dogmas and to discover what surprises there might be within patterns of thought that no one had taken the trouble to examine before with serious critical attention.

As he presented himself to the world, Veblen was a sort of sternly detached diagnostician whose task was to examine the faults and flaws of a system and to indicate what sort of eventual breakdown might be expected. One of his fundamental ideas, expressed first in the volume called *The Business Enterprise*, was that of an inevitable and enduring conflict between the captain of business and the productive machine of which he had set himself up as operator and guardian.

Veblen saw this captain of business as a whimsical tyrant who invented difficulties in the execution of a fundamentally simple operation, that of producing the goods and services required by a known market. This demigod of economic affairs started and stopped production willfully. He created shortages and surpluses so that he could conveniently manipulate prices. Through the system of credits, he rigged the market in such a way that special profits were forever finding their way into his pocket.

The captain of industry showed himself to be a whimsical tyrant also when he deliberately emphasized the vast distance between himself and those over whose lives he exercised economic domination. (It was in *The Theory of the Leisure Class* that Veblen zealously examined this unconscious sin of pride.) Simple men must expect and be content to have strict limits put upon their ability to satisfy their needs. For his part, the captain of business exhibited a princely indifference to limitations of any kind. When such men built themselves houses larger than were needed to give a maximum of comfort, when they filled those houses with servants who could not function efficiently because there were too many of them, when they decorated those houses with art objects upon which artificial high values had been fixed—in all of these activities they indulged in "conspicuous waste," the purpose of which was to place them in a special category as the "honor men" of our civilization. The dazzling evidence of their power was supposed to make them immune from criticism.

Essential to Veblen's system was the distinction that he made between industry and business. The legitimate object of *industry* is the manufacture and distribution of goods needed by the community which industry serves. In Veblen's view the object of *business* is to make the whole process of manufacture and distribution seem as complicated as possible so that few men dare, because they are overawed and dazzled, to challenge the system.

Veblen had a dry, epigrammatic way of half revealing, half concealing his contempt for these complications. He wrote, as he probably spoke, with a sort of Norwegian drawl, well suited to his ironic style.

"Here and now, as always and everywhere," he stated in *The Instinct of Workmanship*, "invention is the mother of necessity. . . . Any technological advantage gained by one competitor forthwith becomes a necessity to all the rest on pain of defeat. The typewriter is, no doubt, a good and serviceable contrivance for the expedition of a voluminous correspondence but there is also no reasonable doubt but that its introduction has appreciably more than doubled the volume of correspondence necessary to carry on a given volume of business or that it has quadrupled the necessary cost of carrying on such correspondence."

This curious man who sat in obscure alcoves defying with his aloof scorn the captains of business was born in Cato Township, Wisconsin, in 1857. He occupied an uncomfortable position in a large family. As sixth of twelve children he was neglected in the family circle, and neglect was his portion all his life.

When he was eight years old the Veblen family moved to Minnesota and settled down among other Norwegian immigrants as farmers. At seventeen, young Thorstein managed to enter Carleton College, and after being graduated taught for a year at an academy in Madison. Feeling the need of a more thorough preparation for his work as a critic of society, he went to Johns Hopkins, and later to Yale, where he studied philosophy and social theory. He was miserably unhappy during those years. To support himself he taught in a military school where he was despised as an alien. He fumbled uneasily with his adopted language and spoke it with a thick Norwegian accent. The contempt with which he was treated entered into his mind and lodged there, a painful weight upon his spirit.

But a more bitter experience was still to come. With a fine academic title to put to his name, he still found no place in the world he wished to make his own. There was no teaching assignment for him anywhere. He returned to Minnesota to live on a farm in the midst of a family which probably assured him in looks, if not in words, that all the pretensions in which he had indulged by going year after year to school had fallen away from him at last, and that he was exposed as a failure. The farmer's son had had come home to the only job for which he was fit, that of a hired man under the direction of others who had trained themselves sensibly to do their own job, not that of their betters.

For seven years he lived in that exile from his work. No mystical belief in the numeral seven is needed to persuade one that it was during that period of bitter growth that his task was really done. The writing came afterward; but the discovery of his method and the formulation of his ideas must have been accomplished as he trudged through the bitter loneliness of those years.

It was unfortunate for the prestige of his work that Veblen should have acquired in his isolation quite so much of personal spite. The contempt that had lain so long in the background of his mind like a load of useless concrete, he began to deposit chunk by chunk in his heavy paragraphs of critical analysis. What made this method worse was that he performed these acts with an air of ironic, rather languid indifference that seemed priggish, almost unmanly. Alienated by his ideas, his confreres were alienated also by his manners; they felt entitled to reject both on the pretense that both were bad. A man with Veblen's gift for phrase-making might, if his temperament had happened to be more genial and forgiving, have driven the steel of his beliefs home much more successfully. But the boor was dismissed from the tournament of economists through he was the strongest, most original fighter among them, and could also have been the most deft.

His entry into the academic world came at last in his own Middle West when, after still another postgraduate year at Cornell, he became a fellow at the University of Chicago. His sponsor at Chicago cannot ever have understood Veblen's ideas very well; he happened to be one who subscribed, in all reverence, to belief in the sainthood of the business man, appointed by God to lead the people. Yet he supported Veblen through many a difficulty and saw him advanced finally to the post of assistant professor.

But bitterness was working in the mind of this man still. He sought compensation for his unhappy past by alienating most men. He allowed women to express their regard for him in ways that were designed to disturb an academic community where professors are supposed to float in disembodied ecstasy, above suspicion of any carnal inclination. At last he was obliged to leave Chicago, and went in turn to Leland Stanford and the University of Missouri. In 1918 he gave up the idea of trying to live in a position of armed truce with the academic world, and went to New York, where he lectured at the New School for Social Research and helped to edit the *Dial*.

The end of his life was as dismal as its beginning. His only steady income came to him as a gift from a former pupil. Magazines rejected his articles. His admirers were scattered, and he had nothing in the least like a set of disciples. His life ended, along with the life of an era, in 1929. But he did not survive quite long enough to see the drama of the stock-market crash which so many of his theories had tacitly predicted.

Now his bitterness, his personal feuds and scenes are either forgotten by most readers or quite unknown to them. His influence becomes steadily more pervasive, more certain to endure as long as there is need of sharp criticism to deflate the pretensions of the ill-educated.

Veblen was very surely the product of the conditions of life in Wisconsin and Minnesota. He himself did not enjoy his heritage, but it was of the sort that belonged to all the Norwegian immigrants of the region, strong, stubborn, and unyielding. Nor did he enjoy those seven years on a farm near Northfield, Minnesota. Yet they shaped his mind in the lonely detachment that such a mind needed in order to make an uncompromising bold attack upon the very foundations of an economic system. If Veblen had not studied it from a distance during so long a time, he might not have seen its weaknesses with such clarity.

KNIGHT-ERRANT OF SOCIAL LEGISLATION

"I was reborn when I entered Wisconsin," Professor John R. Commons writes in his autobiography, called *Myself*.

That rebirth did not occur until he was in his early forties. Already he had had many teaching experiences as sociologist and economist. Already he had served on several important commissions investigating the problems of trade-unionism and the background of strikes. But it was at Madison that he found himself for the first time in a completely congenial atmosphere. There he entered into the pragmatist's heaven, a place where there were plenty of problems to solve and a sympathetic atmosphere in which to solve them, not by abstract theoretical rule, but by the application of realistic common sense.

In those early days of the century the elder La Follette was busy reforming the state and snatching its government back from the hands of the outraged bosses, who imagined vainly that they had got rid of the nonsense about democratic practice. La Follette was undertaking also to adjust inequalities of taxation, to remove an intolerable burden from the backs of farmers and to require the railroads to carry a just share of the load.

Professor Commons, who had always believed that the task of

the economist was essentially that of acting as adviser to leaders, found himself in the exact place where he longed to be. He had some splendidly strenuous years during which he rushed back and forth between his classroom and the statehouse, serving in both settings precisely as he was best fitted to serve. Appearing before his students in the role of a latter-day Socrates of the economic field, he teased their minds with questions and challenges. He gave them assignments that sent them to investigate for themselves the practical working out of economic principles in the lives of men and women. At the statehouse he helped La Follette put through his famous civil-service commission law, thereby helping to write the death sentence of boss rule. He served on an industrial commission and was many times before the legislature, carrying to the makers of laws an economist's view of the basic principles involved.

In the course of all this highly practical application of economic theory Professor Commons was, of course, developing a broad concept of his own concerning the scope and significance of his subject. Having had so active a finger in the shaping of many programs which, under his guidance, had been put into actual practice, Professor Commons was bound to be a very different sort of thinker from the economist who isolates himself in the immaculate confines of an ivory tower to experiment with pure theory in an artificially limited field of study. Inevitably it became Professor Commons's life work to try to widen the scope of economics once more to include at least glimpses of political science and sociology as "branches of political economy." Greatly daring, Professor Commons did not hesitate to mention the concerns even of ethics when he discussed the problems of his science.

What he evolved was a system called "Institutional Economics," a theory of social organization that gives greater attention than neoclassical economists allow to the cohesive force of customary and collective behavior. Society, as Professor Commons sees it, is a "going concern" operated in accordance with human designs. Its functioning is based on the idea of "willingness"; that is, the voluntary choice of the human will-in-action to direct economic activity toward an increase in the future output of goods and services. According to the social purposes that dominate the thought of the time, this human will-in-action can be controlled either to the end of giving those goods and services to the nation as a whole or to the end of acquiring a large share of the national output for particular individuals or groups.

Our capitalistic system, in Professor Commons's interpretation, is such a going concern dominated by expectations of the future. It has passed through the phase of "employer capitalism" and reached a phase of "banker capitalism." Now it is destined to make further progress in one or the other of two possible directions. It may develop into "reasonable capitalism," based on the idea of protecting community welfare, or it may degenerate into a dictatorship of the Fascist type.

It is here that Professor Commons boldly introduces the ethical concept. He has had wide practical experience in adjusting the differences between combatants in strikes of various kinds. He believes that it should be possible to persuade sensible men, like those with whom he has already dealt in disputes between employers and workers, to adopt in each unit of society a code of "reasonable practices." Such a code would protect community welfare by working for "the highest attainable idealism that is found in going concerns under existing circumstances." Professor Commons has wanted nothing to do with distant intellectual ideals of the kind out of which Utopias are fashioned. But he does believe that as social intelligence becomes better organized all the managerial principles upon which society operates will be employed for the expansion of the general economic welfare.

Professor Commons has occupied the uneasy position of the liberal whose views are neither radical enough for the Left nor conservative enough for the Right. He does not please his fellow economists either. His insistence upon the voluntary character of the relationship between man and the economic world tends to throw discredit on those sacred and immutable laws in which the neoclassicist finds his authority. When he substitutes the idea of collective action, in control of individual action, for that of the sacredness of individual liberty, he also tends to undermine the ruggedness of individual enterprise. It is clear that his colleagues find distressing and untidy his willingness to let economics flow over into sociology and ethics. In all of these habits of thought he has been unorthodox and unacademic. He does not greatly care, for he can afford to let his reputation stand on the fact that his influence upon the social legislation of our day has been greater than that of any man in private life.

Commons has resembled Veblen in that he is a critic of the capitalist system, and also in that he has little intellectual sympathy with the effort of the economists to force upon the world the belief that theirs is a science based on thoroughly known and unalterable natural laws. But he has been utterly unlike Veblen in his way of putting his views before the world. Veblen was sour, contemptuous, aloof, antisocial. Commons is generous-minded, humble, companionable, co-operative. It is his favorite boast that his students have done most of his work for him. In compiling his studies, such as that of the labor movement, he has incorporated the findings of everyone who has worked with him in the most modest capacity and has said in effect to his students in his classes: "I am not a man but a syndicate. I exist to express you."

He has always been a man of the great world rather than of the study. He has demonstrated the sincerity of his belief in the principle of collective action in control of individual action by collaborating with political leaders, lawmakers, commissions, anyone or any group that has been interested in the objective of broadening general social welfare.

Again, it is characteristic of the "Wisconsin idea" that it should have developed, out of its impulse to reform the world, two men who approached that goal by exactly opposite routes. Veblen showed the hard, cold, negative aspect of the critical spirit; Commons has shown its malleable, warm, affirmative character. Out of similar views and preoccupations Veblen could evolve only a destructive method, while Commons has undertaken always to translate his ideas into immediate creative service to the people of the society in which he so vividly lives.

When he wrote his autobiography in 1934, he was still an extremely jaunty old gentleman. He was already more than seventy years old. His wife and four of the six children born of their marriage had died before him. A son who had served with distinction in the first World War had come home a victim of shell-shock and finally had disappeared. Yet despite all of these tragic reminders that the end of even the most excellent and useful life must inevitably be lonely, Professor Commons summoned up out of the curious and attractive recesses of his pragmatic mind a genuine and unforced gaiety. A pleasant epilogue to one chapter of Professor Commons's curiously dramatic life was written when his eldest son, after suffering for many years from partial amnesia, emerged out of his own private limbo to be reunited with his father.

Professor Commons recalled for his own pleasure images out of the past, which he quickened to life with a creative touch that was soundly and shrewdly artistic. There was his father, a backslider from Quakerism who had a kind of lifelong love affair with Darwinism, until in his old age the mysterious charms of spiritualism and Christian Science wooed him away. The elder Commons loved to sit among his tobacco-chewing, tobacco-squirting Indiana friends, swapping yarns, ideas, and properties. He was a survival of the barter age and could never adjust himself to the era of money and credits. Once he came into possession of 360 acres of land in the incredibly rich Red River Valley of Minnesota. But he swapped this property for a printing office, where he was really happier. The end of his tradings was that of a certain, often repeated parable for children: he had nothing. But while he lived on timberlands in Florida, he and his sons had such a magnificent time as only the crackers could properly appreciate and only Marjorie Kinnan Rawlings could describe. Perhaps it was Professor Commons's stories about life among the crackers that sent Marjorie Rawlings from the University of Wisconsin to rediscover Florida.

And there was the mother, militantly a Presbyterian, militantly an Anti-saloon Leaguer, militantly an intellectual. She had been graduated from Oberlin, and there her son must go, though she had to take roomers and boarders to provide him with the means. Nowhere does there exist a better portrait of the humble priestess of the American cult of the excellent life than in Professor Commons's study of his mother.

Best of all, there is the portrait of Professor Commons himself in all his early experimental phases. He was a resourceful and untiring pragmatist from the start, despite the poor health that was forever tumbling him into a ruin of nerves at the most inconvenient moment. He seems to have combined some of the most dramatic features of Tom Sawyer with those of the village neurotic. It is a mixture as unorthodox as most of Professor Commons's blendings in the economic field. But it worked rather well for a man whose job in life was to be that of trying to reconcile the ways of the gods of the academic world with those of men in industry and in legislatures.

Early in his youth Commons learned the printer's trade, and he worked at it, off and on, through all his college years. Some of his Tom Sawyer experiments in rugged individualism gave him his first insight into the principles of collective action in control of individual action. For his fellow printers managed to put him down when he proved to be just a shade too resourceful.

Even in his love of baseball he showed a curious blend of academic curiosity and practical energy. It was Herbert Spencer (of all people!) who tried to demonstrate the scientific impossibility of throwing a curved ball. And, determined to disprove Spencer, Professor Commons in his youth threw one of the first curved balls. Even the great Babe Ruth and the immortal Lou Gehrig, all unconsciously, owed something to his pioneering.

He is a fine democratic figure, hearty, experimental, ready always to try again, unafraid of inconsistency. The rights and privileges of academic godhood he has always put away with a reckless gesture. Graduated by indulgence of his professors at Oberlin—that is the citation he claims for himself. A failure at one academic assignment after another until he found the technique of confiding to his classes all his doubts and of making his students fellow conspirators in his many sins of inconsistency! Out of these long, patient explorations of the humble paths that workers must tread have come many adjustments, many compromises, many small agreements that work.

VITAMIN VISIONARY

Stephen Moulton Babcock was born a hundred years ago, and he was already a young man in his teens at the outbreak of the Civil War. Yet he lived on into the last decade and his name is associated with one of the most epoch-making of modern scientific discoveries. The radio announcers who indulge in fine frenzies (every hour on the hour) about the marvels of our time, such as vitamins, would perhaps be a little chagrined to know that the truth about these benevolent substances did not spring from the mind of a strictly twentieth-century chemist in a strictly twentieth-century laboratory. Snobs of modernity would expect of a man born in 1843 no more chic a contribution to human knowledge than, at most, a small technological improvement in the cotton gin. But Babcock's physical vitality covered more than eighty years and his intellectual vitality covered a much wider stretch, the distance between ignorance and knowledge.

Babcock was born at Bridgewater, New York, and had his early education at Tufts College. He taught for a brief period at Cornell and presently went to the University of Göttingen in Germany, where he took his doctor's degree. He returned to Cornell once more as a teacher and later was chemist for the New York State Agricultural Experiment Station.

But, like John R. Commons, he was reborn when he entered Wisconsin. There he was permitted to follow the hunches of his exploring mind and to admit quite openly that he believed in very little that he had been taught.

One of the beliefs of the time which he felt inclined to put far, far away was that any diet containing the proper balance between proteins, carbohydrates, and the rest of the known substances of nourishment was as good as any other. The Germans felt, even then, their cold, fanatical love of *ersatz*, and were determined to find artificial foods that would do quite as well as natural ones. Babcock, who was a hearty, natural, spontaneous man with a love of laughter and sports and all free and gracious things, felt an instinctual distaste for this cheating and contriving.

He belonged in an atmosphere like that of Wisconsin, where so much of the population devoted itself to the tasks of growing natural foods. And Wisconsin had the greatest need of him.

Babcock arrived in the West at a moment when there was a crisis in the dairy industry. Farmers were dissatisfied with creamery prices because no premium was allowed for high quality. Dairymen retorted that farmers were adulterating their milk. In angry deadlock, the two groups hurled accusations at each other while a promising source of income for the state dwindled.

What Wisconsin needed, and in a very great hurry, was a simple test for butterfat. Only when the quality of milk could be accurately measured might the feud be expected to end. But many scientists had tried to find such a test and each had abandoned the effort in disgust at its complications.

Babcock found one. For months he devoted himself to this problem exclusively until it was solved. With characteristic nonchalance he strolled into the office of his superior, Dean A. W. Henry, and announced that the thing could be done by using a specific amount of sulphuric acid, which rendered soluble all solids not fat while the heat evolved in the mixture melted the fat and allowed it to rise to the surface. By this test, samples of milk could be tested and graded quickly and with unfailing accuracy. Today the Babcock test is essentially unchanged.

It was a characteristic also of his high-spirited dedication to the doing of a job that he was quite uninterested in any profit that might be made from his discovery. The technique of the test could easily have become Babcock's private property. For the use of this reliable and inexpensive method the dairies of American and foreign countries might have been required to pay him millions of dollars in royalties. But that kind of low cunning made no appeal to Babcock. In his genial and generous-minded philosophy, the discoveries of science belonged to the world. To anyone who had the wit to want it he gave the formula gratis.

The Babcock test revealed also the intimacies of the performance of an individual cow. Slackers were exposed and excellent animals identified for special admiration. The fortunate result was the development of better strains. The cow, that best and most eugenically cared for of domestic animals, owes something of her present-day splendor to Babcock.

Many things about the secrets of human functioning interested him also. One of his important contributions to human knowledge was in the field of metabolism. Babcock, feeding insects on an exclusive diet of fur, discovered that the inner workings of their bodies managed, even out of so dry and fuzzy a table d'hôte, to produce the moisture they needed. Babcock's notes on this phenomenon contributed fundamentally to the conquest of the un-known in this field of study.

He came finally to grips with the problem of disproving the faith reposed by his German teachers in chemical foods. Working with a group of colleagues, he showed first that conventional food analyses had gone decorously round and round in a circle, really demonstrating nothing about how an animal takes nourishment from food. It was discovered by experimentation that a cow dis-charged from its body as much in the way of energy content as it had taken in. Then in a patient, long-range, closely controlled experiment Babcock and his colleagues began to study the prob-lem of diet from its very beginning.

They divided a herd of experimental heifers into four groups of four each. The first was fed on an exclusive diet of wheat and wheat substances, gluten, and roughage. The second had a similar diet based on corn; the third one based on oats; and the fourth, a table d'hôte composed of smaller quantities of all these foods.

Quite soon it became apparent that while the corn-fed creatures thrived and flourished, the wheat-eating heifers seemed un-happy and dissatisfied. They rolled their heads and lolled their tongues. If they could have spoken they would undoubtedly have complained of general lassitude and of seeing spots before the eyes.

These findings were noted as interesting but inconclusive, and the experiment continued. The heifers were bred with a healthy bull. Babcock, having had the nudge from his imagination that there was something wrong with wheat as an exclusive diet despite its very proper theoretical value as nutriment, wanted to put it to a fuller test. If it could produce life then it ought to be able to sustain it.

But once more the wheat diet proved to be disastrous. The corn-fed animals went through their full terms of gestation and brought forth fine, sturdy young that took to their own legs and their mother's teats with enthusiasm. But the wheat contingent grew daily more pathetic throughout the whole period. Their young were in a neurotic hurry to be born, but survived only a few hours or days after premature delivery. One well-shaped bull was born dead. Wheat stood convicted of inadequacy as an exclusive diet.

There was one more test still to be made before the point could be regarded as demonstrated. One of the cows that had been fed on wheat until she was lean and wretched was put on a corn diet. Straightway her body filled out, her coat became glossy and she was a credit to the herd once more. One of the complacent, corn-fed creatures was transferred to wheat and all at once, like a heart-broken female in a Victorian romance, she began to sicken and die.

The truth had been established at last that there was something in corn besides its known chemical elements that made animals plump, content with their environment, and adequate to all the responsibilities of their experience. Dissimilarly wheat, though it contained all that the German chemists would require of it in the way of nutritive value, lacked something that an animal needed to be whole, and without which it could not be expected to pass on its life.

The discovery of vitamins was still several leaps of the imagination away. But a start had been made.

As Commons has proved himself to be the perfect democrat of the economists' round table, Babcock was the perfect democrat of the laboratory. Neither man wanted anything but the opportunity to work at the job for which he felt himself to be fitted. The results of his study he gave freely to the world. Neither added up out of his work the private treasure that the slightest touch of cunning might so easily have brought him. They spent their lives in a sympathetic environment, searching, discovering, sharing.

They were alike in several curious ways. Commons is living a long life, and Babcock had his eighty years and more on earth. Both were cheerful, gregarious, unassuming. And both loved base-ball. They were boyish spirits who grew old and wise and became enormously useful without losing their innocence or their enthusiasm.

ANALYST OF THE FRONTIER

Unlike Commons and Babcock, Frederick Jackson Turner did not need to be reborn to enter Wisconsin. He was born there in the first place, at the town of Portage, which has been for many years one of the most persistently, patiently, minutely described of Wisconsin communities. Zona Gale was also its citizen and she made it the setting both of her cheerful *Friendship Village* stories and of less optimistic interpretations like *Birth* and *Miss Lulu Bett*. It was appropriate that a son of Portage should, when he turned scholar, have brought forth one of the most dramatic ideas as to why America chose unconsciously to develop as it has developed.

When one writes that Turner's contribution as a teacher and thinker is based on his idea of the importance of the frontier in our native history, one has to expect to see the eyebrows of the younger critics make a supercilious dash for the hairline. Lips that may, after mature reflection on the part of their owners, be too polite to put the question, seem none the less to shape the unspoken challenge: "What of it?" It is, of course, the fate of all men of insight to have their ideas catch up with them. After seeming for a time bizarre and advanced, theories become, the moment everyone has accepted them, just a little quaint and old-fashioned. "Old hat!" say the bright young men concerning all the intellectual wear that once infuriated the conservative with its *outré* audacity. But when Professor Turner stepped up, at the age of thirty-two, to show his new creation before a meeting of the American Historical Association held at the World's Fair in Chicago in 1893, it was a very glossy and impressive hat indeed.

Dr. Charles Beard has distilled the essence of Turner's ideas into these salient sentences:

1. *"The existence of an area of free land, its continuous recession, and the advance of American settlement westward explain American development";*

2. *"American social development has been continually beginning over again on the frontier";*

3. *"The frontier is the line of most rapid and effective Americanization";*

4. *"The frontier promoted the formation of a composite nationality for the American people";*

5. *"The advance of the frontier decreased our dependence on England";*

6. *"The legislation which most developed the powers of national government, and played the largest part in its activity, was conditioned on the frontier";*

7. *"Loose construction [of the Constitution] increased as the nation marched westward";*

8. *"It is safe to say that legislation with regard to land, tariff and internal improvements—the American system of the nationalizing Whig Party—was conditioned on frontier ideals and needs";*

9. *"This nationalizing tendency of the West . . . transformed the democracy of Jefferson into the national republicanism of Monroe and the democracy of Andrew Jackson"; "the most important effect of the frontier has been in the promotion of democracy here and in Europe. . . . The frontier is productive of individualism";*

10. *"So long as free land exists, the opportunity for a competency exists, and economic power secures the political power";*

11. *"The frontier developed the essentially American traits—coarseness and strength, acuteness, inventiveness, restless energy, the masterful grasp of material things, lacking in the artistic but powerful to effect great ends";*

12. *"The closing of the frontier marked the end of 'the first period of American history.'"*

Today critics of Turner's theories are inclined to believe that, like most inventors of tight systems of thought, he tried to explain too much in terms of his own particular vocabulary. At the very moment when he was insisting on the strict "individualism" of the frontier, the agrarian crusade was creating its various forms of fraternal co-operation, the basic idea of which was that of mutual dependency.

But if the complex character of American development cannot be reduced to quite the orderly pattern that Turner sought to put upon it, at least the fact that restless men were forever rushing into rich, uncrowded corners of the American world to help themselves to the best of its resources and then push on has had an undeniable effect on our native temperament and on the culture that has been evolved to satisfy the essential needs of that temperament.

From the social point of view, the fortunate characteristics of the frontiersman's psychology were his energy, his adaptability, and his imaginative insight. He created a plant for the service of a rapidly growing community, and he did it in record time. The unfortunate aspects were the haste with which he improvised his way of life and the lack of a sense of responsibility that he felt toward a particular bit of land. As a devotee of the idea of getting on, he could abandon, without any feeling of loss, his loyalty to the soil that had served him well but could serve him no longer. In his seeking and rather greedy imagination, heaven seemed always to lie on the other side of the mountain, and what he did in the country through which he passed to get there scarcely mattered. The frontiersman did not linger in his cities to give them beauty or even a look of permanence. He was but a stranger there; the heaven (of the resources still to be grasped) was his home.

It has been pointed out frequently that grandsons of the most rugged of our pioneers often show pale, apprehensive, and decadent faces to the world. This may be partly because their education lacked the sense of social responsibility that it might have had if the vigorous founders of American families had stayed in one place, thrust their roots deep into a particular soil, and identified themselves creatively with one community.

Even today some Americans show the restlessness and neuroses that their training cultivated in them. Behind the closed frontier they struggle with a suffocating claustrophobia, and dream of escape to a new, free world. After the present war we shall have our restless groups whom travel has inspired with visions of opportunity to be grasped in lands across the sea. The "great open spaces" of Australia will attract them irresistibly.

Fortunately for the development of Wisconsin and Minnesota there were mong its citizens men of solid character with ambitions that vaulted less high than those of the frontiersmen. After the pilgrims had passed on to the heaven on the far side of the next mountain, the sober men who were left behind worked hard to pull their communities together into livable ones where there was useful work to do in the mines, in the forests, and on the farms.

Turner's ideas may seem less dramatic than they once did, and less reliable, but anyone writing today who tries to answer the questions: "What is an American? And why?" is, in a sense, his disciple. Turner asked those questions first.

FIRST AID TO LIVING LITERATURE

The importance of Joseph Warren Beach as a representative of ideas lies in the fact that he has dared to apply the method of scholarship to an appraisal of the writing of his contemporaries. His scholarship has never been called into question among his colleagues. He is intimately acquainted with the hallowed shrines and his work on a figure like Wordsworth, for example, has the profound respect of the academic world. Philosophy ever has had so great an attraction for his exploring mind that his book called *The Concept of Nature in Nineteenth-Century English Poetry* is of equal interest as analysis of abstract thought and as criticism of literature.

It is a desire to interpret the thought of our time that has led Joseph Warren Beach into the consideration of the work of John Dos Passos, Ernest Hemingway, and Erskine Caldwell. He brings to the task a scrupulous concern for absolute standards of excellence. In *The Twentieth-Century Novel* and *American Fiction, 1920–1940*, he has examined the impulses that animate the writer today and make him a very different sort of person, both in thought and in technique, from his Victorian predecessor.

He has shown such things as how the author has abdicated from the throne of judgment. Indeed, the conscientious creative artist has departed completely from the stage to seek a dramatic method through which his characters may seem to act upon one another in absolute independence of their creator. Even when the interior of the mind is the scene of the drama, it is, as Joseph Beach has pointed out, still the character who speaks, not the author.

Writing today, particularly in America, in his opinion shows a strong sociological tendency. The novelist is concerned with the values that men seek to enthrone as arbiters of human behavior. Yet their seriousness has not led them back to the high and aloof perches of the Victorian oracles. Each writer has sought his own means of presenting his beliefs effectively, without rhetorical display, but with a subtle appreciation of the æsthetic means that can best serve his own kind of emphasis on ideas.

It is the task of a critic to show even the artist himself how his instinctual equipment has prompted him to work and what instruments of communication he has invented. The critic studies these instruments with detached and scientific perception, making their use more evident. No one else has done this for the literary artist of our time with the sympathy, the justice, the fully rounded perception of the trend of a whole school of writing that Joseph Beach has shown. He is unique among critics and commentators today. The best among such men and women possess gifts of human understanding and taste and shrewdness. What almost all of them lack is a sweeping view of the whole history of letters which can show clearly how contemporary writing follows the continuity of the tradition of communication. And what all but a very few lack is a set of principles by which a man's work may be accurately measured in relation to the values that it attempts to present. Because he is a philosopher who believes in scientific method, Joseph Beach has lifted the criticism of contemporary letters far above the level of gossip and self-exploitation where it so often is allowed to languish.

A description of his critical method should not be allowed to sound austere. His seriousness does not exclude brilliance and wit of style. Joseph Beach is a man of letters who controls a wide range of literary means. He has written many charming poems, of sensitive and searching quality. He is the author of a novel, *Glass Mountain,* an interesting demonstration of how a critic puts his theories to work when he assumes the role of a creator. The informal essays contained in the volume called *Meek Americans* are models of grace. Their themes, developed with an air of innocent and light-hearted casualness, actually comment with warm and humorous perception on some of the most dramatic crises of human relations.

Joseph Beach was born at Gloversville in New York. He did his undergraduate work at the University of Minnesota. Having earned his A.M. and Ph.D. degrees at Harvard, he returned to Minnesota as a member of its English department in 1910.

Inside and outside the academic world Professor Beach is interested in the whole drama of human society. Minnesota reserves a special niche for him in the gallery of its creative people because he has done so much to direct the course of its thinking.

COMMON SENSE AND GENIUS

For nearly thirty years the greatest Shakespearean scholar of our time taught at the University of Minnesota. During that period the beliefs of Professor Elmer Edgar Stoll took root in the minds of the leading teachers of the world.

He was not receveid at first with unreserved enthusiasm. Indeed, the stately kings of criticism waved this audacious begetter of new ideas from before their sight. Quietly, but very firmly, he refused to be dismissed. His monographs, his papers read before learned societies, his essays contributed to scholarly publications developed with ever more and more certainty of purpose a new approach to the interpretation of genius.

The startling novelty of Professor Stoll's approach lay in the fact that it was the direct one. Nineteenth-century criticism had found all manner of pleasant, ambling, circuitous paths by which to come at the meaning of *Hamlet* or *Othello*. The inclination of those innocently resourceful thinkers who had seized upon the work of Shakespeare as their private preserve for scholarly scouting, trapping, and hunting was to regard the plays as a sort of mysterious and magical wonderland of ideas in which the faiths and fears of all centuries, past, present, and future, were herded.

In this curious game refuge you might, if you were sufficiently wary and cunning, trap an exquisite doelike little allegory of the previous century or perhaps a great, wild, snarling anticipation of the whole Freudian psychology, escaped from the twentieth century.

This impressionistic method of reading into the work of an Elizabethan poet the ideas, tastes, and preoccupations of every century but his own seemed to Professor Stoll a great deal too ingenious. Being a man of enormous erudition with a knowledge of literature that ranged through all ages and through virtually all languages, he had a sense of the continuity of the writing tradition. He was far less fond of mysteries than the *exalté*, but only half-educated, thinker is inclined to be.

Professor Stoll chose as his task that of relating the genius of Shakespeare to his time.

Shakespeare, he reasoned, was a practical man of affairs, writing for a London audience. Certain familiar traditions of the stage had to be respected. Writing for a popular following which he must please if he wished to continue to be popular, Shakespeare sensibly adapted his genius to the literary conventions of the period.

The fresh current of common sense let into the stuffy atmosphere of conventional scholarship by Professor Stoll had the effect of blowing away many of the stale and unwholesome concepts about Shakespeare's æsthetic motives and philosophic meanings. It was no longer necessary to knot one's brows over the problem of Hamlet and to decide whether he was merely a vacillating creature with sensibilities that weakly drained away his power of will or a thoroughgoing neurotic with an Œdipus complex.

Hamlet, in Professor Stoll's interpretation, is the typical Elizabethan hero. He has a task to perform. It must be made to seem urgent in the first scene, yet the execution of it must be delayed until the last, because that was the way in which Elizabethan plays were made. Indeed, it is the way in which solid plays are made today. The body of the text is devoted to the necessary elaboration of the narrative, underscoring the seriousness, the dignity, and the difficulty of the duty that the Prince had laid upon himself. Correctly understood, Hamlet emerges not as the uncertain and even timorous shirker of responsibility, but as the essential man of action. Shakespeare's play shows Hamlet resourcefully buffeting and beating down the obstacles that tradition, superstition, and intrigue throw in his way.

Similarly Professor Stoll has shown that scholarship plunges into a jungle of quite imaginary difficulties when it tries to twist the character of Iago into something that can be made to fit a behavior pattern outlined by a modern psychiatrist. It is not in the ingenuities of the "hostility" motif that the clue to an understanding of Iago should be sought. He is, in fact, the perfect example of the Elizabethan villain, a highly conventionalized figure, well understood by the audience of the time. Villainy was the métier of the villain, and Iago went about it with a resourcefulness that Shakespeare's following loved to watch.

Professor Stoll has insisted that modern criticism waters down the interest of these Elizabethan plays by failing to accept the fact that they were the products of the mood, the mores, the æsthetic preferences of their day. We misread the plays and then marvel at the enigmatic wonders of our misreading.

Two equally sentimental impulses have tended to defeat a proper understanding of Shakespeare's genius. The first is the confused desire to find a cozy identity between literature and life. But, as Professor Stoll has patiently pointed out again and again, the purposes of literature are blurred by such an interpretation. Literature is selection, arrangement, treatment of the materials of life according to a conventionalized æsthetic plan. It should be an illuminating comment on human experiment, not a full, factual report, a sort of Gestapo dossier.

The other limitation is our latter-day desire for the soft drink of consistency. Elizabethan audiences took their emotions "strong and mixed."

Within the common-sense limitations set by his theory, Professor Stoll's studies have been inspired by the subtlety of his own mind and the depth of his own poetic appreciation. He has refused to consider Shakespeare as a prophet, oracle, or modern psychologist, because he believes him to have been none of these things. His stimulating critical gift has been devoted to interpreting Shakespeare as a dramatist and poet of genius.

Professor Stoll, born at Orrville, Ohio, was graduated from Wooster, took his A.B. and A.M. degrees at Harvard, studied at the University of Berlin, and received his Ph.D. from the University of Munich. He came to the University of Minnesota in 1914 as professorial lecturer, and in the following years was made professor. He retired from teaching in 1941.

Gradually, over thirty years, the beliefs of Professor Stoll seeped down through the layers of prejudice, through the rocky, hard, and inert acceptance of the dead theories of the past. His principles penetrated at last even the most stubborn minds. All at once there was general acknowledgment that he is the finest of living Shakespearean scholars and a no less brilliant interpreter of Milton and other gods of English literature.

Logan Pearsall Smith has expressed the widespread belief of scholars: "Professor Stoll has applied his sanity, his enlightened manly common sense and also his great learning to . . . many problems [and] brushed aside much sophistication and academic cobweb."

13

SING, REGIONAL MUSE!

THE WORD "REGIONALISM" first came into popular use as a term intended to describe the impulse of novelists to tell, in more or less precise detail, how their own worlds and their own people seemed to them. Having been given a name, regionalism straightway became a cult, and a great many people seized upon it with the religious fervor of converts. Much that was either silly or overintense was written in misguided dedication to the new faith. But there has been a long tradition of legitimate regionalism in American writing, and of that solid kind Wisconsin and Minnesota have had their share.

By legitimate regionalism one means the sort of interpretative writing that shows a man putting down roots deep into the soil of his own place; that takes account of essential geographic and economic differences between one way of life and another lived in a distant region; and that acknowledges the influence upon social behavior of peculiar local conditions.

In Wisconsin and Minnesota, regionalism has explored the same general themes that have declared themselves in the economic crises and political adventures of the states. Novelists have dramatized the firm, persistent pressure for reform exercised by men like Ignatius Donnelly and Robert M. La Follette. Fiction reflects the readiness to experiment cheerfully, though seldom violently, with minor revolutionary movements in politics. Our story-tellers have been preoccupied with the physical ugliness of towns and the meagerness of the social tradition left behind on our soil as the migratory pioneers have stamped across the land in search of ever wider prospects and bigger profits. The study upon which our regionalism has concentrated is that of a community trying to pull itself together to find a basis for prosperity and a basis for self-respect after the passing of the first phase of wild and raucous exploitation.

This kind of regionalism is quite different from that which has tended, in some meager minds, to make of local prejudice something resembling an evangelist's brand of religion. That naïve interpretation has held feverishly to the view that the heavenly muse does herself over with protean variability each time she crosses a state line. The conviction has seemed to be strong in the true believer's heart that when one of the inspirational sisters finds herself in Wisconsin or Minnesota, she wearily gets out her make-up kit and prepares for a lugubrious session celebrating the sorrows of the soil and of the soul. The costume assigned to our local muse is a decent, though shabby Mother Hubbard. She sings exclusively of ruined wheat fields, and she sings of them with a strong German or Swedish accent.

It is inevitable that more sober writers have wished to divorce themselves from such follies of cultist dedication. They have sometimes been moved to deny that they were regionalists at all. But in the spontaneity of their interest in the life that they know intimately they have continued to be regionalists in spite of themselves.

A certain cosmopolitan awareness of the world as a whole has prevented such writers from being concerned greatly with dialects and accents, with costumes and mere local peculiarities. Rather, their interest has centered upon the crises of conduct produced by the circumstances of a particular way of life, bringing passion into play. Attention has been not upon the setting, but upon the man in the setting; it has spent its skill less in decking out character in quaintness than in stripping character down to find its universal and cosmopolitan essence.

This has been the impulse even of a writer like Sinclair Lewis, who has always taken the sidelong look of satire at human experience. It was for evidence in support of a sweeping generalization that Lewis looked when, in *Main Street*, he examined the mean and meager parochialism of the small town. Again, when he scrutinized so shrewdly and ruthlessly the shabby and concessive social values dramatized in *Babbitt*, Lewis was seeking a truth of universal applicability.

These are Sinclair Lewis's two Minnesota novels. The community of his birth unquestionably sat for its portrait in each. Though neither study is gratifying to the kind of vanity that expresses itself in chamber-of-commerce literature and tourist-bureau booklets, our citizens have admitted with a mixture of humility and masochism that these sketches are recognizable, at least as lively caricatures. But it was not to display Minnesota in a curious light that Sinclair Lewis wrote *Main Street* and *Babbitt*. From a familiar background he simply took familiar types and characteristic conflicts. The task that he set himself was to make the crises in the lives of the Kennicotts and the Babbitts seem typical of similar crises in the lives of similar men and women everywhere in America.

Lewis has long since ceased to be a regionalist in any strict sense of the term. During his middle period his themes grew broader. In *Arrowsmith* he undertook to interpret a man's conflict with the exactions of his profession, in *Dodsworth* a man's conflict with the whole European tradition, and in *It Can't Happen Here* a man's conflict with the ideas and technique of dictatorship. Recently his themes have shrunk once more so that in *Bethel Merriday* he seems like nothing but a belatedly stage-struck innocent, and in *Gideon Planish* like a pamphleteer deriding, in an irresponsible frenzy of witty, sometimes brilliant inventiveness, a whole realm of honest American thought and experimentation.

Sinclair Lewis is regionalism's brightest son in the sense that he made the news of an American village seem worthy of universal attention, his report upon it worthy of the Nobel Prize. But his program would not satisfy the more mystical exponents of the doctrine, for he has undertaken to interpret many regions far from home, and has even sinned the sin of Henry James by living out of America and writing about *principesse*.

The same cosmopolitan outlook modified the regionalism of

two other writers, both of whom have lately died, but whose books will be rediscovered by succeeding generations for many years to come.

Charles Flandrau was one of the most ingratiating and highly cultivated American writers of our time. He must continue for long to occupy a unique place in our literature because he was the last survivor of the genteel tradition and one of the few latter-day men of letters to make a reputation almost exclusively as an exponent of the art of the informal essay.

Flandrau might have said of his experience as an artist what Max Beerbohm actually did say of his own: "My gifts are small. I've used them well and discreetly, never straining them, and the result is that I've made a charming little reputation." Flandrau's debut was made very early when, while he was still an undergraduate, he published a volume called *Harvard Episodes*. These remain the best stories of college life ever written by an American. They examine the trivia of adolescence with insight, tenderness, and a steady glow of wit. To this affectionate study "of a very small corner of a very big world," Flandrau added as pendants two other studies of student life, *The Diary of a Freshman* and *Sophomores Abroad*. In the second of these the theme began to seem so small to the author that he left his book unfinished. The beginning chapters lay in the obscurity of a magazine file for many years until one of the staunch devotees of his gift rediscovered them and chaperoned them into print.

Viva Mexico! Flandrau's frequently reborn classic of travel literature, came about almost accidentally when he went as a visitor to a brother's coffee plantation and found his imagination caught up by the drama of the peon's gift of varying languor with violence. Again it was a small corner of a big world that he chose to examine. Because he responded sensitively to certain fundamental traits of the primitive mind, his essays, set down casually and without thought of offering a definitive interpretation of Mexican character, have exercised a persistent fascination upon readers.

At certain productive moments of a literary career spread scantily over forty years, Flandrau wrote enough other essays to fill two small volumes, *Prejudices* and *Loquacities*. These have to do with a St. Paul childhood, with the era of the bustle, with a winter in Majorca, with the more fabulous and dismaying uses of the English language—with anything, in fact, that happened to engage his interest. To the most unimportant theme Flandrau could impart a special kind of grace; he conferred significance on many minute matters out of the richness of his humorous insight.

Flandrau's own theory of writing was that human intelligence was spread in a thin layer over the surface of the globe and that therefore one place was as good as another in which to study the working of man's heart and mind. He wrote comparatively little about Minnesota, and his contribution to the history of regionalism is slight. But it may be of importance to observe on the basis of his unique career that any region may at any time whimsically take the impulse to produce a perfect cosmopolitan. There should always be room in the philosophy of the regionalist for that delightful possibility.

The career of Scott Fitzgerald showed curious similarities of pattern. He began writing when he was a schoolboy in St. Paul. His debut was made when he was still in his early twenties with a novel, *This Side of Paradise*, which was in part a study of college life. The book gave him immediate success and widespread reputation. In St. Paul he first observed, at very close range, the type of brilliant and lordly youth with whom he was always to be preoccupied. As he proceeded to explore the larger fields of disillusionment, the spiritual confusion of "the lost generation" and the rootlessness of the expatriate on the Riviera, figures from Minnesota kept crossing his large stage. In his work the interests of regionalism and of the cosmopolitan spirit had spontaneous fusion.

In his most satisfactory novel, *The Great Gatsby*, Fitzgerald introduced a young man from Minnesota into the crazy pattern of life on Long Island during the Prohibition era. Gatsby, the millionaire racketeer, wooed for his wealth by all the hangers-on of a confused social world, is revealed slowly and pathetically as a prince of wistfulness. He longs to be accepted into that golden world of grace and insolence which is occupied so serenely and so securely by Fitzgerald's lordly young men. One of these, the narrator, is a former citizen of St. Paul.

Yet the underlying theme of all Fitzgerald's work was that the security of the rich boys whose portraits he liked to paint was not satisfactory to them and could not keep them from slipping into weariness, emotional squalor, and the overwhelming conviction of being damned. As his own life became a tangle of tragedies and disappointments, Fitzgerald made frequent public confession to belonging to the fallen-angel contingent.

It may seem strange that a community the history of which has been as short as that of Minnesota should have produced so brilliant a representative of the gospel of despair as Scott Fitzgerald. One is tempted to indulge in the fanciful notion that Minnesota yielded to a stern duty in creating him. Having imagined herself as a microcosm of the great world of letters, it seemed necessary to dramatize in one of her sons the doomed character of the unproductive life.

Like Lewis, Fitzgerald finally turned his back on the scene of his younger days to become the complete cosmopolitan. Just before he died, his great talent burned fitfully but brilliantly once more. In *The Last Tycoon* he had begun a novel that promised to be the first serious analysis of the art of Hollywood. Even in its unfinished form it is strikingly shrewd and searching. The bright young man from Minnesota who had spent his life examining the frustrations of the idle ended his life by writing about the complexities of the most modern of the arts. He had gone a long way from St. Paul. Yet the best of his work contained a significant comment on the life of Minnesota. Many a promising grandson of the pioneers turned decadent because he had inherited no solid tradition to which he could dedicate his talents. The Riviera and Hollywood took such men because they found it impossible to become interested in rebuilding the society of which their ancestors had run up a hasty framework.

Grace Flandrau is another of the cosmopolitans who are regionalists in spite of themselves. A tireless explorer in time and space, she is, by training and natural curiosity, disinclined to take into her sphere of vision fewer than two good-sized continents at a

DOG TEAM AND SLED NEAR GUNFLINT LAKE, MINNESOTA

BRINGING A DOE INTO CAMP-NEAR ELY, MINNESOTA

time. In *Then I Saw the Congo* she has explored the African jungle. In *Under the Sun* she has explored the mind and the senses of the white man succumbing to the influence of the jungle. Yet she constantly returns to themes that are at least incidentally regional in character. In *Being Respectable* she employed the accent of drawing-room comedy to protest, politely but emphatically, against the retrogression of a community like St. Paul into an out-of-date and rigidly conventional kind of social life. In *Indeed This Flesh*, an intensely sober and earnest novel, she psychoanalyzed a son of the pioneers who in his effort to rebuild the society of which he was a part found himself painfully handicapped by an oppressive sense of sin. The local scene and its people gave these novels their special character and in them Mrs. Flandrau lights her own "little fires of reform."

You would not expect to find so politically adventurous a state in possession of a fixed and unchanging political creed. Minnesota has writers who champion staunchly and untiringly every shade of opinion. Marking the boundaries of political thought from left to right are Meridel Le Sueur and Margaret Culkin Banning. Mrs. Banning, a resident of Duluth, often uses the background of a small prosperous city, very like her own, as a setting for dramas intended to show that social adjustments can be made comfortably within the established pattern. Miss Le Sueur has used the past labor troubles of Minneapolis as a point of departure for the assertion, in rhapsodic prose, that everything must be changed as quickly as possible.

The best of Miss Le Sueur's work is contained in the volume *Salute to Spring*. It includes a story of great beauty and charm, "Annunciation," which demonstrates skillfully how a social theme may animate fiction without ever being blatantly stated or obtrusively insisted upon. Mrs. Banning has broadened her interests, during wartime, to include excursions into non-fiction intended to further our friendly relations with our neighbors in South America and our allies in England.

If the question were put: "What has life been like in Minnesota from the pioneer days until now?" there would be a chorus of answers—shrill, quizzical, hysterical, solemn, no one agreeing with another. Martha Ostenso has taken a disconsolate view of the failure of pioneer hopes in *The Mad Carews*, and a more refreshed and resolute one in *O River, Remember!* William McNally, in *The House of Vanished Splendor*, has pointed out that our soil seems appallingly to quicken the process of decay, so that a family of rugged pioneers may deteriorate by the third generation into a group of conscientious drunkards and anemic spinsters. In *The Roofs of Elm Street* he regards the story of the successive invasions of the region by different racial groups, with appreciation of both the drama and the economic significance of the movement. In *Earth Never Tires*, Darragh Aldrich offers comforting evidence that the vitality of the pioneers still is preserved in their descendants. In *Prairie Fires*, Lorna Beers dramatizes certain recent phases of the agrarian crusade. In *A Humble Lear* she undertakes to reconcile the disappointments of the pioneers with a reasonably optimistic view of human experience. She admits the worst about life on our soil, but persists in the faith that any man of normal vigor would wish to relive his life exactly as it had been. In *Wind without Rain* Herbert Krause has painted a grimly realistic picture of contemporary farm life, yet he also reveals the influences that help the resolute to survive.

Certain members of the Minnesota writing fraternity reject classification. Dagmar Doneghy writes in *The Border* not of the local scene, but of her native Missouri. Her talent is a sensitive one which Minnesota would be glad to claim. Brenda Ueland, in her autobiography called *Me*, has told the story of how the daughter of a Norwegian pioneer did herself over into a glittering Greenwich Village sophisticate and then returned to the home of her childhood. Glanville Smith, a literary descendant of Flandrau, is one of the few men on the American horizon who seem able to breathe life into the informal essay. He sprang to recognition with a sketch about the Minnesota woods where the Finns picturesquely maintain their native customs. In his most recent work, *Many a Green Isle*, he uses his highly personal gift to invoke the enchantment of Caribbean scenes. Elizabeth Reeves has written novels of adjustment, the quiet charm of which might belong to any American scene.

The Minnesota tradition is enriched by the memory of three other men whose influence survives them. The poetry of Arthur

Upson, the criticism of Oscar Firkins, and the novels of O. E. Rölvaag belong on library shelves that will never be permitted to become dusty. Arthur Upson, author among other things of the University of Minnesota hymn, is known to many a visiting celebrity who knows little else about Minnesota. The architectural neatness of the prose of Oscar Firkins housed some óf the most readable of contemporary criticism. The largeness of Rölvaag's spirit as revealed in *Giants in the Earth* and *Peder Victorious* is an enduring monument to the Scandinavian-American tradition which he celebrated.

Rölvaag would loom large on any literary horizon, for he had those qualities of heart and mind that identify a major figure. His insight was deep, his compassion broad. His scene and his people took on the proportions of his own gift of perception. The flaccid generalizations of the novel of the soil became sharp and piercing with conviction as he restated them. The undisciplined, swooning sensibilities of which so many prairie stories were made had the tension and terror of the great crises of the spirit thrust into them by Rölvaag's firm, unwavering hand. His Scandinavian farmers were no strong, silent men facing doom with the remote resolution of granite statuary. They were variable creatures, with all the quirks and oddities of human goodness and weakness in them. His pioneer women were not all models of self-sufficiency. Indeed, his most appealing and pathetic portrait, that of Beret in *Giants in the Earth*, shows the disintegrating influence of a pervasive sense of guilt.

From the design for the novel of the pioneering West, Rölvaag swept away the clichés, tore out the clutter of reiterative, dismal decoration, and made room for the living of richly imagined people whose characters were simple in outline but subtle in detail, strong yet never quite strong enough. His tragedies were uncompromising, but at their best they were also calming, for they did nothing to rob doomed human nature of its dignity. His books had the serenity of the temperament which enabled him to sit one day on the banks of Lake Nokomis in Minneapolis and tell a group of friends that he was soon to die. He was not tense or self-conscious as he talked that day. He offered, simply as a matter of general interest, the observation that when a man realizes he may be watching a sunset for the last time, he enjoys it with a heightened awareness. He had that heightened awareness always. And his books tower over those of his contemporaries in the giant stature of their author's spirit.

Rölvaag was born and educated in Norway. He wrote his books in Norwegian, leaving translation to others. His command of English, which was quite good enough to permit him to be a valued teacher at St. Olaf College, he fastidiously rejected as insufficient to the demands of literature. Rölvaag offers an example of the international character of Minnesota letters. His best books deal with its scene, but they deal with transplanted people, and in a foreign tongue.

Writing in Wisconsin shows a similarly complex pattern. In the past there were fine figures like John Muir and Hamlin Garland who wrote eloquently of the wilderness in which each lived as a child. In keeping with his taste as a naturalist who had a lifelong love affair with mountain peaks, Muir wrote of wild Wisconsin in terms of sights and sounds, and he wrapped up his memories in the warm phrases of rhapsody.

Hamlin Garland, born in the Wisconsin village of West Salem in 1860, was, to begin with, conscientiously and copiously the chronicler of life in the region. In *Main-Travelled Roads* and *Prairie Folk* he stated, often with great bitterness, the harsh terms on which the pioneer had to live his natural and his economic life. All the work of his youthful period was concerned with people who worked too hard and received too few rewards for their labor. The issues of the agrarian crusade were dramatized with a fierce, uncompromising vigor that was sometimes crude but always appealing. His early short stories belong to the literature of protest at its most spontaneous.

Later he parted from his rebellious past. His autobiographical studies grew mellow, his politics conservative. At one time he even thought well of Mussolini. When he died in California, his interests had broadened and been dispersed through all the realm of time and eternity. Experimentation with the occult took up his mind, and the fresh, fierce, concentrated rage of his radical youth was gone. In a cloud of fine white hair and beard, he looked like a prophet turned passive and genial. But those who had admired his militancy regretted the transformation of a rebel into a minor mystic.

Zona Gale of Portage was one of the best-known and most popular of Wisconsin regionalists. Her career offers a curious and touching example of how the creative impulse sometimes takes possession of a person who would have been glad to escape its demands. Zona Gale was a frail and exquisite little creature who seemed always a little too tired to be doing the strenuous work she had in hand. The discrepancy between her delicate appearance and the interests to which she gave herself sometimes disturbed the unsympathetic. At a woman's suffrage meeting early in the century one of her suggestions irritated a leader of the more militant type. "What are we going to do," this suffragette mocked bitterly, "about our little Miss Zona Zephyr?"

But she was a Gale for all that, a descendant of a resolute pioneering family which had helped to shape the destiny of Minnesota as well as of Wisconsin. Her opinions and her faith influenced many people at the University of Wisconsin, where she was a regent, and in her own city of Portage, where she became a kind of seeress among the young intellectuals, liberals, and æsthetes.

She wrote a great deal about her own community, vacillating nervously between the patient, hopeful, and distinctly sentimental tone of *Friendship Village* and the wry-lipped wistfulness of *Miss Lulu Bett*. This latter story of a sensitive woman submerged in the midst of the vulgar and cruel banality of an American home which made her its slave caught the fancy of the American public in the midst of the *Main Street* period. Lulu Bett's two grotesque flings at romance made her also a figure that the stage could use. The novel became a play, the play a film. Curiously enough, *Miss Lulu Bett* was simply what was left over after the cutting of a much better book of which comparatively few readers know. *Birth* is a big, ambitious novel dealing with many aspects of the cruelty of village life, which puts premiums on success, conformity, and colorlessness and regards with a corroding suspicion any hint of individuality.

The sharpness of observation that makes *Birth* a much more moving, because it is a more believable, experience than *Main*

Street was lost to Zona Gale in her later books. Their themes trailed off into vagueness. Symptomatic of her inability to know what impression she wished to create was the impulse that made her call one of her books *Faint Perfume*.

Zona Gale had many disciples whom she generously encouraged. Some of them, as their own strength grew, found it necessary at last to repudiate her. Such a young writer was Margery Latimer, author of *We Are Incredible* and *This Is My Body*. In *Guardian Angel* Margery Latimer wrote brilliantly and cruelly about the high priestess of a Wisconsin town who, with a great sense of virtue, destroyed the initiative and independence of her followers. The contribution to regionalism made by the Portage school of letters was that of introducing psychoanalytical method into the study of village types. Margery Latimer, Karlton Kelm, and others of the group demonstrated with a kind of tense ferocity that the prairie country, too, has its victims of frustration and hidden hostility.

Glenway Wescott, born on a Wisconsin farm, offers a dramatic example of what happens to a sensitive and observant young writer when he embarks upon an odyssey into the great, tormented world. Wescott's early books *The Grandmothers* and *Good-bye, Wisconsin* examined with a young man's intensity and a poet's discrimination the realm and the people of his youth. The cadences of his prose sought to evoke the sights, sounds, smells of the rural scene; sought to dramatize the cycle of folk life, the groping of the young, the questionings of the middle-aged, the surrenders of the old. He was ever preoccupied with the story of life as desire, thwarted, distorted, unfulfilled; yet his characters were ones that seemed entirely at home in the uncomplicated external world of Wisconsin.

His most recent work, *The Pilgrim Hawk*, is still concerned with thwarted and distorted desires. Like all of Wescott's work, it has grace and originality of style. But the pattern has become delicate and complex. The characters torment themselves in exquisite and complicated ways. Wescott's long residence abroad and his commitment to discipleship under Somerset Maugham have made him a kind of honorary European. Like Scott Fitzgerald, he has moved far away from his native scene. The cosmopolitan touch is upon his work, showing itself in the careful precision of the craftsmanship. No one would suspect *The Pilgrim Hawk* of having been tossed off in a frenzy of eagerness to get something said. It has been labored over with dedicated zeal of a Flaubert.

Wescott is an artist in the same sense that Flandrau was. The doing of the job is the important thing, not the prestige, the attention, the adulation it may bring. Flandrau used to be congratulated upon the delightful spontaneity of his style. "The only spontaneity I possess," he once retorted impatiently, "is the kind that comes from sweating blood for forty-eight hours at a stretch."

As proof that Wisconsin is able to produce anything out of its abundance, one may point to Edna Ferber busily wielding the shuttle of her facility. She has woven her way through many an American scene, including that of Wisconsin, where she lived as a child and where she had her preliminary education for a writing career. Her first published novel, *Dawn O'Hara*, described the glittering journalistic Bohemia of Milwaukee, where Edna Ferber herself worked as a young newspaper woman. In *Come and Get It* she returned to Wisconsin for her background. The novel dramatized the strenuosity of the lumbering days when everyone was coming and getting the state's resources of pine.

The journalistic gusto that is the most noticeable feature of Edna Ferber's work in fiction was a tremendous asset in helping her to find an audience. She has told over and over again sophisticated and knowing versions of the rags-to-riches story which, in the days of its innocency, America loved. There is still an audience for this success story, and Edna Ferber repeated it once again in her most recent novel, *Saratoga Trunk*. There, however, the method seemed to have become almost completely mechanical, and the book contained few of the disarmingly human and gracious scenes that illuminated moments of her earlier work.

But Edna Ferber has made one contribution to American writing that seems likely to have permanent value. It is her autobiography, *A Peculiar Treasure*. The book is so superior to all the rest of her work that it suggests the possibility of Miss Ferber's having maintained an almost grimly gay pose throughout the whole of her career. If her tongue was lodged in her cheek as she wrote all those novels, stories, and plays, her performance sets an all-time record in marathon endurance contests. However that may be, the portrait in *A Peculiar Treasure* of a sensitive, suffering, resolute Jewish girl with her face set firmly against any impulse to yield to the weight of intolerance is a moving and impressive one.

Early in her autobiography Miss Ferber paints the picture of racial prejudice as it reveals itself in a small Wisconsin town. Here it plays the role of village idiot—slack-jawed, lunging, bored, and trivial in its cruelty. This passage offers a shock to those who have thought of race riots as being crimes of the great cities. The villages, too, have their miniature circuses of meanness. Yet the very vividness of Miss Ferber's little study in Jew-baiting serves to emphasize the fact that such episodes are not characteristic of the life of the region. I can think of no other incident from regional writing to set beside it.

Of all the company of regionalists, August Derleth is the most resolute, the most profoundly convinced follower of the faith. He lives in a small Wisconsin town, studies its scene, its contemporary population, its history, its legends, its mores. Of these absorbing interests he makes his novels, his poems, his journals, his short stories, his historical studies—the whole body of his work. In a series of novels of which a representative one is *Wind over Wisconsin*, he has undertaken to dramatize, period by period, the whole of what he calls the "Sac Prairie Saga." His project, which is to find in his village a microcosm of the American world, should exhaust all the possibilities of the gospel of regionalism in literature.

Mr. Derleth is a large and vigorous young man with an appetite for exploration which appears to be utterly inexhaustible. He exults in his own copiousness, and boasts that, though many influences have been brought to bear to keep him from writing so much, none has yet succeeded. His shelf of works is long and it grows each year by two or three volumes.

The Universities of Wisconsin and Minnesota have acted as magnets to enrich the literary life of the communities. They have drawn to themselves, in temporary or permanent association, such

American writers as Mary Ellen Chase, who was for several years at Minnesota, and William Ellery Leonard, who lived out his long life at Wisconsin. Maine is the background of Miss Chase's *A Goodly Heritage*, but souvenirs of the Minnesota residence creep into her writing. As a Latin scholar, a poet, and a student of psychological crises, Professor Leonard made a unique niche for himself in American letters, though the comment contained in his work on life in Wisconsin is purely incidental. In *Two Lives* and *The Locomotive God* he ranged challengingly through all the country of the mind and heart.

Gladys Hasty Carroll, whose literary country is Maine, also had a Minnesota moment. Helen Constance White, author of many historical novels, products of careful scholarship, is a member of the English staff of the University of Wisconsin. Samuel Rogers is her colleague in the French department and he gives his holidays to the writing of fiction (*Dusk at the Grove* and *Flora Shawn*). The essential character of his work is derived from a sensitive feeling for human society rather than from preoccupation with any particular locality. Mark Schorer went out from Wisconsin to Harvard. The excellent beginning in fiction that he once made may have a second phase in which Wisconsin will be more deeply explored.

Walter Havighurst and Warren Beck belong to the Appleton school of letters. Appleton is the town in which Edna Ferber lived during a period of her childhood. She appears to have enjoyed herself there so little that in one of her plays, *Stage Door*, she avenged herself upon it by having a character "dwindle, peak and pine" of boredom in its society. Mr. Havighurst and Mr. Beck have felt much at home there. Indeed, if only Miss Ferber's girl in the play had thought to enroll at Lawrence College, Appleton, and to take one of Mr. Beck's courses in English, she might have had so stimulating a time that she would not have had to desert her husband and rush back to Broadway.

Warren Beck has written some of the best short stories of the past decade, but they can hardly be called regional. Each one is concerned with a small personal problem of universal significance rather than with a community problem of local significance.

Walter Havighurst has been more genuinely a regionalist, using the background of his native state in fiction as well as in several non-fiction studies.

Writers with many different kinds of interests have gone out from Wisconsin on odysseys that have taken them far from their childhood scenes. But often they turn back, in imagination, to write about the past. Sterling North, serving as a critic first in Chicago and later in New York, has paused now and again to write such nostalgic novels as *Ploughing on Sunday* and *Night Outlasts the Whippoorwill*. Ray Stannard Baker has divided with an alter ego to which he assigned the pseudonym David Grayson an apparently inexhaustible appetite for experience as editor, diplomat, and biographer. He gave his own name to a witty and charming souvenir of his Wisconsin youth called *Native American*.

A group of contemporary poets of the first importance are identified in one way and another with these states. Robert Penn Warren, for example, is a member of the faculty of the University of Minnesota. Kenneth Fearing and Marya Zaturenska attended the University of Wisconsin as students. But these are pilgrims out of other worlds, and one finds in their work few souvenirs of their temporary homes. The subtle, searching intensity of Warren's mind may yet find a theme in Minnesota as he has previously found themes in Tennessee and Kentucky. Marya Zaturenska seems to be preoccupied with generalizations upon human experience that have little to do with particular places. Kenneth Fearing's strident, ironic rejections of the shallowness of the average life seem to have been inspired by the people of the great cities.

It is different with poets like Horace Gregory and Frederick Prokosch, both of whom were born in Wisconsin. Recollections of the past creep frequently into their work. Gregory writes of his university remembering "the campus of our hearts" with its

> *oceans of maple spray, green harbored, flowing*
> *against the sky. . . .*

He thinks of a friend dead in Portage, where "the slow mile of dark catalpas and the river" wind "inland to Mississippi waters."

His imagination reminds him of how "the corn leaps toward the pale north star."

Prokosch's poems contain similar souvenirs. In *The Carnival* he speaks of how "the brooding child still dwells in our blood." This early self reminds him of the setting of his youth,

> . . . *the blazing orchards and the release*
> *Of streams and the fifty jubilant scents of a valley*
> *And the hood of snow on the roof and the rushing*
> *torrent monstrous, eternal. . . .*

There have been other wanderers through the literary tradition of these states. Thornton Wilder was born at Madison. Majorie Kinnan Rawlings attended the university there. But Wisconsin can scarcely claim credit for them, any more than Minnesota need accept responsibility for Westbrook Pegler, who prepared for a crabbed maturity during what appears to have been rather a crabbed youth at Lake Minnetonka, near Minneapolis.

Of the making of books there has never been a pause from the very beginning of the history of these states. Out of their policy of persistent communicativeness has come much that is characteristic of the region, much that is characteristic of America, and much that is characteristic of the country of the human mind.

14

THE CREATIVE IMPULSE
IS INDESTRUCTIBLE

THAT THE IMPULSE to create art is an anemic one, stirring fitfully in the breasts of unmanly æsthetes, is a misapprehension that the unsympathetic hug perversely in their ironic minds. Nothing could be farther from the truth. When one explores the history of painting in Wisconsin and Minnesota, one is impressed chiefly by the stubborn virility of the desire to create. No other interest, faced with the chilling unconcern that greets the work of the painter, would have the hardihood to try to survive. But the artist, drawing upon hidden reserves of vitality, lives on in the bleakest environment, bounded on the north, east, south, and west by mis-understanding, condescension, irony, and indifference.

It would not be surprising if an inspection of the pioneer world where people were more concerned with getting roofs over their heads than with finding adornments for their walls were to show no early impulse to create art. People lived life ruggedly at first hand; one can understand very well that they might find no time to interpret its forms in the abstract terms of composition. Yet that was not what happened on the frontier.

No sooner had the way through the wilderness been opened than men with sketching pads, brushes, and canvas began to pene-trate to the farthest known corner, attracted by the wonders that the diaries of the explorers had described. They lived the harsh life of the untamed world, and lived it with energy and relish, as their own vivacious diaries exhilaratingly show.

The first ones among them enrolled as "official artists" in exploring parties sent out by the government. In the early years of the last century Congress seems not to have felt quite the same uneasy distaste for painters that it had learned to cultivate a century later, when with a mixture of indignant rage and ribald incredulity it brushed away the men and women of the WPA projects as though they were so many infuriating insects.

With Major S. M. Long, Samuel Seymour went into the wilderness in 1819 to make records of conferences with the Indians and to set down literal notes about the topography of Mississippi River bluffs and the rugged shore of Lake Superior. He seems to have had a modest notion of his responsibilities, for he made no effort to introduce either liveliness of device or corroborative detail into his summary sketches of the wilderness.

After him there were many others who came into the region during the next thirty or forty years to perform the same sort of task. The drama of helping the Indian to vanish was of enormous interest to the citizens of the East. They wanted to see what he looked like in his final moment of splendor as he sat in full regalia and played the role of war chief for the last time. The artists ranged all through Wisconsin and Minnesota, following the rivers from settlement to settlement, recording moments of the buffalo hunt and of the traditional dances as well as glimpses of the gentle aspects of Indian domesticity.

They were an enterprising and resourceful group of men, James Otto Lewis, Seth Eastman, George Catlin, John Banvard, Frank Mayer, and Henry Lewis. Their work seems naïve today because it was done with much more concern for literal accuracy than for interpretative richness or completeness. They did not work under favorable or even safe circumstances. Once an Indian whom J. O. Lewis had drawn in profile made the threatening complaint: "You have left out half my face. Put it in or I'll scalp you on the spot." Sitters then were difficult in the same way as they are now, but they had an even more alarming degree of forthrightness. To get down quickly what he had seen was all that Lewis could hope to do with his "rude materials." He knew the limitations of his work, but he asked indulgence for the inadequacies of his craftsmanship out of respect for the authenticity of his picture of frontier life.

Seth Eastman was a graduate of West Point who as an officer at

Fort Crawford and Prairie du Chien, and at Fort Snelling, near St. Paul, made topographical sketches of the region intended especially for the War Department. Like the best of the primitive painters, Eastman saw the drama of Indian life with the intuition of a precocious child. He knew little of perspective, and he had no sense of composition, but his figures plunged into action with a headlong fervor that compensates for their lack of subtlety in the organization of material.

George Catlin, who has been called "the Audubon of American Indian painting," had, like the man whose model he followed in every detail of a painter's progress, an almost religious dedication to thoroughness and accuracy. His object was to record all that text and pictures could make permanent of the costume, the mysteries, the anecdotes, and the history of the various Indian nations. He accomplished precisely what he set out to do, for his pictures are exciting. They must be looked at with what Elinor Wylie called "the hard heart of a child." Typical of their naïve vitality is one in which a rider to the buffalo hunt looks over his shoulder with an air of jaunty unconcern as a great, shaggy, bedeviled, infuriated beast is about to gore his horse from the rear. The buffalo's tongue hangs from his mouth like a bloody banner. Any properly receptive heart must be filled by this picture with a small boy's unregenerate love of brutality.

Like Audubon, Catlin took his exhibits to England, where the fashionable world drew in a deep breath of his vigor and lionized him appropriately. In Paris, too, he found a following at Louis Napoleon's court.

John Banvard adds to the story of art in Wisconsin and Minnesota a curious and unique note. He made it pay. There was a moment in the 1840's when America, yearning in its soul for the moving pictures which had yet to be invented, fell madly in love with the "panorama." Banvard dashed off four hundred and forty yards of canvas depicting the beauties of the Mississippi. This phenomenal masterpiece of patience he exhibited in public, unrolling the work across the stage from one great vertical cylinder to the other. It was valued in its day for "fidelity and truthfulness to nature," and a great many people went to see it, including the Queen of England. (Banvard, following the example of the other wandering artists, took his panorama to London.) But before he had achieved the distinction of a royal command performance, the artist had had what was probably a greater satisfaction, that of persuading the citizens of Boston to surrender fifty thousand dollars at his box office. Among his distinguished customers was Longfellow, then engaged in writing his poem *Hiawatha*, which described a region he had never seen. In his diary of the year 1846 Longfellow wrote: "I see a panorama of the Mississippi advertised. This comes very apropos. The river comes to me instead of my going to the river. And as it flows through the pages of the poem, I look upon this as a special benediction."

In 1850 Frank Mayer, upon the same search for accurate images of the wilderness country, tried to get an official commission to paint the signing of the treaty with the Indians at Traverse des Sioux. He failed to find any sort of backing for his trip, but he came anyway to make sketches of Little Crow, of Indians lolling before their lodges, of the overworked Dacotah "Tawechew" ("squaw" is not the word that the Dacotah uses for "wife," Mayer observes a little pedantically), whose feet, despite the constant service exacted of them, remained, for him, as beautiful as those of the Venus de' Medici. After his journey through the wilderness Mayer returned to the East. From Annapolis, where he finally set up his studio, he sent many persuasive letters back to Minnesota urging that he be given a commission to do a great painting of the treaty scene. But the legislature refused to be beguiled and at long last paid a niggardly two hundred dollars for a small study which, in its curious, huddled innocence, hangs today in the Minnesota State Historical Society. The irony of the artist's life is rounded out in the epilogue, which finds Frank D. Millet painting a decoration for the new State Capitol of Minnesota, following Mayer's general plan though it modifies the composition, making it seem more dramatic and less confused.

Still another of these reporters in paint made the Mississippi Valley his "run." Henry Lewis came to America from England in 1836 and, after settling in St. Louis, began exploring and exploiting the wilderness country. In 1849 he visited the Mississippi, the St. Croix, and the Chippewa Rivers and painted the scenes about Fort Snelling and Fort Crawford. He improved upon the enterprise of Banvard by doing a panorama just twice as long. After making a grand tour of Europe in the Audubon fashion, he finally decided that it was time to submit his strenuous talent to academic discipline and settled down in Düsseldorf. The German city was to Americans of that time what Paris was later to become, and only if one had the stamp of the Düsseldorf school upon one's work could one hope to be recognized as authentically or even legally an artist.

Souvenirs of the creative impulse are to be found in the Historical Society buildings of Wisconsin and Minnesota, in the Minneapolis Institute of Arts, and in private collections of the region. The interest of these studies is great, for, though the style is confused and naïve, the pictures reflect the spontaneous response of sensitive people to the wilderness world. The very faults of composition correspond to the ironies of the scene. The dark density of the forest, the brilliant, almost electrical blue of the sky—these contrasts dominate the palette; the thick, set look of wooded country, the emptiness of the prairie—these striking opposites declare themselves in stretches of a picture's composition that are either huddled full of detail or left barren of interest. The reporters on canvas were a lively lot, vigorous, adaptable, and above all capable of astonishing patience and endurance. If Catlin or Banvard were to have his irrepressible vitality exploited in the way that our contemporary rhapsodist Donald Culross Peattie has exploited Audubon, we might have a new theme of hero-worship ringing sonorously through another series of best-sellers. But perhaps one recitalist who devotes himself to "singing in the wilderness" is enough.

The art history of the latter half of the nineteenth century in Wisconsin and Minnesota is not devoid of interest, though its features are much more stereotyped and commonplace. There was, for example, a drift of portrait painters across the continent, leaving behind in Wisconsin and Minnesota a deposit of "likenesses." Artists, too, followed the course of empire as it took its westward way. They paused in the region long enough to record the features of the grim and stalwart pioneers, who seem to have been quite willing to have themselves presented in settings of synthetic grandeur. These owed much more to the British tradition of what the background of a portrait should be than to any effort to suggest the actual environment of the country. Thus Solomon Juneau, founder of Milwaukee, was painted with glimpses of Xanadu or some "fairy land forlorn" visible over his left shoulder. The portraits would have been more interesting today had the background really suggested something of the Wisconsin village, elbowing its way into strenuous commercial existence.

Within an amazingly short time of their actual beginnings, these pioneer communities were undertaking to lay resolute hands on culture, in order, as a traditional story of Chicago puts it, to "make it hum." Lumber barons in Minneapolis and successful industrialists of Milwaukee were dashing abroad with critical advisers to buy up pictures for their mansions. Sometimes they were well guided; sometimes they were quite simply cheated. In some instances the acreage of a composition seems to have appealed to the amateur collectors, who were used to the great open spaces of the wilderness. The results of their excursions to import works of art were various. But at least these manifestations of what Veblen calls "conspicuous consumption" kept an awareness of art uninterruptedly before the citizens.

It was not alone by importation of European pictures, however, that interest in art survived. There was also the importation of men to give the creative impulse a direct blood transfusion. Of these figures Henry Vianden of Milwaukee was typical. He came to America from Cologne in 1849, presumably to escape from interference in the practice of his faith as a Roman Catholic. He lived, in the beginning, the typical existence of the pioneer, farming for subsistence while his other interests awaited the moment of leisure. He continued to grow food all his life, though he very soon became a highly valued and protected figure of the Milwaukee community. In the rather aggressive fullness of his masculine vigor, he walked ten miles from his farm to the studio where he painted and taught his students. He helped Milwaukee to remember Europe by sitting long hours at a time in a *Weinstube*, where he presided majestically over discussions with his cronies. He appears to have been a kind of genial bully who "loved first nature and after nature, art." He painted the dark grandeur of trees with patient and persevering attention to the outline of every leaf. His students were frequently rebuked for skimping the splendor of these "kings of the forest." Milwaukee took Vianden to its heart and actually bought his pictures, so that in the end he was able to live by art alone. "Cast iron" was the phrase his less reverent students came finally to use in describing his style. Eventually his vogue passed. But Vianden in his time represented a vital tradition.

Long after his death his students continued to preserve his tradition. One of them, Carl Marr, returned to Germany to become head of the Royal Academy in Munich. Robert Koehler, after his apprenticeship with Vianden, studied in Germany and became at last director of the Minneapolis School of Art, where he helped to mature the talents of many Minnesota painters. Like Vianden, Koehler lived the life of the out-of-doors whenever he could escape from his studio. In that he was preoccupied with social subjects his work was typical of the combination of interests that was characteristic of Milwaukee in its earlier days. And in his refusal to sentimentalize and prettify subjects of portraiture, he anticipated a tradition that was to become general after him. He might define a background in so perfunctory a manner that a head seemed vaguely and incompletely to take shape out of a kind of vaporous gloom. Yet he caught firmly and held candidly to the essential characteristics of a subject, so that his portraits of men who have been long dead seem much more alive in spirit than many glibly competent, deliberately superficial, modern portraits.

In the beginning of the present century Americans, in Wisconsin and Minnesota as well as in the rest of the country, were fairly well agreed that if you were seized upon by the impulse to create, you must immediately prepare to undergo "sea change into something rich and strange." Art was a mystical rite as well as a personal adventure, and you went to Europe to woo it. If you were a painter you went, of course, to Paris, where a ludicrously rigid convention required you to follow a routine that was already out of date when Puccini set it to music. You grew a beard, wore sandals, ate breakfast at the Deux Magots, spent many hours at the Dôme discussing abstract form, changed your name to something that sounded vaguely French, and tried dutifully to degenerate in a direction specifically prescribed by the tradition of your favorite painter.

Wisconsin and Minnesota sent many of their talented men and women to follow out this generally depressing and unrewarding routine. The trouble was not that students failed to receive stimulation from exposure to Paris or that they learned nothing from their teachers. Despite the silly artificiality of this masque of artists, it did succeed in communicating the mysteries of technique to men who, at that time, were less likely to have acquired proficiency at home. But still it was unhealthy for the American artist to be so completley cut off from the public that should have been his and to have no organic link with his own world.

The potential buyer of pictures tacitly recognized the inappropriateness of exporting American painters at the moment when they were in the midst of the heat of their creative youth. He expressed his disapproval (perhaps quite unconsciously) by declining to acquire the work of such young men and women. If he were to have a painting of the rooftops of Montmartre or an etching of the prostitutes in the Place Pigalle, he preferred to have such subjects treated by a "right down regular" Parisian painter rather than by the clever but unstable boy who had gone out from Minneapolis or Milwaukee only a few years before.

Still the export trade in artists continued. If a man of talent proved to be either recalcitrant or sluggish and simply remained at home, a committee of well-meaning citizens would resolutely raise a fund and ship him abroad, almost by force. He was supposed to take refreshment from Paris and Florence. When he returned, the same committee gave a tea at which his new work was exhibited. Dear old ladies swept through the studio giving all of thirty seconds to the inspection of each item in turn. Happy in the consciousness of having done their duty by art, they hurried on to the next engagement murmuring: "Oh, I do think he's improved so much!" At the fiftieth utterance of that trying formula the artist turned pale and crept away behind a screen, from which shelter he could not be enticed again all afternoon.

And no one bought any of the artist's new work despite the gratifying improvement! When the upright citizens of Milwaukee, Minneapolis, and St. Paul wanted family portraits painted, they brought on someone with a reassuring accent, the fashionable artist of the moment who had been having a great success in New York.

The first World War interrupted the pilgrimage of young men to Paris, except, of course, as soldiers. But in the end the 1917–18 season augmented the prestige of France as the stronghold of the arts. Not until the depression swept the world did the American artist decide to come home and stay home. The depression, as the critic Forbes Watson has pointed out, was a blessing in disguise. It forced government to recognize the plight of the artist. It transformed a country that had had a vague, cautious, and snobbish attitude toward the painter into one that bought the work of its own citizens as no country has ever bought before.

Like every other community in America today, that of Wisconsin and Minnesota has a colony of painters who take their subjects from the scenes about them. Edmund Lewandowski paints the tramp steamers of Lake Michigan. Dewey Albinson is concerned with the mystery and violence of scenes along the north shore of Lake Superior and with the drama of open-pit mining. Tom Dietrich catches from his studio the glimpses of American social life that he records in his water colors. Clement Haupers finds a rolling rhythm that satisfies his expansive temperament in the sight of a Minnesota highway plunging through wheat fields. Gerrit Sinclair's quiet colors find less vehement but equally satisfying values in the local scenes of Wisconsin. Robert Von Neumann likes the sturdy figures of Great Lakes fishermen. Having a similar taste for the monumental, Santos Zingale seeks out his models among the potato-diggers of a Wisconsin farm.

All these men would probably deny vigorously that they are regionalists. They fear any suggestion that they have fallen into the deadly sin of being merely illustrative. Only form, color, composition interest them, they insist. But it is still a fact that Cameron Booth, when he looks for material to be used in any of the various styles with which his highly analytical gift has prompted him to experiment, has always been able to find what he needed in a corner of a Minnesota farm. The young painter who rejoices in the name of Forrest Flower has been able to work with inexhaustible spirit all over his palette even though it is always the Wisconsin land-scape that supplies the basic inspiration.

Opportunity for putting personal signatures upon fragments of the Wisconsin scene or the Minnesota scene has been explored by many painters of highly individual spirit. Adolph Dehn, one of the best known of the artists born to the region, is perhaps chiefly responsible for the image—tidy set of buildings placed in the midst of a fat farm—that rises in the minds of most people at the men-tion of Minnesota's name. Unlike Dehn, Syd Fossum frequently thinks of his native state in terms of the proletarian struggle. He likes to lend the vigor of his talent to the rebuke of mean streets and shabby urban compromises. Caleb Winholtz insists upon be-ing completely objective in his water-color treatment of similar scenes. Bob Brown, prowling city highways, seems always to find some wild, humorous, poetic secret in their vistas.

A sense of form, like beauty itself, is in the eye of the beholder. While temperaments continue to vary greatly, treatments of the physical scene may be expected to vary quite as widely. Josephine Lutz, painting the old houses of Stillwater, finds a sort of brooding architectural grandeur in them. William and Angela Ryan, work-ing in what appear to be masculine and feminine versions of the same style, dwarf the whole community of Stillwater into the neat pattern of a child's toy village, set on toy hills. Lowell Boble-ter has an intense feeling for the individual character of his native place. Into an etching he manages to thrust the heavy, firm impact of a cold night, giving one the sense that this is indubitably Minne-sota and unmistakably January. George Resler's etchings make of the juxtaposition of streams and hills in Minnesota something that might offer a proper setting for a Grimm fairy story.

The themes of farmland, prairie, and lake shore run variously through the work of the artists of the region. Schomer Lichtner is preoccupied by the sense of movement and finds appropriate ma-terial in the stirring of wind in a cornfield. Howard Thomas has an obsession with water, and the shore lines of Wisconsin's great and small lakes supply him endlessly with subjects. Mac Le Sueur is, for the most part, the pavement child, and he explores the theme of cities tirelessly.

Because any region so various in background must be a sort of microcosm of the whole world of temperament, the community of Wisconsin and Minnesota has produced many painters who are completely unconcerned with their immediate environment. Women seem to woo the personal touch in painting more persistently than men do. Wanda Gág, born in Minnesota to a painter father who specialized in great, gory panorama views of historic crises, has turned away from this sort of stern reality to invite her humorous imagination. She and her sister, Flavia, who works in a similar style, lend an engaging fairy-tale quality to their sidelong glimpses of our human life. Their wit is gracious, warm, and wholly feminine. Clara Mairs is a more compassionate version of Peggy Bacon. She likes to paint the droll and grotesque, but seems always to be touched by the human idiocy that she exposes. Frances Greenman is a brilliantly witty and sophisticated painter who puts a touch of mischief into even her portraits and lets her wicked gift of insight rip devastatingly through satiric studies. Ann Krasman is a painter who hides away poetic comments within her subtle treatment of simple themes.

The highly personal painters among the men of the region are more deliberately challenging. Alfred Sessler is the local Breughel. He takes his subjects from such crises in the lives of the underprivileged as a derelict's worried effort to retrieve a cigarette butt from the gutter. Karl Priebe is devoted to charming small excesses of whimsicality. Dissociating his talent very firmly from anything resembling regionalism, he paints sinuous Negresses, bathing the dark tones of skin in a wash of moonlight blue. He frames such curious conceits in elaborate Victorian frames painted white. This, surely, has very little to do with life in broad, free, and far from secret Wisconsin.

Government sponsorship in the days of the Art Projects resulted in the production of many objective interpretations of the interests of Wisconsin and Minnesota. At Ely, Minnesota, one of the gateways to the mining country, Elsa Jemne has decorated the walls of the post office with vigorous and dramatic re-creations of the lives of the men who go down into the pits. In the Memorial Union Building on the campus of the University of Wisconsin, James Watrous has slyly recaptured the riotous comedy of the Paul Bunyan legends. Men like Charles Thwaites and women like

Ruth Grotenrath have used their gifts for working with monumental forms to make a permanent record of the industrial and social preoccupations of Wisconsin. John Steuart Curry, imported from Kansas to be the state's official regionalist, has spread broad and genial glimpses of agricultural country over the corridors and classrooms of many campus buildings. Painting has ceased to be a studio rite performed in secret and become a part of the life of the people.

Wisconsin and Minnesota have maintained normal and lively relations with the great world of art. They have kept at home, to train new generations of artists, such teachers as Emily Groom, and have sent out to other centers such teachers as Erle Loran and such portrait painters as Paul Clemens. They have found occupation among their own citizens for sculptors like David Parsons and Alonzo Hauser and have contributed sculptors like Paul Manship to the cosmopolitan company of craftsmen. They enroll among their soldier and sailor artists such vigorous young painters as Lester Bentley, Richard Jansen, and Warren Beach. Strenuously and fully they lead the life of our time.

There is a curious parallel between the artistic and the economic history of these states. The first men who appeared in the region armed with brush and palette came chiefly as explorers. They did not intend to stay; all that they wanted was to get quick impressions of the country's breadth and richness. Their psychology was exactly that of the advance agents of the fur trade.

On the second wave of invasion came the exploiters. They were also visitors and transients. It was their purpose to paint portraits of the men who had prospered in the region. When that chore was done they moved westward, dutifully following the movement of expansion. They left no tradition behind.

Today's artists, like today's loggers and today's farmers, give themselves unconsciously to the task of pulling our society together and of filling the gaps in its culture left by the rampaging pioneers. They are creating a tradition and, though they stubbornly reject the idea of belonging to a "school," they are creating their tradition out of the materials of their own scene.

Despite the fact that the government once set an excellent example by buying the artistic work of its own citizens, it cannot be said that individual collectors show a tender and nourishing attitude toward the artist who is creating this local tradition. People with money to spend for pictures are still inclined to look nervously toward the great centers where the art market is thought to be steadier and safer. When the patrons of the arts in our region feel a momentary need of a portrait painter, they usually import one. The artists of Wisconsin and Minnesota are encouraged cautiously, intermittently, and with a vague interest clouded by distrust.

No doubt several generations must pass before a community as young as that of Wisconsin and Minnesota can be coaxed out of its timorous retreat from any sense of responsibility in matters of taste. The Art Projects helped to give prestige to the work of regional artists. We saw that their work, on the walls of post offices and schools, looked quite well, after all. But there is still much to be done to make a small community accept its artists.

Fortunately the creative impulse is indestructible. Though individual workers may crumple and surrender, there are always new recruits, bursting with *élan*. They keep the tradition alive.

15

A DAY IN EREWHON

WITH ACCIDENTAL TACT the bus company helped me to approach Taliesin in just the right way and at just the right hour. I stepped down into the little country road that skirts the Wisconsin River at eight o'clock in the morning when the dew was still heavy in the rank grasses covering the hillside. The freshly washed shine of a late September day made the world look new. The world also looked uncrowded, almost unused. The day was Sunday, and there seemed to be no movement but my own along the highway.

All this was as it should be, for Taliesin is not of this world. It is an idea, an abstraction, a fine, unbelievable dream brought to reality in wood and stone on the brow of a Wisconsin hill. It is something out of a Utopia imagined by Samuel Butler and brought into actual being by the resolute determination of another creative genius, Frank Lloyd Wright. It was as though the bus had traveled from Madison not to the post office marked Spring Green on the Wisconsin map, but deep into Butler's Erewhon.

As I rounded a turn of the road, I saw the buildings which express the very essence of Frank Lloyd Wright's architectural theory. A dwelling should look like the scene of which it is a part. It should seem to spring spontaneously into being out of its setting. Wood and stone should be the wood and stone of the place, and the line of the building the line that nature herself has followed in making her pattern of earth and vegetation. A house should be a harmonious feature of a poised, fluent, rhythmic composition, not a scar on the landscape.

That is the way with Taliesin. Its stone might be the outcropping of the cliff itself; its weathered wood and sand-colored stucco have the look of nature's own face. The buildings fold themselves gently around the brow of the high hill like a natural growth, following its line, echoing its rhythm.

I missed the proper road and clambered up over the face of the hill, through the dew-soaked weeds and over the ledges. At the top I stopped to draw my breath in middle-aged respiratory pain and felt a suddenly renewed and youthful delight. Behind the crown of buildings that the "shining brow" of Taliesin wears is an open space at the top of the hill. From its height the land stretches far away in soothing prospects on all sides. The country is folded into many hills and valleys that give the panorama a look of rolling, almost of romping, liveliness. Below, one catches a glimpse of the silver thread of a creek and, farther in the distance, the broad expanse of river and sand-lined shore.

Taliesin is a Welsh word which means "shining brow." It is pronounced as it is spelled, the "e" and "s" forming a syllable that gives the name a sort of sibilant sigh in the middle.

In these hills Frank Lloyd Wright was born, three quarters of a century ago, and to them he has returned from all his troubled, turbulent journeys. It is as though his creative impulse, which came to being in this place and which was dedicated first to the idea of expressing in architecture the beauty of the natural form of this scene, must constantly renew itself in the midst of the Wisconsin hills.

Frank Lloyd Wright has told his personal history fully and without reserve in his autobiography. It is, very surely, one of the great records of literature, having the candor, the challenge, the the intellectual vigor, the prophetic urgency that characterize the *Confessions* of Rousseau. These qualities in Rousseau have made the nervous wince all through the centuries, and the same qualities in the mind of Frank Lloyd Wright have made our generation wince, too. But when Frank Lloyd Wright has been dead long enough so that his utterances no longer have any interest as scandal, the fundamental importance of what he has had to say can be properly appraised, and the enduring, revealing value of his æsthetic theory will be clearly understood.

His autobiography describes, always in the mood of challenge and often with the accent of indignation, the various phases of his lifelong war against compromise, concession, commonplaceness. He left the University of Wisconsin with his work toward a degree in engineering incomplete because he felt that academic training was designed to put the creative impulse into a straitjacket of outmoded rules. He left his place with the firm of Louis Sullivan, a bold innovator and visionary in his time, when he found that he could accept no one as his master. He left his first wife when he began to feel that domesticity and suburban respectability were encouraging him to repeat himself architecturally, like a man grown senile and garrulous before his time. He left America when he found that there was no ready acceptance here for the new ideas and the driving passion behind them that he wished to express in his architecture.

The pattern of these rejections and the passion behind them were the true expression of the man. For many years Frank Lloyd Wright was in bitter rebellion against the whole of organized society. He is in rebellion against it still, though the tone of his repudiation is now more mellow, and even his sweeping denunciations sound humorous and genial.

The first great dramatic success of Wright's career came when he built the Imperial Hotel in Tokyo. To provide against the probable dangers in a country periodically rocked by earthquake, he evolved his famous cantilever principle, which balances the weight of the floor on central concrete supports just as a waiter balances a tray on his fingers. The advantage of this principle to a waiter is that it enables him to maintain the equilibrium of the tray in the midst of the swaying rhythm of his body; the advantage to an architect in Japan is that it ensures the poise of the building in the midst of the swaying disturbances of nature.

Science collaborated with imagination in the discovery of that principle, and a bold spirit put it to the test in defiance of the ribald disbelief of all builders whose imaginations were bound by tradition. Then presently an event confirmed the truth that Frank Lloyd Wright had discovered. An earthquake came, a particularly disastrous one, and in the midst of the ruin all about it the Imperial Hotel stood secure on its supports.

In the public mind the dramatic event confirmed Frank Lloyd

Wright's title to the rank of genius. Unhappily the title often has carried with it as many inconveniences and pains as it has carried honors and privileges. It proved to be so with Wright. Though his work came to be more and more in demand among responsive and courageous patrons, it was no triumphal highway strewn with laurel and bay along which he moved. His outspoken challenges to orthodox architects have made him many enemies. His domestic affairs have always managed to become public scandals. To top off the trials of his middle years, the depression all at once made of architecture a forgotten profession. Though Wright's reputation was known all through America and far beyond it, he was in the early 1930's one of the most distinguished members of the unemployed.

It was at that moment, when so many men were seeing their plans disrupted violently, that Wright created his famous Fellowship of Taliesin. Out of its studios have come, even during a period when building has been handicapped by every obstacle that has ever impeded development, some of the most brilliantly original structures in the world. At Racine, Wisconsin, Wright built an administration building for the Johnson Floor Wax Company which forgot all the grim austerities of such workshops and emerged instead as a great luminous bubble of glass. At Ardmore, Pennsylvania, there is a group of homes so cunningly designed around a core containing the communal services of an apartment building that each unit, with its private entrance, seems to have the spaciousness and seclusion of a separate house. In Minneapolis there is a low-cost home that has woven all the advantages of Taliesin into its design. Topping a hillside, it achieves a curious unity with the scene, blending equally well into the green of summer, the parti-color of autumn, or the white of winter and taking the out-of-doors indoors through its walls of glass.

Taliesin has produced designs to blend into every different aspect of the varied and changing face of America. There is a home the units of which are all variations on a circular pattern that echoes and emphasizes the roundness of the hills in which it lies. There is another home, called Wingspread, in which the several units dedicated to different phases of the daily life fan out as though from the body of a bird. To this kind of building, designed to express the special character of the land on which a structure lies, and designed also to fulfill and satisfy the individuality of the owner, Frank Lloyd Wright has given the name Usonian. He has borrowed it from that prophet of better worlds to come, Samuel Butler.

Fundamental to the theory upon which Usonian architecture rests its case is that ours is a land of great variety, great beauty, great abundance, and great spaciousness. These characteristics should be reflected in our building. Centralization is an outmoded feature of a rapidly changing economy. The skyscrapers are like tombstones lining the rows of the great cemeteries that are our cities. In place of these perversions Wright offers a vision of the urban community of tomorrow which he calls Broadacre City. An actual model of it has been set up in his studio. It shows how a whole community may be considered as a work of art; how it may utilize the modern advantages of quick motor travel to defeat the vulgar, squalid huddle of the city of our time; how schools, markets, factories, hospitals, parks may be strategically placed, like climaxes in a great harmonious composition. The homes of Broadacre City do not elbow one another on forty-foot lots as though America were a meager and ungracious land, but each will have its acre of ground. In the midst of that seclusion a man may learn to be himself, at peace with his neighbors and with his world.

Broadacre City is a vision, but it reflects what Frank Lloyd Wright has seen in the promise of the Wisconsin hills and realized in the beauty of Taliesin.

Standing on the peak of the "shining brow," I remembered all these things about Frank Lloyd Wright's history. I remembered, too, how he had sprung from a long line of Welsh ancestors who had always been preoccupied with teaching and preaching. It took three generations of Unitarian ministers to produce his uncle, Jenkin Lloyd Jones, who went out from these same hills to fight in the Civil War and later, as founder of a church in Chicago, to fight his private civil war for the principles of the brotherhood of man. It took as many generations or more of idealism, at once maternal and militant, to produce Frank Lloyd Wright's aunts who founded the Hillside School in these same green hills of Wisconsin. The Lloyd Jones sisters were pioneers in the idea of progres-

sive education. It was once said that no intolerance could equal
the intolerance felt by those stalwart women for intolerance. Near
Taliesin stand the buildings created by Frank Lloyd Wright to
house his aunts' school. Since their death what was once Hillside
has been incorporated into the campus of Taliesin. Much has happened in those hills and is happening still.

On that day at Taliesin I crossed the grassy plot and knocked
at the door of a wing above which I had seen smoke rising. A
young man came to greet me. He was Ken, he said, one of the
apprentice architects of Taliesin. His dark skin and straight black
hair made him look rather like an Indian. He would tell Gene,
Mr. Wright's secretary, that I had come. Gene appeared from the
kitchen, where he had been supervising the preparation of breakfast. Slender, tall, and fair, he kept popping in and out of my
Taliesin day with a kind of hyperthyroid eagerness, always a
little breathless from his many duties, but always poised, pleasant,
and informative. Ken took me on a brief tour of the buildings
while Gene went to announce me. Taliesin is a maze of many turn-
ings, of open courts and subtle, half-disguised entrances. At every
turn there are souvenirs of Frank Lloyd Wright's long residence
in the Orient—delicately carved Japanese panels set casually into
the glass of doors; the subtle blues and greens of vases set along the
shelves; statues of Chinese and Japanese goddesses in attitudes so
lithe and eloquent that they achieve everything but motion and
seem to lend their beautiful poise to the rooms themselves.

The chief living-room seems (by benefit of the cantilever principle) to spring lightly from the brow of the cliff and to soar above
the trees. "An airplane room," Wright himself calls it. Huge fire-
places, the native stones of which have been carefully not "dressed"
in the manner of the conventional mason, manage to look like the
outcroppings of the cliffs themselves, and everywhere glass doors,
panels, and partitions let autumn come crowding indoors, bringing red leaves and bright berries. The natural and the civilized
have been made to lie down together in millennial harmony.
Rough stone floors are strewn with tawny rugs through which
Oriental designs in light blue weave their way.

Back on the hilltop, outside the dining-room, Ken and I awaited
the arrival of Frank Lloyd Wright. When he appeared, it was a

little like a royal progress. His party came threading its way across one of the open courts and then up the steps—first a charming-looking girl in her teens, the youngest child; then Olgivanna, Wright's wife; then Frank Lloyd Wright himself, with two apprentices bringing up the rear. The entrance, completely uncalculated though it was (any family at a summer resort going en masse from cottage to the dining-hall would have looked the same and yet utterly different), seemed to call for muted music in the strings just off-stage. There are people who cannot move without giving off the glitter of drama, and Frank Lloyd Wright is one of them.

At seventy-odd he is still a handsome and vital-looking man. His color is healthy without any extravagant excess of ruddiness. His white hair is no longer so abundant as to give him the look of æsthetic fervor that is mildly disturbing in some of his photographs. Indeed, his photographs scarcely look like him at all, for they catch the challenge of his individuality and give it a twist that suggests fretfulness or even truculence. There can never have been very much of either at the basis of his character, for a kind of habitual geniality, which is seldom learned late in life, informs all of his talk. He smiles (and disarmingly) when he calls the world a great blunder and society a great fool.

There is little about his dress that marks him as the artist, though on a chilly fall day his neck and head seemed to emerge out of a chrysalis of jackets and shirts. The layers of his costume lay in a neat pattern of gray upon blue, blue upon buff, buff upon white. He looked, in fact, like a highly cultivated European such as one saw, in a less turbulent day, strolling along the boulevards of a Riviera town. Here in the Wisconsin hills, a worker among workers, a man who has never owed anything to the European tradition and has never admired it greatly, he managed somehow to have a look of Antibes about him.

At Taliesin he is as surely "the master" as Michelangelo and Raphael were masters of the disciples in their studios. Even at breakfast on a Sunday morning, when he glances down the length and across the breadth of the T-shaped table his eye has the authoritative glint of one who is used to gathering up an audience. After the meal his voice automatically rises a little, and automatically all the apprentices, their wives, their children, and their friends turn deferentially. It is as though an invisible tripod has been moved into place. The fumes begin to rise, the oracle begins to speak; the young heads nod in ardent agreement, and ripples of approving laughter sweep through the room.

For it is an epigrammatic and far from enigmatic style that Frank Lloyd Wright has devised for himself as oracle. He loves balance, poise, a neat antithesis in his sentences, as he likes them in his architectural forms. His spontaneous feeling for structure makes him an admirable extemporaneous speaker and he seldom pauses, never stumbles or gropes. Only an artist with words could say: "We slip blindfold and softly to our doom." Sentences like that flow steadily from Wright's tongue at an hour of the day, and on a day of the week, when it is very nearly universal for men to wrap themselves up in a surly and inarticulate somnolence. The truth about Frank Lloyd Wright is that he has done himself over into an uninterrupted seminar. Somehow he has managed to solve the technical problem of being always at his best.

He has a great deal to say about doom. The present system of education is doomed because it suffocates rather than educates. If he were Rockefeller he would buy up all the colleges in the country in order to close them and end their pernicious influence. The economic system is doomed because it has inverted itself and put its base ludicrously on top. Money has become not merely a convenience, something to be used toward interesting ends, but an end and a power in itself. The machine civilization is doomed because "the man" has been forced to become the slave of the machine. Perhaps the whole Western world is doomed, for the millions of the East begin to show signs of imitating our aggressiveness, and with their vastly greater potential strength they could easily prevail against us.

At breakfast doom is presented as cheerfully and casually as though it were a hot buttered roll.

But for this desperate outlook a cure is not lacking. It is to build Broadacre City and put democracy actually to work in it. Salvation must not be sought through the imitation of the ways of Fascism, Communism, or Socialism. It can be found only in the evolution of a native economy and a native culture entirely our own. The folly of our failure to prepare for the future and of our

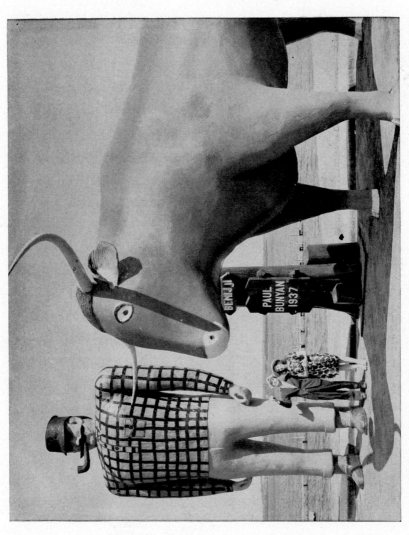

PAUL BUNYAN AND BABE, THE BLUE OX, AT BEMIDJI, MINNESOTA

MODERN LOGGING NEAR INTERNATIONAL FALLS, MINNESOTA

stubbornness in trying to accomplish impossible things by dangerous expedients Wright shapes into the epigram: "You can hammer
red-hot steel, but you can't hammer dynamite."

It would be unfair to a man of Frank Lloyd Wright's courage
and candor to suppress any item of the credo which he utters with
complete lack of reserve. Even though the impulse might be
friendly, though it might spring from a desire to present him sympathetically, it would be unfair. He has expressed his views with
unabashed completeness to representatives of the Federal Bureau
of Investigation, meeting them eye to eye, question to question,
challenge to challenge. He has walked with a representative collection of his ideas into the Washington headquarters of Robert
Sherwood and spread them out for all the Office of War Information to see. The color and the shape and the sharp edge of his ideas
are all well known. They must be seen and touched here as indi-
cations of the temper of one man of influence.

Frank Lloyd Wright does not believe in the objectives of this
war. He says: "It isn't the old Germany that I knew and loved
that has gone to war. It isn't the old Japan that I knew and
loved that has gone to war. Nor is it the old America that I knew
and loved that has gone to war." He would stand above the battle,
rejecting the idea that we are engaged in a crusade, remembering
our own past faults and blunders, hoping that in the heat of the
struggle all that has been false to his own notion of democracy
may be burned away in preparation for a new beginning.

All through breakfast and later, in his private quarters, far into
the afternoon, I argued with him about what seemed to me the
central paradox of his philosophy. He believes in individualism, in
the dignity of man, and in his right to a full, free and harmonious
life. Yet he rejects the idea that a first requirement for the safety
of his own Broadacre City must be the destruction of the German
and the Japanese philosophies which are not based on a belief in
individualism, are not concerned with the dignity of man, and
deny his right to a full, free, and harmonious life.

I could come to no other conclusion than that Frank Lloyd
Wright lives in Erewhon. And Erewhon has no foreign policy. It
is sufficient unto itself and it puts strict limitations upon John
Donne's belief that "Every man's death diminishes me."

But if the Wisconsin hills were Erewhon, even if there were no war, Frank Lloyd Wright's design for the harmonious life would be something that anyone could admire. At Taliesin he has staked out a section of Broadacre City, and within its limits he and his disciples lead a life that does credit to the spirit of man, to the variety of his aptitudes, to the depth and breadth of his sensibilities.

The design is based on the idea of work, of self-sufficiency. Taliesin is a farm, five hundred acres and more, under intense cultivation. The fields of wheat, alfalfa, barley, and oats band the hillsides in the neat strips of contour farming. It gives the young apprentices satisfaction to realize that science is in league with art in this matter of serving nature. For contour farming fulfills the harmony of the scene, looking as attractive as it is virtuous. Taliesin has one hundred and fifty cattle, forty of which are milk cows and the rest steers. It has five hundred chickens, one hundred and fifty pigs, and an enormous vegetable garden. Out of the fruits of the soil which they themselves work, the people of Taliesin draw their nourishment. Their daily life is no fine-spun theory, dreamed away in a studio; it is organically linked to the fundamental laws of existence.

The whole pattern is a crowded, yet unhurried, improvisation. The apprentices are at Taliesin to learn architecture, and they work at its theoretical and practical problems for many hours of every day. But the academic work can be set aside when a climax occurs in the routine of the farm. In haying season all the boys work with the pitchfork. If new buildings are needed for the animals, the apprentices work along with the professional masons. They take their turns in the kitchen, at waiting on table, making beds. When the time comes for the whole group to move to winter quarters at Taliesin West, near Phoenix, one of the boys may go the whole distance between Wisconsin and Arizona by motorcycle to prepare for the coming of the rest. It is an experiment in community living that works harmoniously within the limits of its well-organized self-sufficiency.

Time slips away deceptively at Taliesin because there is so much lively and challenging conversation. When Wright and I had sat talking for a long time, Olgivanna came to take her husband riding in the gig. At breakfast she had looked handsome in a yellow suit and purple blouse. The trace of an accent in her low-pitched, musical voice underscored her rich individuality with a little flourish of foreignness. But now she thoroughly looked her Montenegrin background. She wore a flowered white skirt that flowed about her with a subtle liquefaction, a tight-fitting jacket, and about her square-shaped face a brightly embroidered handkerchief. The peasant touch somehow emphasized the fact that Olgivanna is not a peasant at all. Her father, as Wright likes to remind himself and others, was a justice of a high court in Montenegro. There was a little flurry of discussion over the ride in the gig. Wright was loath to go, liking indoors better on a day when the autumn air had a tang of adolescent briskness and rudeness to it. But Olgivanna knew her mind. With a soft, almost maternal persistence she put him into the two-seated gig and drove him away.

So I went for a tour of the farm with the apprentices. There is no midday meal at Taliesin on Sunday, but the young men and I drank milk and ate bread and butter in the kitchen before we started. In the theater which was formerly the gymnasium of the Hillside School, we looked at films that experimented with the theory of making abstract composition fluent and animate. To the music of the *Danse Macabre*, lines and squares twisted themselves into fascinating patterns on the screen. Later the young apprentices gathered around the piano and romped over the whole field of musical composition from Bach to boogie-woogie.

For an hour before dinner everyone at Taliesin goes his own way. Mine led into a guest room, where I turned the pages of the books on the shelf and found that most of them came from the Hillside School. Holding Spencer's *Principles of Education* in my hands, I had a touching glimpse of those earnest Lloyd Jones sisters firmly pushing and prodding ignorance and intolerance back into their black lair. Yet they were armed only with the improving works of the Victorian thinkers.

Dinner at Taliesin is a great occasion. The lights are on in the living-room now. They glow out of hidden places, from behind a cluster of fall leaves, or along a shelf, picking up first the outline of an Oriental vase. Everyone dresses in order to acknowledge the right of an evening meeting to a touch of formality. The women wear long skirts; the men have exchanged the smocks of the studio or leather jackets of the farm for the shirt, tie, and suit of conventional dress. Wright wears a high collar of surprising turn-of-the-century rigidity. The meal is served on individual tables set before the guests ringed around the room. Wright's sisters have come across the field from their houses near where the old family buildings stood. There is an atmosphere of the gathering of the clan, as clans have gathered on Sunday evenings in native society from its beginning.

The dinner is good and there is the native wine of Wisconsin. Talk flows pleasantly, with a current of conviction carrying it a little faster perhaps than is usual in dinner-table conversation.

Afterward there is music. Half of the apprentices play instruments, and they form themselves into trios for Mozart and quartets for Beethoven at the most casual suggestion of a preference from the listeners. It is not true, of course, that this music wells spontaneously out of some effortless source of inspiration. It is the result of many hours of conscientious rehearsal. One hears the young men hard at it as one wanders through the rooms of Taliesin on a Sunday morning. There are greater surprises still in store. The orchestra plays Purcell; the chorus sings Palestrina; and one of the young men has revived the art of "the soft recorder," the ancestor of the flute which, in Shakespeare's and Milton's time, invited "the Dorian mood."

At Taliesin they have turned over all the civilizations of the past to find what pleases them. They have also projected their imaginations into the civilization of the future, and the apprentices conduct their private experiments with every sort of interest, occupation, adornment that may be needed in Broadacre City. One of them has set up a loom to weave the hangings for tomorrow's walls and windows. Another has gone daily to a sliver of a shop in Spring Green to teach himself printing so that he may set up his own press and experiment with the type, the typography, and the formats of tomorrow's books.

Integration, harmony, unity, organic wholeness—these are words and phrases that are forever on Frank Lloyd Wright's tongue. In the beguiling atmosphere of Taliesin they are not mere abstractions, but the principles of a practical program for living.

FATHER OF THE SKYSCRAPER

NOTHING COULD DEMONSTRATE better the sprightly willingness of our culture to contradict itself than the contrast that exists between two of the most striking and influential architects of our time, Frank Lloyd Wright and Cass Gilbert.

Cass Gilbert was born in Zanesville, Ohio, but made his home in St. Paul for many years during the period when his artistic theory was taking shape. There he attended Macalester College before going to the Massachusetts Institute of Technology to receive his diploma. In St. Paul, too, he did all of his early work, returning in his later years, a world power in his field, to add some characteristic footnotes to his career.

Frank Lloyd Wright has been just as closely identified with Wisconsin. He was born in Richland Center, a typical small town of the region, and he lives his superb baronial life today on his hilltop only a few miles from his birthplace.

The two men were born within a decade of each other, Gilbert in 1859, Wright in 1869. All the influences about them have been similar. Yet there could hardly be a greater dissimilarity than exists between the impression which Gilbert left upon his world when he died in 1934 and that which Wright is making today.

Gilbert was fundamentally a classicist. He believed that architecture should be a sort of summation of all the ideals of beauty that the cultures of the past have added to the richness of tradition. When he designed the Woolworth Building in New York, Gilbert did not hesitate to introduce Gothic motifs, emphasizing the vertical line, achieving, by the addition of color to the thin shell of his structure, the look of shadowy depth which the medieval cathedral had by virtue of the thickness of its walls. Gilbert once used the charming, casual, almost accidental design of a Normandy inn as his model for a modern hospital for children. Toward the end of his life he still followed the same principle of judicious borrowing. The Greek spirit survives in the façade of the Supreme Court Building in Washington.

Wright, for his part, rejects the past; he has been little influenced by it; his eyes are on the future.

Gilbert has been called "the father of the skyscraper."

Wright regards the skyscraper as a kind of monstrous perversity.

Gilbert was a man of the great world. He was honored by the academies of his own country and of England. In appearance he satisfied the most exacting notion of what an ambassador to the Court of St. James's should be. Except for the fact that in writing and speaking he habitually split his infinitives, he might have been created by Henry James.

Wright today looks like an aging poet. He is a rebel and a prophet, satisfied to live apart from the world and let those who find themselves in sympathy with his views come to him as disciples. Until society has come around to his way of thinking in everything, he intends to be antisocial. There is no trace of the concessive spirit about him anywhere. He likes to antagonize his fellow architects. He baits them with every stinging word that the resourceful mind of a poet can suggest. He prides himself on his enemies, and might easily have modeled himself on a design suggested by James McNeill Whistler.

The only comment that the culture of Wisconsin and Minnesota would seem to make on the curious circumstance of having fathered two men so alike in their sturdy, manly impulse to serve art, so utterly unlike in all their ways of doing so, is: "Do I contradict myself? Very well, I contradict myself." It is the privilege of a growing tradition to do so.

Cass Gilbert had a vigorous and resourceful hand in the creating of modern America. Souvenirs of his work are scattered all the way from New York to Arkansas. As a specialist in public buildings (the capitols of three states are his and so are Federal structures of importance in New York and Washington) he had enormous influence on taste. One of his most sympathetic critics, Royal Cortissoz, has written: "The groundswell of his career . . . had its origin in classical ideas. . . . His were the characteristics of a designer who drove at refinement, simplicity, just proportions, in short, the elements of the grand style. . . ."

What might be called the architectural costume of the nation has been made graceful and gracious by his touch. But it is not as original as the audacity of the skyscraper might make it, at first, appear to be. There are borrowed lines in the Gilbert style, as there are in any style that puts its emphasis on tradition and proceeds upon the assumption that the development of a new form is a historical matter, not one of pure inspiration. Gilbert seemed to believe that modern America should build by adapting the serviceable ideas that in the past had resulted in handsome, impressive structures. Ignoring the æsthetics of functionalism, he built office buildings that were overblown Gothic cathedrals, and set up a court of justice in a temple suitable for the worship of the pagan gods of Greece.

But there is reason to believe that Cass Gilbert was not, in spirit, profoundly dedicated to the tradition of the skyscraper. Responding on the occasion of his receiving a Gold Medal for Architecture from the Society of Arts and Sciences in New York, he said:

". . . It is not my intention to acclaim the skyscrapers . . . or to condemn them—they have faults as well as merits. In some respects and in some localities they are entirely suitable, in others not, and when I see the long shadows cast even at noon on a winter's day, I sometimes wonder if the light and air their occupants enjoy compensate for the sunlight their neighbors lose. . . . We have carried concentration too far; we must begin to think in terms of decentralization. Think it out."

This was said when Cass Gilbert was at the very height of his renown, just three years before his death. The blunt order to his colleagues contained in the last three words of this passage suggest that he was ready to welcome a change even though it meant a turning away from all that he himself had represented.

Perhaps he and Frank Lloyd Wright might have met with more harmony than discord in their talk. For Wright's Broadacre City

is merely a plea for decentralization of the kind for which Cass
Gilbert had begun in his later days to long.

A little tour of St. Paul to inspect the examples of the work done
during the years when he was practicing architecture as one of its
citizens shows that he did not at the outset of his career assign his
talents to the glorification of a particular style. Instead he experimented widely, sometimes on a lavish, sometimes on a most modest
scale. Indeed, he sought to do what any young architect must,
which is to satisfy his client's taste and not get too far outside the
confines of his client's pocketbook.

What is probably the earliest extant example of his work is a
little frame house standing high above a street which once was
fashionable, but is fashionable no longer. It is a quite indescribable
structure, not because of its complexity, but because of its featurelessness. Belonging to the early shoe-box style of architecture,
there is nothing to be said of it except that it has survived for a
comparatively long time and done its duty as a shelter.

In contrast is a large, handsome red stone house on Summit
Avenue that improvises a kind of splendor on a shallow plot of
ground along the edge of a bluff. It is a little difficult for the modern imagination to follow the theme of the façade. A "gay nineties" notion of majesty seems to be principally involved, as the
design leaps from the motif of a solid Romanesque arch to that of
a turreted tower, without benefit of any unifying scheme. It seems
to be an accumulation of architectural ideas, in much the same way
that English castles and country houses, rebuilt from century to
century by residents with different tastes, are accumulations.

But the two best St. Paul examples of Cass Gilbert's art represent also the wide range in his interests and his skills. The Capitol
is his, and it is set very nobly and resolutely on a rise of ground
from which it takes its proper prominent place in the profile of the
city. It is flanked by a state office building and the home of the
State Historical Society in an area the whole pattern of which Cass
Gilbert helped to plan. The district still wants more clearing away
of shabbiness, but it is a good start.

The Capitol, following the plan of the parent building at Washington, with a dome crowning the central part and the wings of
the House and Senate on either side, manages, despite its general

conformity, to achieve distinction. Its wingspread is genuinely serene and confident. It looks like a hall of deliberation, having none of that huddled, collapsed, blunted look that makes some of the state capitols mere vulgar caricatures of their parent.

The other building is as modestly and subtly gracious as the Capitol is boldly a statement of the idea of authority. Built originally as a church, it has the slenderest and most graceful of spires reaching up with unassertive aspiration from the peak of the roof. But what is chiefly attractive about it is the way that it folds itself around the base of a hill. A gracefully curved stone stairway leading to the front door is tucked in around the pavement of a broad highway that swings in an arc past the façade of the building.

Seldom has a designer managed to get so much of charm out of what might have seemed like a completely unsympathetic site. A building constructed without an intimate feeling for the character of the land itself would have seemed to retreat in fright against the hill, drawing its toes timidly away from the surging traffic.

Cass Gilbert's church does nothing of the kind. It seems to spring as spontaneously out of its setting as Frank Lloyd Wright's Taliesin seems to emerge from its shining brow. It manages even to dramatize quite touchingly the idea of the church at the side of the road, belonging close to the flow of human life and still a little withdrawn from it—easy of access, yet offering seclusion and shelter.

17

"REJECT ME NOT"

❦

THE MINNEAPOLIS SYMPHONY ORCHESTRA is only a little less than half a century old. Its concerts are given in the huge Cyrus Northrop Memorial Auditorium on the campus of the University of Minnesota. On Friday evenings between early autumn and late spring, audiences of nearly six thousand people crowd in to listen to samplings from the whole of musical literature, beginning with Bach and coming down to Shostakovich and the realm of experimental moderns, including those of our own community.

On the first floor the audience is as fur-bearing and orchidaceous as cosmopolitan groups of art patrons usually are. The men show a tendency to use the war emergency as an excuse for not changing from business suits to dinner coats, but the women are still enclosed in shimmering envelopes of silk and outer wrappings of mink. In the balcony faculty members of the university and professional musicians of the Twin Cities gather in the front seats, while students with scores open on their laps fill seats that reach so far away from the stage that an occupant has the impression of being in the next street.

It is not easy to reach Northrop Auditorium on a winter night in Minnesota. A disgruntled patron has been heard referring to the campus under such circumstances as "that American edition of the Nevsky Prospekt." But come blizzard or thaw, come a half-dozen competing attractions in the form of prize fights, political rallies, foreign policy addresses, and plays by George Kaufman, the campus is crowded on symphony night, and the two huge ramps beneath it purr with the anticipatory eagerness of a vast menagerie of hungry cats.

Half a century is far too long a time to maintain a pose, and the taste of the Twin Cities for symphonic music is certainly no pretense. Indeed, the singing Scandinavians of Minneapolis and quartet-playing Germans of St. Paul had their private societies for the purpose of performing *Messiah* and the works of Mozart before they had anything else in the way of entertainment or any paved streets by which such entertainments could be reached. Music was an immediate and spontaneous need, and when "two or three were gathered together," it began to be performed. It is no accident that one of the oldest of civic institutions in Minneapolis, one which is half the age of the city itself, should be a symphony orchestra.

The first conductor, the late Emil Oberhoffer, was everything that tradition requires a musician to be. He looked rather as though he might have been specially created to be an interpreter of the more exquisite inspirations of the genius of Debussy. Indeed, his particular talent lay in exploring the delicacies of the most refined and intellectual forms of music. In his younger days he had been obliged to conduct a band, and he was happy later to take refuge from the thumping declarations of public park music in the subtleties and intricacies of French composition.

Oberhoffer was tall, slender, and elegant. He conducted women soloists onto the stage with an Old World ceremoniousness that gratified all the drama-lovers in the hall. His fine head and neatly chiseled features were topped by a chestnut toupee which he brushed into a superb and reassuring semblance of leonine vigor. His innocent aptitude for dramatizing the role of the conductor was like a graceful flourish with which he embellished his thorough and unchallengeable musicianship. He built the orchestra into a solid and admirably disciplined organization. Oberhoffer earned the gratitude with which he is remembered. Though his community sometimes found him limited in range, it respected his complete integrity as an artist.

His successor, Henri Verbrugghen, was a Belgian by birth who had zigzagged his way to America along a circuitous course that led him through Scotland and Australia. He had picked up en route a wholehearted catholicity of taste and an earnest desire to please his audience, no matter what sort of audience it might be. He was the orchestra's patient, friendly drillmaster. With a love of teaching and a conscientiousness that nothing could interrupt or deflect, he demanded a high standard of excellence of his individual performers. To the men with whom he worked for a decade and more he was never the imperious, tantrum-swept maestro but the affectionately cherished "old man."

Electrifying is the only possible adjective to use of the effect created by the arrival of Eugene Ormandy as conductor of the Minneapolis Symphony Orchestra in 1931. He had his training as a young violinist in Budapest, and made his debut before an orchestra at the Capitol Theater in New York. The feeling for the platform, into which he had been thoroughly trained by the very atmosphere of his native country, had been disciplined into a technique by the challenge of pleasing the untrained listeners who gather together in a movie house. Fresh from that experience, Ormandy came to a community that cared genuinely for serious music. The opportunity was a real one for Ormandy. Into it he poured all of his gift for creation, all of his youthful eagerness, all of that surging rhythm which seems to be the inheritance of normally constituted Hungarians.

Under Ormandy's treatment the color of the orchestra brightened; the texture became rich and full. More beautiful sound issued out of the Northrop Auditorium than its patrons had ever heard before. Whether Ormandy played a Strauss waltz with all the centuries of a city's tradition of gallantry and gaiety crowded into it or a Bach prelude and fugue, measured out into the precise purity of its abstract form, he seemed always to put exactly the right means at the disposal of the music. His tone could be lush and sensuous, almost insinuating, or it could be chastely reticent and correct. Youthful as he was in his Minneapolis days, fond as he was of a gay man's pleasures, all the way down the scale to the elaborately contrived practical joke, he knew how to control his high degree of sprightliness and how to make himself the medium of the music.

A man from Minnesota chanced to be in New York at the time when conversation among music-lovers turned upon who was to be Stokowski's successor at Philadelphia. "I'm sorry to say," he remarked, "that I have heard it is to be our conductor, Ormandy."

All about him eyebrows shot up as though they had been clicked by a central switch. "But why should it be Ormandy," everyone in the room wanted to know, "when there is So-and-so and So-and-so and, if it comes to that, even the great So-in-so?" Ormandy has been in Philadelphia many seasons now. When anyone from Minnesota mentions in Philadelphia that he remembers Ormandy well, again the eyebrows click up. The accompanying look seems to say: "What curious delusions of grandeur these people from Minnesota have!" The Philadelphia legend now appears to be that Ormandy sprang full-fledged from the brow of Stokowski. It doesn't greatly matter to the man from Minnesota. He knows what he knows.

Dimitri Mitropoulos is the present conductor of the Minneapolis Symphony Orchestra. The eastern seaboard has also heard him. Mitropoulos is by birth a Greek, and he had plans for taking Minneapolis to Athens or bringing Athens to Minneapolis until the war ended his hope of joining the threads of his artistic life. In his secret mind he still nourishes those hopes, no doubt, for he is a mystic by temperament, a man who once thought of becoming a priest and who looks rather like a William Blake angel all done up in evening clothes.

Mitropoulos has the agelessness of the mystic. The completely bald head that he presents to an audience when he is conducting would give a stranger no clue to his age, for the tense, youthful vibrancy of his body belies any suggestion of venerability. He is actually in his early forties, but his priestlike mask of detachment conceals even the usual signs of middle age.

The most conspicuous feature of Mitropoulos's style as a conductor is a kind of hyperthyroid drive of nervous energy. He might be suspected of having swallowed a dynamo that throbs relentlessly within him, threatening to shake his frail-looking body to pieces. This is not to suggest that there is any false histrionism in his platform performance. It is, in fact, reticent, dignified, and impersonal. Nothing but his tremendous fervor is evident in the quivering eagerness of his approach.

The Minnesota public has received under him a full and exhaustive education in the literature of music. Mitropoulos's own taste is highly eclectic. He likes and interprets with enthusiasm any type of music that seems to him to show a rewarding degree of musical intelligence and musical *savoir-faire*. Sometimes he has brought out of obscurity compositions by the lesser masters which patrons of the concerts feel should have been left to gather dust on the shelves. More frequently he has explored the unknown realms of modern composition, drawing his audience along after him either in delighted and wondering surprise or in panic and open revolt. Mitropoulos feels that it is good for us to have our minds broadened by things untried in harmony and song, even though we may feel inclined to rebel at the instruction.

The Minneapolis Symphony Orchestra frequently travels, and it is particularly welcome in the neighboring cities of our own region, which feel that their enthusiasm has helped to nourish its tradition.

"Reject me not into the world again," Edna St. Vincent Millay once urged in a plea addressed to a symphony of Beethoven. A large and representative group of Minnesota citizens know precisely what she meant. For as long as many of them can remember they have been able, at regular and frequent intervals, to escape the crowding anxieties and apprehensions of daily routine, and to give the spirit, oppressed by many cares, the bulwark of music.

18

ESCAPE OF THE OLD ADAM

No MASS MANIFESTATION of the impulse of our region to entertain itself is more typical than the State Fair. Both Wisconsin and Minnesota have such festivals. They are Gargantuan affairs including very nearly everything in the way of excitement, wonder, awe, and terror that has ever played upon the human spirit as it seeks, in its robust and challenging way, to enlarge the range of experience.

A catalogue of the fine sights and pleasures planned to make the community "less forlorn" should include these:

A roller-coaster of such size, speed, and villainous design that it may be counted upon to unnerve any but a monster of fortitude;

A piece of modern farm machinery so complete that in harvesting the wheat it does everything an agriculturist could ask of it except to curse loudly at the gambler in grain futures;

A prize boar of enormous solidity whose bulk is contained in an envelope of such glowing flesh that it cries out to be painted by Rubens;

A heroic statue of the governor of the state, modeled in butter (this exhibit not available in war years);

A horse show where sleek and elegant animals, only a little less haughty and superb than their high-hatted riders, are put through traditional maneuvers as formal and stylized as those of a ballet;

An art show where every influence from that of Maxfield

Parrish to that of Salvador Dali is evident in the canvases of the local citizenry;

A freak calf with an extra pair of legs worn, as though in reckless abandonment to some whimsical dictate of chic, at the front shoulders;

A horse-racing contest, which ceremoniously observes among agrarian democrats all of the formal routines of the sport of kings;

A honky-tonk area, complete with fat ladies, flame-swallowers, fake hermaphrodites, Indian villages, peep-shows, tours of wonderland, fun houses;

Acres of barns in which gentle and unsurprised cows lie, each in her own cubicle, like ladies of the harem, immaculate and stupid, surrounded by family souvenirs testifying to excellence of pedigree;

Other barns clamorous with the sound of prize cocks and hens, all glittering in feather and full of challenge;

Improving exhibits of butterflies, the fish resources of the region, models of wild life, conservation programs;

And, rounding back to the innocent, fearsome, ferocious motif of the start, ferris wheels, merry-go-rounds, and toy trains.

Such community enterprises have always been a part of our American program of fun and self-improvement, as they were part of similar programs in England long ago. The tradition goes on and on, modified by native conditions and blown up in size to satisfy our passion for bigness.

In Wisconsin the State Fair is held at Milwaukee, in Minnesota at St. Paul. During the week of the festival all roads seem to converge upon the Fair Grounds and all traffic turns with concentrated, cheerfully controlled energy toward one focal point. Everyone forgets other interests, to live, with whatever overtone of fervor or irony may suit his temperament, the life of the fair.

Sophistication has not enveloped the atmosphere of these spectacles or allowed their homely charm to be swallowed up in commercialism. There is still a kind of spontaneity about a State Fair. Church groups of the Twin Cities undertake to balance the budget by setting themselves up in tents to serve chicken dinners to family groups. Amateur barkers, who are deacons in their moments of greater decorum, vie vehemently with one another in

ST. PAUL IS ON THE MISSISSIPPI

MINNEAPOLIS IS PROUD OF ITS PARKS

MILWAUKEE TAKES ADVANTAGE OF ITS LAKE MICHIGAN SHORE

DULUTH AND LAKE SUPERIOR, LOOKING TOWARD WISCONSIN

an effort to lure hungry customers off the wide highways and into their booths. In great whitewashed temples dedicated to domestic science, judges address themselves solemnly to the task of deciding which contestant has preserved the best pickles and made the most creditable apple pie. The preoccupation of the whole spectacle is evident in its cozy confusion of homemade comforters, jellies, folk art works, and contests specially planned to encourage the farm arts of boys and girls.

Out-of-town visitors always arrive in family groups. Phil Stong's shrewd and clever novel *State Fair* dramatized the adventures of such a group—father, mother, son, and daughter—broadening their emotional as well as their scientific outlook. But families of the cities also move as a unit. One sees them wandering up and down the highways together, going in and out of exhibits in mass formation, breaking rank only now and again in an effort to dissuade the more explorative elements from entering the mildly distressing sideshows, re-forming to go on and see the pigs. Absent-mindedly they take on amazing consignments of foodstuff—hot dogs, orange pop, cracker-jack, peanuts, mountains of a strange confection that looks like pink-tinted cotton batting. For eight hours or more this pilgrimage moves back and forth across the grounds. It may last far into the night as the family trudges dutifully to see spectacles in the grandstand that dramatize in fireworks some familiar natural disaster or some recent earth-shaking battle. Then at a final rollcall faces blurred with fatigue are counted, and the family swings into one of the steady lines of traffic raying out across the city to turn again home.

To anyone living in Wisconsin or Minnesota the first State Fair is a milestone in his personal history. It looms clear and vivid in the midst of the murky scenes of childhood like an initiation into the world of wonder, a first adventure beyond the garden gate. Many a full-grown man remembers his own rendezvous with ecstasy in the midst of the steaming heat of the Fair Grounds and the elbowing urgency of crowds. Across the years he can still hear the far, sweet enchantment which the pathos of distance creates out of the shrill symphony of the fair, the clang of the bell warning that the merry-go-round is about to start, the tinkle of the carrousel, the blended hoarseness of the barkers' voices shouting their incantations, the mooing in chorus of hundreds of mildly bewildered cows, the trumpeted orders of the judges at the race track.

Perhaps the perfection of this experience can be expected to come only once in a lifetime. But many a man has had the delightful adventure of recovering it three or four times over, vicariously, in the lives of his children. It is paradoxical but true that ecstasy is never more gratifying than when it comes at second hand. The radiant face of a five-year-old girl or boy meeting the world of wonder at the Fair Grounds holds all that the human spirit can ever capture of pure delight. The State Fair must seem like a place of miracles also to the full-grown man who finds that, at the cost of a dollar or two, he can satisfy all of the needs, passions, and whims of another human being. From generation to generation the fascination of the fair does not diminish. Unconsciously, each visitor goes out to discover the world and, one way or another, he is seldom disappointed.

The criticism has been made frequently in the past that Americans as a group and as individuals go to their pleasures solemnly. There is little reason to hope that we shall hear less of that sort of thing in the future. More Europeans of the cultivated, analytical, and garrulous sort are coming to us than ever before. They are quite ready to describe how superior they are in their talent for gaiety. Indeed, not the least acute aspect of the refugee problem is the question of what to do with the attractive woman psychiatrist from Vienna who observes, with a glitter in her eye, that American men do not know how to flirt. That sort of challenge could easily lead to trouble.

Yet a glance at the "play spirit" as it manifests itself in Wisconsin and Minnesota does not indicate that it is sluggish or lacking in spontaneity. Many a town of the region has its special community festival that springs out of the tradition of its own way of life. In the extremely jovial community of Bemidji, for example, the citizens regularly recall their logging days in a Paul Bunyan celebration.

On the shore of the lake, in a conspicuous place at the end of one of the main streets of the town, stands the figure of legendary Paul himself. He rises up eighteen feet tall and is made appropriately of steel and concrete. Gaudily painted in keeping with the logger's fancy in dress, Paul smiles out genially upon the community of which he is the patron saint. Beside him stands Babe, the Great Blue Ox, painted as he should be. In the beginning, the figure of the ox was anatomically accurate and complete. But the bad boys of the community took an understandable delight in sneaking up under the cover of darkness to ornament Babe in a ribald and noticeable way. In the end the conscript fathers of Bemidji met in solemn, special session and voted to have Babe altered.

It is part of the celebration of Paul Bunyan Week for all of the robust men of the town to let their beards grow so that they may look like authentic lumberjacks. When a man stops shaving he automatically stops feeling regimented. To neglect the razor is the first declaration of independence that suggests itself to the vacationist. In Bemidji this simple act of renouncing discipline has the effect of raising the level of jollity by several degrees. At no time in the year is Bemidji a smug or stuffy place. It is both a summer and a winter resort, and long since it has learned to play its role of host with high spirit and imagination. But during Paul Bunyan Week, when all of the citizenry are wearing stubby beards as though this were a sprouting of the aggressive impulse, the citizens' spirits soar to new heights. Viennese psychiatrists with cases to prove are invited to go there at their own risk.

In older communities public festivals seem usually to spring out of religious celebrations. Sometimes, as with the Mardi Gras of New Orleans, they spring a very long way. Prolonged hilarity precedes and shadows the period of penitence. The celebration of the Mardi Gras is a way of compensating oneself in advance for the piety and virtue one vaguely hopes to display during Lent.

Young communities like ours do not go such a long way about to find an excuse for ribaldry. Our festivals are reflections of an interest in our own historical past. It is typical of the whole region to take a great interest in its beginnings. Many a town of Wisconsin and Minnesota had begun to care for its history in the womb, so to speak, before it really had any. The first official gesture, after incorporation proceedings had taken place, was to form a historical society.

Stillwater, Minnesota, is such a community. It was a center of the lumber industry in the region, and once thought itself destined to be a great and thriving center of trade. When the last big drive went through, Stillwater settled back with a sigh into being just an attractive town perched picturesquely on the terraces of the St. Croix Valley. It is enormously paintable, and many an artist has lingered comfortably in it for months at a time to make compositions from its tiers of streets rising one above another, the caves along the shore of Lake St. Croix, the charming old houses. One of the most curious of the latter is a pocket-sized edition of the Alhambra which a lumber baron who had traveled and seen the world was once inspired to build. The same man fulfilled the destiny of the too recklessly expansive world power when, finding himself suddenly ruined, he borrowed a quarter from a neighbor, traveled by bus to St. Paul, engaged a room at the Ryan Hotel, and shot himself.

But Stillwater once showed the gusto and extravagance of which monuments like the local Alhambra and a picturesquely ruined old brewery are the souvenirs. In its annual Lumberjack Festival it remembers those days. Women flounce happily through the streets in the trailing costumes of the 1880's and '90's. On every street corner, in the hotel lobby, and perched on a stool at the soda fountain one encounters an "Adelina Patti," dressed in the elegance of the concert stage to recall the fact that the singer once visited Stillwater in the days of its youth. All the bars are clamorous with the shouts of men who have released themselves from the control of humdrum respectability by putting on the gaudy checks of lumberjack shirts. For a night or two Stillwater follows the ancient principle of discharging resentment against restraint in a planned and decorous saturnalia.

The interest of the occasion is not, however, solely that of imitating for a night the careless freedom of the lumberjack. Every hall, every public building, every show window in the Main Street stores, contains exhibits designed to dramatize Stillwater's past. And on the lake in daylight the old sports of the lumberjacks are revived amidst a great histrionic fervor such as the lumberjacks, who were all of them actors *manqué*, would have applauded.

It is the fate of most public carnivals to become commercialized. But where they invite the active participation of great numbers of the whole public, in events that occur out of doors, spontaneity is apt to reassert itself despite all earnest efforts of exploiters to enroll the play spirit as a means of advertising soft drinks, patent fasteners, underwear, and breakfast foods.

In St. Paul the Winter Carnival remains hearty and raucous and boyishly absurd after many years of intermittent re-enactment. Every generation, though not every year, of St. Paul's history has seen a Winter Carnival. The war once more has caused a hiatus. But Boreas Rex is only biding his time until he seizes his throne once more.

The best features of the Winter Carnival dramatize simply the coldness of Minnesota and the opportunities that that coldness offers for skiing, coasting, and skating. The story is told in terms of melodrama and low comedy. It has nothing in common with the spirit that a slightly mystical and very misty-minded Broadway director once declared that he had discovered in Maxwell Anderson's play *Valley Forge*. "You cannot grasp its significance," he told his cast, "until you have made yourself feel the fourth dimension of cold." The cold of the Winter Carnival in St. Paul has no fourth dimension. It is enough that its tingle and excitement produce a sense of well-being such as the community experiences en masse only once a year.

Fundamentally the pattern of the Carnival is that solid and useful one of a legendary hatred between ice and fire. Each year a King Boreas is elected to dramatize the power of the North. He is always a prominent citizen of goodly port who looks well in ceremonial robes. His duty is to ride through the streets frequently in full regalia, graciously acknowledging his subjects; to crown the queen who is elected after a great deal of tense campaigning among the friends of pretty stenographers; and finally to hold his castle against the storming of the followers of Vulcan, god of fire and traditional enemy of Boreas.

Vulcan and his hordes, in costumes of black and scarlet, go masked throughout the week. It is their privilege to break into the most solemn sanctums of industry to humiliate bank presidents with their impudences and to kiss all of the secretaries on sight. Black smudges mark kissed cheeks and sometimes bald heads. These invasions create inexpensive diversions of an afternoon for all the office workers who crowd into the private quarters of executives to see these audacious thrusts at dignity.

Last scene of the eventful history of Boreas's brief reign is the storming of the palace. This structure stands sometimes in the center of town, sometimes near the Capitol, and again in a park on the outskirts of town. It is an architectural oddity built up of great blocks of shining ice illuminated from within by red and blue and purple lights. Stout citizens in mackinaws and ski pants return, for the moment, to the days of their youth and rush the fortress, armed with snowballs. It is part of the traditional routine that the palace must dutifully surrender until another year when another Boreas Rex reigns, high, wide, and handsome.

All through the Carnival a mood of mild indulgence prevails. Wearing a special costume, which identifies him merely as a member of this or that business institution, a man feels a little unlike his everyday timorous and cautious self. It is as though he wore a disguise, and under its protection he is less inhibited, more genial than is his custom. If he is caught and tossed in a blanket by other noisy citizens he does not permit his dignity to suffer. When he sees a troop of boys from the meat-packing district lunging through the streets singing:

> *Let's go, let's go, let's go now*
> *South St. Paul and hook 'em cow . . .*

he sometimes yields to the temptation to join them. The ancient principle of allowing the old Adam, for a period, to escape from the tight confines of civilized respectability in a mild approximation of the orgy is thus innocently served.

Wisconsin and Minnesota are important centers of interest for all who are devoted to winter sports. They have the longest and the highest and the most audacious ski slides. St. Paul has always prided itself upon its contribution to the art of ice-skating. The experts who make the skates of the great Sonja Henie have always lived among us, ignoring the slyly seductive gestures that would lead them elsewhere. The St. Paul Figure Skating Club has developed many a national champion of the rink. It puts the tiniest children of Minnesota on skates. In the strange, fascinating fantasies which its choreographers devise, one sees babies of four break from eggs, playing newborn chicks in delightfully impossible Easter programs, to go sliding and gliding away with magnificent virtuosity. St. Paul cannot give up its skating even in summer. When the August "Pop" concerts begin, the Figure Skating Club sweeps onto the artificially iced arena of the Auditorium to the orchestral accompaniment of Strauss waltzes. These cool and competent performances help the sweltering, beer-drinking citizens temporarily to forget that the thermometer stands at one hundred degrees above zero.

Minneapolis, having more lakes than St. Paul (two in everyone's back yard is the modest exaggeration of the facetious), concentrates on swimming as its official sport. The dubious inspiration came to one of its citizens to call the annual summer festival of the lakes an "aquatennial." It is not difficult to detect the influence of that special language invented by Billy Rose at the time of the New York World's Fair when he presented his "aquacade" with "aquabelles" and "aquabeaux"—all, no doubt, in the best "aquataste." The Minneapolis celebration draws to itself all of the most accomplished swimmers, from "Tarzan" Weismuller himself down to the newest of his disciples.

These large, well-organized, officially endorsed manifestations of the play spirit actually draw the greater part of the community and of all the neighboring communities into a mass movement in favor of fun. But the annual rejection of sobriety does not by any means exhaust the capacity of the region for amusing itself. In little halls of towns and villages all over Wisconsin and Minnesota groups of people having the same national heritage are forever gathering to revive the games and songs and dances of the old country. Swedes in a kind of pure and dedicated fervor meet to dance the robust steps of their highly athletic forebears. Ukrainians assemble in costume to sing the fine songs celebrating the beauty and fertility of their native land. Bohemians, Serbs, and Greeks rush into public parks for picnics, one of the chief purposes of which seems to be to determine who has preserved the most Gargantuan appetite for a particular native dish. Even the Mexicans, while they represent the least large of special groups among our citizens, come bravely together for fiestas though these are likely to become a little limp under a sun that glares in a different way from the sun of their native country.

The youth of our region, though it is as staunchly dedicated to the American art of "rug-cutting," though it loves the songs of the Hit Parade, and though it can chant all the words of the "Pistol Packin' Mama" of the moment, no longer rejects, in the nervous fear of being thought inferior, the traditional songs and dances of its parents. No doubt the International Institute of St. Paul and other organizations like it have done much to make young people think well of their heritage. For when a community chooses to reserve a few afternoons and evenings out of the year for the special purpose of honoring, in a "Festival of Nations," the graces and the skills of the countries from which America has drawn its peoples, the risk of seeming like an outsider has been replaced by the gratification of seeming gay and gifted.

No similar credit, perhaps, is due Wisconsin and Minnesota for the fact that their Chippewa and Sioux preserve the ancestral traditions. Indians everywhere have a quietly persistent way of keeping their customs alive. But at least a flutter of applause may be permitted Minnesota for the gesture of forbidding any but Indians to take stone from the Pipestone quarry. The place, now a national park, has an impressive history. Legend fixes it as the spot where the Great Spirit created man, and the dark red quartzite is believed to be the flesh of the first Indians, hardened by the waters of the great flood. For years the tribes fought for possession of this sacred ground, coming at last to an agreement to hold it in common as a neutral place of worship. Today its specialness is no less scrupulously observed. From it the Indians take stone for their pipes of peace while white tourists look on, wishing perhaps that they had a sacred place from which they could take similarly comforting symbols of peace to come.

One of the most spectacular of Indian festivals in Minnesota is that of the wild rice gathering at Glendale. Quite in the traditional way the Indians paddle into the swamp to thresh the rice heads into the canoe. In the evening the age-old ceremonial dances are enacted. A great symbolical drama of the harvest draws the whole Indian community into its action. The old men bend grimly over their drums; a chorus of men's and women's voices chants out the ancient stories of the tribe; colorfully dressed girls dance slowly in a circle; and then, at the climax of this allegory of a people's resurgent strength, the young men in fiercely brilliant costumes suddenly rush into view, their faces mysteriously hooded in fur-trimmed headdresses, their feet stamping out a rhythm that rises to a great climax of triumph.

Everywhere in our region the people have found ways of letting the old Adam escape in moments of relaxation, to display without reserve his pride in strength, in skill, in vitality and wit and appetite. And his imperishable sense of well-being is good to see.

❧ 19 ❧

"SHORT RETIREMENT,
SWEET RETURN"

❧

THE POET Milton, whose genius is chiefly associated with breathtaking expressions of the great austere crises of the spirit, once took time out from his major preoccupations to toss off the perfect description of the homeliest of adventures, a vacation in the woods.

In *Paradise Lost* he was casually inspired to write:

> *For solitude sometimes is best society,*
> *And short retirement urges sweet return. . . .*

Few even among the most completely urban of creatures can have failed to experience occasionally the need to drop from their shoulders the burden of apprehensions and tensions associated with their daily lives. Fifty weeks are quite enough in which to rise to the brassy order of the alarm clock, gulp a cup of coffee (to the accompaniment of urgent pleas, warnings, and invitations to wisdom issuing out of the radio), jostle other worried people on the way to work, and juggle the items of an office routine for eight hours crowded with exacting commonplaces.

Fifty weeks are enough in which to devote one's evenings to the forays, the raids, the last of defensive stands which pass for pleasure at the bridge table. Anyone will recognize Milton's "short retirement" as the traditional two-week holiday and his "sweet return" as the satisfaction of showing to office colleagues a face dyed a fine fumed-oak shade and of telling them great tales

238

of wall-eyed pike caught and others that got away, of bear seen prowling, and of deer glimpsed in a forest of virgin pine.

On the border between Minnesota and Canada, from the North Shore of Lake Superior reaching west-by-north to Rainy Lake, lies a region that offers one of the last and one of the best glimpses of the unspoiled American wilderness. Here is a vast unpopulated region without towns, farms, factories, industries, any of the things associated with the necessary but exhausting pulsations of civilized life. Through it twists a chain of connected lakes filled with small and large wooded islands. White pine and Norway pine, spruce and balsam push their way down to the waters' very edge and lift their blue-green splendor high overhead. Jack pines spring picturesquely and precariously out of the cliffs that border the shore, and the withered-looking trunks of the cedars bend over the water to show the fernlike delicacy of their green branches. Wall-eyed pike, northern pike, and pickerel are abundant in the lakes. Ospreys circle over the water to dive for their dinner, and eagles swoop down to rob them of their catch. The woods beyond are hospitable to wild life. The recesses deep and silent offer shelter to moose and bear and porcupine, to deer and partridges, to warblers, woodpeckers, and hermit thrushes, to timber wolves and beaver.

This world is still what it has been since the beginning of the time when earth began to sustain life. Even today it must be explored with some of the audacity and resolution that took the French fur-traders and the English explorers over it. There are no de luxe approaches, for highways reach only the edges of the area. Travel, after one has penetrated into the heart of this country, is over water, with portages around the falls that link the lakes on their different levels.

Pierre Gaultier, Sieur de la Vérendrye, traveled through this country in the early years of the eighteenth century, looking for the Sea of the West. He, his four sons, a nephew, and a company of fifty—all dedicated to the idea of serving France by outlining a new highway over which its New World trade could travel— paddled through these lakes and camped on these islands. The pattern of land and water that they saw is unchanged today, and the composition of wind and bird call and murmuring water which they have heard has had no dissonance of urban life added.

Alexander Mackenzie would still be at home here. He was the blunt trader who traveled west across this region, leaving his name on modern maps as discoverer of the Mackenzie River. The introduction to his journal warns the reader to expect no ecstasies of description, no embellishments added to factual observation, and there are none. But his descriptions of the portages and rapids, chasms and cliffs would be perfectly suitable for use in a modern guidebook, so little has the restless activity of modern man altered the silhouette of this landscape.

It has been a struggle to preserve this country in its virgin state. In the great stretches of forest beyond the lakes the lumbermen worked long ago, and they are eager to enter it again to take the stands of virgin timber that were inaccessible before or somehow were not worth the trouble of felling. Other commercial interests yearn covetously for the right to put in the lakes and rivers dams that would turn the whole region into a vast swamp. Other busy and resourceful minds cannot give up brooding over the possibilities of further exploitation if roads and highways were introduced into this wilderness. They forget that, had highways been in existence, the wild life would have retreated long ago in alarm, and the wilderness would have surrendered its natural beauty to the eloquent urgings of signboards telling how life begins with one's introduction to a particular candy bar, cigarette, or soft drink.

The Quetico-Superior Council has fought off those who wish to exploit the last wilderness. The Quetico National Park on the Canadian side of the border and the Superior National Park on our own have collaborated on a program of conservation. The Isaak Walton League has made the struggle one of its major interests.

So the wilderness lies there still, seeming to bridge the centuries that lead back into the past. It bridges, too, some mystical chasm lying between our modern mood, composed so grimly of tension, determination, and distrust, and another realm of the spirit in which the air is easier to breathe. The wilderness is a place, one discovers, where each day's need may be satisfied, not without effort, but without the constant prodding of fear that demoralizes urban life.

At each stage of the journey into the wilderness one drops still another item of one's excess baggage of chronic anxiety. From the town that is nearest to the edge of this refuge from civilization the trip into solitude is made first by truck to a prefatory lake; across that long, narrow body of water by launch; over another "portage" (once more via a truck that stands waiting on the shore line where deer come down to drink in the cool of the evening), and then at last, when the second lake has been crossed, to the dock of one's destination.

It is clear immediately why the man who loves this alcove of the wilderness has chosen the particular spot one sees from the lake to be his home. His log house stretches its comfortable length through a grove of pines that have never heard the ponderous footsteps of any of the disciples of Paul Bunyan, looking for stately victims. The trees that stand there on the point thrust out between two small bays have presented, year after year and century after century, precisely the same look of velvet richness as they spread their green against the sky. They tower some seventy-five feet above the ground and are slender in comparison with their height. Above a floor of soft brown pine needles they crowd into a deep shade where all sounds are softened into harmonious decorum. There even the truant mind surrenders its last impulse to pulsate with the rhythm of flight and becomes serene.

The trees in this particular grove are chiefly white pine. Their bark is deeply grooved and looks weather-beaten, like the flesh of an old Indian face. The rough surface makes, apparently, a perfect playground for the tiny, impudent red squirrels of the neighborhood. While one stands greeting the scene, two of them curl the flame of their bodies down the trunk of a tree and then in an instant up the trunk of another.

All about one's feet in this grove are trees just beginning their lives—three years, four years, five years old; one can estimate their age by the tiers of branches. They have been set out by the man who loves this place and who has indeed made of it a one-man reforestation project. Back in the woods are the bunkhouses of his crew of Finnish lumberjacks who plant and cut, year in and year out, according to the principles of scientific respect for the resources of the land, pulling out the windfalls, cutting down the dying trees and those weak ones that threaten to sap the vitality of healthier specimens. Always the workmen put back many times more trees than they take out.

The cabin of the man who loves this place hides so reticently in the grove that it can hardly be seen from the water. But when it is seen at last, it appears to have a right to be there, for it follows the lines of the ground on which it lies and is made entirely of the materials of the forest. The logs are full, round ones, of course, not weather-beaten and dead-looking like those in pioneer cabins of the type in which it once was considered wise to be born if you wished to become president of the United States. These logs, treated with a mixture of turpentine and understanding, gleam yellow in the sun, full of health and soundness.

The man who loves this place has given himself room in which to turn around even when he is under his roof. Graciousness is a part of his essential philosophy in taking from and giving back to the wilderness. So he has made his house broad and deep. But all of it is wilderness-made. The panels of the doors are held together by strips of wood fixed in place by wooden pegs. The iron latches have been made in the forge on the hill, and every item of decoration inside is a sample of Indian handicraft. A concession to civilization has been made by using electricity generated by the camp's own motor. But Indian artistry has adapted its skill to this emergency by providing the birch-bark shades for lamps. The stone fireplace, raised half a foot from the floor to give a maximum of comfort and radiation, is wide enough to accommodate a four-foot log.

At an angle from the main lodge, following the line of the bay, is another log cabin containing sleeping quarters for guests. A little veranda runs the whole length of this structure and from it one looks through the grove down to the water across a stretch of ground checkered in the brown and green of pine needles and the more adventurous of weeds and grasses. Each guest room contains a double-deck bunk, the frame of which has been made on the place from the trunks of small trees. The odds and ends of furnishings in both lodge and guest house have the unobtrusive rusticity that testifies to the taste of the man who loves this place and who wishes to keep it all in the uncluttered style of a lumber camp.

One superb luxury his imagination has been inspired to demand and his sense of fitness has been wise enough to grant. It is a great skylight let into the sloping roof just above the hearth. Sitting before the fire on a fine, brisk day, one sees the plumes of pines framed overhead with a particularly gracious kind of intimacy, making one feel neighbor to the sky. And in wet weather, when the tops of the trees toss and the rain beats against the skylight, an occupant of the cabin has two things in one, the warmth of the fire and the sense of being identified with the fine turmoil of the storm.

This place invites one to a routine of swimming, paddling, fishing, stalking wild life (though a camera is the only weapon). The days are crowded with small interests that take a long time in the doing. Half a dozen happenings fill the hours between sunup and sundown. In the wilderness you make yourself a morning meal, fill a canoe with the paraphernalia for a day's fishing, find a bay that you hopefully imagine answers the description of the place where recently some men from Indianapolis made a wonderful catch of walleyes, forget to fish while you watch the tawny glow of a deer's coat appearing and disappearing among the rocks along the shore, pull up on an island for a swim and later to fry eggs and bacon on a carefully improvised stove of stones, lie on a rock to feel indolence seeping into the very marrow of your bones and to catch in your nostrils the faint but highly satisfying hint of your flesh actually becoming toasted, return to your fishing with the modest decision to settle for pickerel—to be rewarded for your compromise by actually catching two; begin to brood about eating again and find, from the position of the sun in the sky, that lo! the morning and the evening are the first day.

This blending of the hours into one serene stretch of timelessness, now lighted by the sun, now covered with darkness, is a phenomenon the pleasures of which can be discovered only in the wilderness. In other places, however earnestly the hours may be dedicated to enjoyment, there are obligations that keep the dial of the clock before one's eyes, there are bells summoning one to meals or warning one that the mail boat is coming or going. But a man on his own in the wilderness, alone or even with a companion, can melt time down into an uncharted, unmarked, and uninterrupted interval of contentment.

His satisfaction is of a purely animal kind, and for once he is unapologetic for the fact that everything in his life turns upon a need that is simple, understandable, and readily gratified. From the fish on the line to the fish in the frying-pan to the fish in the stomach, the round of pleasures seems reliable and sure.

The spirit that has cowered so long under its blanket of protection against life and turned a little grim, a little sullen in its retreat from experience, begins to throw off its hypochondriacal apprehensions. It steps out to greet sensation. And sensation is everywhere. It is underfoot as a man makes his way down to the lake to swim in the early morning. The carpet of pine needles, always soft and pleasant, seems porous and springy under the bare foot. The resiliency is somehow like a note in music, and adds another to the wilderness symphony of sensations.

There are endless discoveries for the eye, like that of learning that the bark of the Norway pine which the experts call red is not really red at all. The effect of color is produced by a combination of the subtlest grays and rusts, with leaves of bark laid over one another so as to make a garment of intricate design. Indeed, for all its dignity and majesty the Norway pine seems always to be dressed for a masquerade as Harlequin. Motley is its wear.

Even rainy weather has its delicious sensations. The wilderness trail leads through dense country, along the edge of muskeg swamps, exactly like the green world into which the pioneers came to log and to dig for ore. One sinks ankle-deep into the soaked earth, thinking what it would be like to be a *voyageur* making a portage across this country with a canoe on one's head, or a prospector for iron facing nothing but disappointment and bafflement at the end of such a day as this spent in the open. The wind gnaws at flesh, making one long for the fire. And then, all at once, comes the reward for the impulse that has sent one out in the unsympathetic weather. The rain and wind have vitiated the warnings of sound and scent to which wild life is ordinarily

ROCHESTER, MINNESOTA, IS DOMINATED BY THE MAYO CLINIC

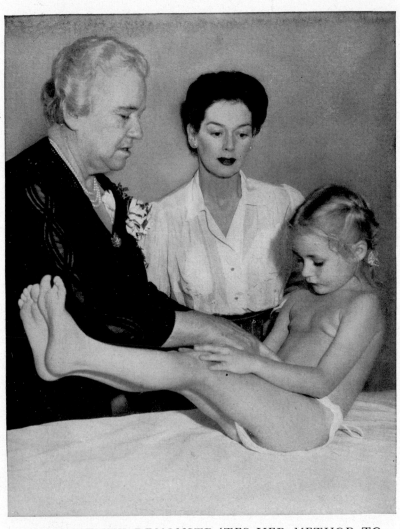

SISTER KENNY DEMONSTRATES HER METHOD TO
ROSALIND RUSSELL, SCREEN ACTRESS

alert. And there on the path stands a doe, so near that one feels able almost to touch the wet velvet of her flank. For an instant one looks directly into the beautiful, unstartled eyes of this incredibly graceful creature. Then with a single bound and hardly a crackle of a twig, she is gone.

On another walk it is the sensation of incredulity that one chiefly feels in an intimate personal interview with a porcupine. Absent-mindedness on the part of both wanderers brings them together. Walking unwarily through the woods one almost steps on the creature. It scurries from the trail and then stands stock-still in what appears to be a moment of worried indecision. The inexplicable circumstance of finding the great moving shadow of a man hanging above it is distinctly displeasing to the absurd little animal, but he decides that inaction is the best short-range policy. It would certainly be the time for quill-throwing if porcupines could satisfy the morbid imaginations of legend-lovers who still believe that quills are thrown. But porcupines have no such athletic talent. They wear their quills simply as armor against their fleeter and tougher enemies.

The porcupine, particularly when it stands in a state of quivering indecision at a roadside, seems like one of the less successful products of evolution. Its adaptation to its environment appears to be somewhat whimsical and uncouth. The small head, armored like the rest of its strange body, manages to look unshaven, unkempt, and derelict. The porcupine rather closely resembles one of those bleary, out-of-focus old men whom one sees degenerating slowly on park benches in the slum sections of large cities. His costume, of course, is very dissimilar. This seems to have been designed by an insane woman of fashion, *circa* 1880. For what the porcupine wears behind is very surely a bustle to outdo any bustle ever conceived. Woodsmen feel no great tenderness for the porcupine because his favorite meal is the tender bark of young trees and, in taking what he requires, he often kills the new growth.

Nor are the woodsmen deeply enamored of the bear. "Lazy, indolent marauders," Joe the foreman calls them. In August they move in closer and closer upon civilization because the time of hibernation is near and they need to put a well-stocked storehouse of flesh about themselves. Going to the camp cooler in the morning, you may find its freshly painted, heavily barred door marked with the clear and unmistakable imprint of a bear's paw. He has smelled the side of beef, the ham, the sausages and bacon hanging inside and has clawed resolutely trying to get at them.

"No self-respect," Joe mutters vengefully as he looks at the paw marks. "He'll eat fresh meat only when he's desperate. Ordinarily he prefers it spoiled. You lay a fresh-caught fish out to tempt him, he'll never take it. But leave it there for three or four days and he'll come back to get it when it's rotten. He'll eat a dead deer when the flesh has begun to decay. And if you kill a bear and bury it, another will come along, dig it out, and eat it. Lots of fellows from the city are hot for bear steaks. We never eat them."

In the lodge is an arrow thrust between the logs. It was used by an expert in archery taking a bear as his mark. Shot at four hundred feet, the arrow passed straight through the bear's body and out at the shoulder.

"That bear never knew what hit him," Joe says. "I was watching and listening. I heard him sort of sigh and then he walked a few feet and lay down. He was dead when we got up to him."

Joe doesn't like the bear's manners, and he seems to disapprove as well of his too easy adaptation to some of the sterner laws of nature.

"You know," he says, as though he were clinching a major point in an indictment of the whole species, "the female bear has her cubs while she's in hibernation. Goes to sleep and wakes up to find a family playing around her."

Joe bosses the crew of Finnish lumbermen who work this one-man reforestation project. He is of Czechoslovakian descent, and he seems to be the most complete and whole of men. He knows this lake and its 3,800 miles of ragged coast line as another man might know his back yard. In his motorboat, the *Scout*, he cruises all day and far into the night, supervising the various projects to which the war emergency has given a tremendous impetus.

The creator of the one-man reforestation project who hires Joe and his Finns has made an agreement with the Canadian government by which he is permitted to go into lands where timber has been logged off and clean up after the commercial companies have completed their operations. These people leave a melancholy scene behind them. Though the law does not permit them to log within four hundred feet of the shore line, bleakness remains where their camps have stood.

It is not worth the man-hours involved to take down their buildings. They leave on the ground the small trees, cut down merely to carve a passageway along which the valuable logs can be hauled to the water. Trees not worth felling stand dying upright, their vitality destroyed by the march of the loggers. And far back into the woods forests of stumps bear witness to the good haul the company has had.

The epilogue to this story is a dismal one indeed. A gray haze of dead pine boughs weaves a filmy pattern of decay over the whole scene. Dying trees, shaken by the breeze, no longer sough or sigh or do any of the things about which the minor poets like to run on; they creak like barn doors. Up the skid-road one comes upon the skeleton of a horse that has died in the service, and for whom a hasty funeral pyre has been built. There he lies, his silhouette still clearly outlined in bone and ash, an unconsumed hoof seeming somehow the most pathetic of all possible testimony to a usefulness that has ended. Farther along the skid-road lies a mountain of tin cans, testimony to the fact that the lumberjacks have lived well if not fussily.

This ruinous scene Joe and the Finns of the private reforestation project will transform into a green and pleasant place once more. They will pull down the loggers' buildings, salvaging whatever timber is still sound, and that is most of it, since the drama of logging is a swift one and allows little time for decay. They will pull out the dead and dying trees. They will haul away the windfalls. All the refuse of the lumber camp will be disposed of decently. Then when the ground is clean and wholesome once more, the planting will begin. Within a few weeks this scar on the landscape will have healed, and within three years no one without map and compass would be able to tell precisely where the loggers had been.

"The trouble with the lumberjack," Joe says, "is that he loves just one thing, to see logs in the water. He doesn't think about what he leaves behind."

Joe sits silently for a moment as the signal of a buck sounds suddenly from a thicket beyond the bay. Everyone waits, tense with interest, for an answer from the doe. But after a moment, when no answer comes, the talk goes on.

"I love to see logs in the water too, by golly!" Joe exclaims.

He sits looking with rapt satisfaction at the raft of fifty logs presently to be floated down to his own orderly camp where a sawmill is part of the equipment. Joe feels as the young man feels whose diploma has just been put into his hand. Here is the evidence that his work has been done well and completely.

"What about moose in these woods?" one asks idly to keep the desultory talk of the camp going.

"We see them, now and then," Joe answers. "But they'll be coming back more and more. This is becoming pine country again and you always find moose where there are lots of needle trees. Deer follow where the leaf trees grow. This country has reached the peak of its deer cycle. As the pines take nourishment from the decay of the shorter-lived leaf trees and get ahead, the moose will come back."

If it can be preserved this wilderness will become, even more than it is today, a haven for the wild animals that civilization has discouraged and driven into farther retreat. No one need grieve over the moose, for he has speed and cunning and has preserved his existence against all odds. He is one of the most curious and ill-favored creatures of creation. Indeed, he might be called the jalopy among animals, seeming to have been put together of the odds and ends of better-designed animals. He is lumpy and out of proportion. His magnificent antlers start him off superbly, but there is a depressing tendency on the part of his body to dwindle, and it becomes almost painfully noticeable in the hind quarters. Still, as he is such an oddity, it will be good to have him back in larger numbers when the pines in their splendor really take over the border country once more.

The Finns who sit about this camp in the evening after the eight hours' work is done are not young men. The boys have gone to war, and the infant of the present crew is in his middle forties. The oldest is sixty. But they are all sound men, hard and muscular and solid. They wear work pants and checkered shirts and bat-

tered hats such as fishermen affect. They have wide-set eyes, suggestive of what science assumes to be their Mongolian ancestry,
but their features are otherwise European, precisely cut, orderly,
producing in several instances a kind of reserved and rather austere
handsomeness.

They are trained to self-sufficiency and silence. They wander
about the camp in the evening hours, gathering together in little
knots of twos and threes for a moment's conversation. Then they
wander again, each by himself, inviting that complete privacy in
which men with uncluttered lives find it possible to pass so much
time. The urban man, who must be forever talking if he is to feel
assured, is at first surprised to discover that these solitary workers
have so little to say about the war. He has seen them huddled over
a battery radio listening to news, but they have almost no comment to make on what they have heard.

"No, they don't say much," Joe agrees on the way back to the
main camp. "But when I take their pay checks up to them, they
endorse them and hand them over to me. Each one of them asks
me to buy him a war bond. Eli—that's the little jolly one—within
a year after Pearl Harbor he had bought five hundred dollars'
worth of bonds out of his wages."

The real social event of the Finn's life is the return from the
woods to bathe. He comes on Wednesday and again, of course,
on Saturday. With him the journey to the *sauna* combines the
interest of a ritual, a sport, and a party. The men are in high spirits
when they arrive at the dock. In anticipation of the pleasure to
come they emerge out of their characteristic stoicism and reticence to behave like adolescent boys, threatening to throw one
another into the lake and snatching at each other's clothes.

The *sauna* is a separate log structure high on the hill above the
other buildings. Several hours before it is time for the bath, Otto,
who is caretaker of the camp, has fired the stove to get the bathroom warm. When the Finns want warmth, they are not half-
hearted about it. They want a temperature of one hundred and
twenty degrees at least.

At this camp the bathroom is painted the traditional white—
benches, window frames, even the logs themselves. In the corner
is a square stove made of sheet iron, standing two feet above the

floor. Stones approximately the size of an indoor baseball cover the whole flat surface. A tier of benches rises against the wall under the sloping roof. There are three of these, each a foot above the other. Large basins to be filled with cold water at the faucet complete the equipment.

Bathers go in by threes or fours. The process is ritualistic, communal, and gay. Having left clothes in the outer room of the *sauna*, a man takes a basin of cold water and climbs to that one of the benches to which his courage calls him. The lowest is for the timorous, the second for the cautious, the third for those who are high of heart and well fortified with audacity.

A dipper goes with you to whatever level you climb. In it you take water to toss on the red-hot stones, two or three feet away. A moment after you have done so a cloud of steam rises, hits the roof, spreads, and finally rushes like a herd of stallions down your nostrils. The first impulse is to choke, gasp, and make for the door in a frenzy of panic. But a glance at the delighted Finns all about you shames you out of the desire to escape. You sit and suffer, every instant an eternity of exquisite anguish. Then, all at once, your body begins to do a fairly creditable imitation of the Fountains of Versailles. At every pore it bubbles with perspiration, which flows down one's back, face, chest, and arms. What was a maddening anguish only a moment before becomes a luxurious delight.

It is permissible, even in the sternest interpretation of the ritual, to dash cold water over one's head in order to make the heat endurable. Then another rush of steam brings another crisis of sweating, and the process is continued for as long as you are man enough to take it.

The Finns have a further refinement in the art of bathing which one must be experienced to enjoy. For them the routine proceeds to a mild fling at flagellation. With fanlike clusters of cedar branches in their hands they beat one another over shoulders and back to quicken circulation. Some of them will lie prone along the benches, their hands tight-gripped along the sides, and invite a really powerful laying on of the cedar clusters. When the beating is over there is no mark on the flesh to indicate what has happened.

For the Finns the bath ends, in winter when there are snow banks handy, with a great, almost canine rolling and tumbling and twisting in the drifts. The amateur is content simply to pull on a bathrobe and dash for the lake. Going down the hill, he weaves a little dizzily, as he might if after dinner he had taken just one more highball than he really needed. It is a pleasant sensation and it brings a deep and long night's sleep.

The water of these border lakes is cold. To enter one of them, say from a warm bed, requires a degree of resolution that is not always available even to the most enthusiastic of swimmers. But when you walk into a lake in the north country directly from a Finnish bath, it is like stepping into your own tub at home. You could relax in it for three quarters of an hour and read improving works of literature, if only the light of the stars overhead were sufficient.

Wisconsin and Minnesota cannot be accused of indulging in parochial self-congratulation when they point out that their northern regions offer an incomparable combination of advantages for recreation: woods, waters, fish, game, resort facilities. Millions of acres of forest land, much of it in public ownership, provide the background for a collection of fresh-water lakes unequaled in the United States.

Here it is the business of a large part of the population to provide entertainment for the vacationist—in summer to plan his canoe trip through a chain of dazzling lakes, in autumn to take him deer-hunting, in winter to escort him on exhilarating journeys behind dog teams, and at all times to feed him well, house him comfortably, and see that he doesn't lose, maim, or otherwise destroy himself. Domestic skill has been broadened to the scope of a large-scale industry, and maternal solicitude has been disciplined into a science. This region, which attracts guests from the farthest reaches of the rest of the country with its promise of pickerel and deer and ski slides and dog teams, has learned the business of caring for these visitors efficiently and well.

With such small excursions and events, the morning and the evening are the second, third, and fourth days of the vacation until one loses count entirely. It is pleasant to give up to the placid contemplation of the enduring simplicities of human existence, attention to which has been recommended in various idioms by all the philosophers from Buddha to Voltaire.

Sometimes in the evening, as one sits before the fire under the skylight framing pine tops and stars, there comes a knock at the door and Otto shuffles in. He is genial and communicative and, as one notes sympathetically, just a little drunk.

"Make company?" he says with a moment's flash of uncertainty. "That never hurt."

Otto should know well that it never hurts in this house. For the man who built it and who loves this place lives like a lumberjack when he is at home here and is delighted to have his fellow lumberjacks about him. But these are foreigners who sit before the fire, and it takes a moment for Otto to make quite sure he is welcome.

Then with a long-drawn, alcoholic sigh he produces his parlor tricks. He pops a wooden cork into a bottle by knocking away, with the greatest ingenuity and cleverness, the ringlet of bark on which it is perilously perched. He demonstrates his godlike strength by making a steel knifeblade sweat under the terrific pressure of his hand. He makes a toy windmill turn this way and that at his arbitrary command. All these are traditional Finnish stunts, learned from his father half a century ago.

But the secret of Otto's showmanship is something that only art can explain. He builds to his climaxes with all the suggestive cunning of a professional vaudeville artist. In his tiny fragments of almost unintelligible English he assures his audience that this trick is so enormously difficult that even he cannot expect to do it always; then he proceeds to do it over and over, each time with an air of tense apprehension, each time successfully. But he is only half professional artist; the other half is small boy, hugging himself with delight at his ability to baffle and confuse.

Finally Otto patters off into the darkness. One follows him out of doors, down the path through the towering pines, toward the black water. Above, the sky is filled with ghostly light. Streamers of pale green are flung across the arch of night. They shake and quiver gently, like curtains being blown by winds of eternity too vast, too subtle, to be felt on one's own cheek. To all else that this vacation has had to give, the superb spectacle of the northern lights has been added in an excess of the natural generosity of the place.

Standing alone under that superb sky, one slips out of one's few clothes and down into the water. Floating face upward, a tiny, sentient particle in the midst of a vast, lovely, unconscious world, one feels as though this were the moment of birth. But now there is no sense of oppression and certainly no terror such as, in the belief of psychologists, the infant's body feels. This experience is healing and good. Into one's spirit there seems to enter the invulnerability of rock, the sturdiness of trees, and the strange illumination of the night sky. The trauma of rebirth is a comforting and dramatic dream.

20

THE HUM OF CITIES

OUR HUMAN FONDNESS for easy generalization finds a sympathetic theme in assigning personalities to cities. "London is a man's town," the old jingle glibly asserts, "there's power in the air." And inevitably Paris becomes a "woman's town, with flowers in her hair."

Anyone with a modest amount of facility could improvise endlessly in this vein, but the whole impulse partakes of the folly of describing the French (an innocent little turn-of-the-century study is said to have done just this) as "a gay people, fond of light wines and dancing." The tendency isn't as utterly innocuous as it can be made to appear. America might have underestimated the Japanese less disastrously if we had not accepted, from David Belasco and other sentimentalists, the vague idea that they were a little yellow people who were strongly addicted to singing arias under the boughs of cherry trees.

Cities do possess individualities, to be sure, since differences of history, of settlement, and of occupation give them essential differences of preoccupation. But these differences are seldom on the surface. They cannot be identified by a visiting lecturer en route between the hotel where he has spent the night and the women's club where he is to give of his wisdom. Park Avenue would dislike having a newcomer assume that some of the blatant, belligerently vulgar stretches of Broadway represent the essential char-

254

acter of New York. Similarly the sweeping comments made on the cities of Wisconsin and Minnesota sometimes make residents wrap themselves up in a brooding resentment. Misunderstanding makes them cherish their oddities just as lonely, troubled adolescents often do.

Minneapolis and St. Paul, the Twin Cities, attract a great deal of attention from those who are fond of devising epigrams according to a simple prescription. Authors of drawing-room comedy used to base their claims to wit upon their ability to fill in the blanks of the formula: "Men are ——, while women are ——." Residents of the Twin Cities long have had to hear glib visitors work on a similar pattern: "I find Minneapolis to be ——, while St. Paul is more ——."

A special mask of indulgence is kept handy in all well-run Twin City homes to be assumed hastily whenever this sort of thing begins.

The naïve notion is widespread that an endless feud goes on between the residents of the two cities. Like the Hatfields and the Coys, they are supposed to mount guard at the barrier, ready, with guns and sullen glances, to defeat any effort at communication.

Actually, a casual visitor would have difficulty in identifying where St. Paul leaves off and Minneapolis begins. The stores and houses on one side of the street in the Midway district look exactly like the shops and houses on the other. Nor is the native dress of the Minneapolitans to be distinguished in any way from the native dress of the citizens of St. Paul.

The residents of the two cities share many facilities, and their interests have been thought by some to be so identical that they ought to merge, making a community of more than three quarters of a million people, the eighth largest urban center in the United States. Our American love of bigness makes this a tantalizing and tempting suggestion. But the two cities, established in a day when each had its special reason for being, have sprawled out so comfortably that it would be difficult to find a center for shopping and for entertainment that would satisfy the residents of both. It is ten miles from Courthouse to Courthouse, and that is greater than any psychological distance that separates them. Not even the Mississippi River really divides them, for both cities have grown up casually on both banks.

In the days of personal journalism, when editors made an art of insult and when libel laws were sufficiently generous to encourage rococo styles in the literature of abuse, the press happily abetted the rivalry of the Twin Cities. It prodded the communities on into battles over the census, into mutual attacks on the honesty of city governments. But these wrestling matches were largely verbal and represented little more than an effort on the part of journalists to contribute to the cause of innocent merriment. Nowadays there are few flashes of such rivalry, and for the most part the Twin Cities live together without spectacular friction, like any two members of a family. They feel for each other the not unpleasant mixture of indulgence and disapproval that has kept the family circle tolerable throughout the generations.

St. Paul is the older twin. Those who have a taste for mild mockery like to recall the fact that despite the sacred name it has given itself St. Paul was conceived in sin. The first settlement on its present site was made, when "Pig's Eye" Parrant, a formidable and unalluring character, was driven off from the vicinity of Fort Snelling because he had made a nuisance of himself selling whisky to the soldiers. Along with him were evicted the squatters who had settled on government land. They moved along the river to a situation that is now near the heart of St. Paul's business district. There Parrant continued to sell his shockingly cut whisky until he managed to cut even his patronage to nothing. He shuffled a little farther down the river, and presently Father Galtier built his church in the very center of what had been the Parrant community. The landing took its name from the church, and the slightly sinister frivolity of being called "Pig's Eye" passed out of St. Paul's tradition.

Or did, possibly, a little trace of it remain? A psychoanalyst of cities might easily believe that he found souvenirs of St. Paul's paradoxical beginnings in its temperament as it exists today. Worldliness and other-worldliness have struggled long and conspicuously for possession of the spirit of the people, and the result has been to produce a community that seems old, experienced, mellow, and humorous. The patina of sophistication lies over its whole way of life.

Equally important in its tradition is the theme introduced so early in its pioneer history by Father Galtier. St. Paul is a Catholic city. On the most prominent point of the highest terrace of the Mississippi stands the Cathedral, looking down on the city below with an air of benediction and also of watchfulness. It is a magnificent pile dominating the skyline, authoritatively Roman in its architectural blending of solidity and aspiration.

Anyone who lives in St. Paul long enough to penetrate below the surface level of banality on which all American cities look alike (neon signs, crowded drugstore windows, chromium bars —these are some of the features of the mask of the city) must come to be aware of this not unpleasant pressure of tradition. Like a much older European city, St. Paul wears the look of its experience. It knows that the world is a sinful place. It knows itself to be sinful. Still, it has settled down comfortably in the shadow of the Cathedral and hopes for the best.

The people who came to settle St. Paul were likely to understand and fall into this way of life. They were the Germans and Irish chiefly, coming to make fur into garments, coming to share in the interest and the profits of the great horse market, coming to make shoes, coming to manage the great industrial empire that sprang up as the forests were torn down.

They built St. Paul as they would have it, the railroads on the first convenient terrace of the valley wall, the business district of the city on the second level, and the residential section on the rim of the bluff overlooking the whole scene. On the two sides of Summit Avenue, the great street of St. Paul's beginnings, the Germans built their stately and complicated houses of brick and stone. They gave themselves fine views of what their industry had accomplished. They lined the thoroughfare with trees, so that while they still lived, these elms and oaks crowded into a shade to give a look of antiquity to their setting.

Within these houses the pioneers lived a spacious kind of existence. The frontier life of this river town was marked by many a sprightly influence. The French, who had lingered on from the earliest period of settlement and attracted immigrants of their own kind, insisted on having good food. The Irish insisted on wit and gaiety. St. Paul, even in its first days, enjoying affluence as head of navigation on the Mississippi, had sophisticated tastes. It went in for banquets of a dozen courses. A host with a proper sense of responsibility had a well-stocked cellar. The frugal house-wife was one who saw to it that enough oysters to last out the winter's entertaining were buried in the snow conveniently near the house.

Knowing that the world is sinful, and being surprised and shocked at no evidence of the frailty of man, St. Paul has some-times winked outrageously at the misbehavior of its citizens and visitors. The jaunty frivolity of its beginning lingered on when it had a government that deliberately sheltered criminals, exacting only their guarantee to commit no crime within the city limits. The city paid quite bitterly for this recklessness when the post-Prohibition breed of criminal became desperate and arrogant. In those days leading citizens were kidnapped every other Friday, the houses of the blameless were splashed with machine-gun bullets in displays of sheer animal spirit, and, by way of climax, John Dillinger shot his way out of an apartment building in an eminently respectable neighborhood. To the residents of St. Paul such manifestations were momentarily oppressive illustrations of the familiar fact that the world is a wicked place. Parrant and Father Galtier were still striving for supremacy.

St. Paul has long since made its peace with civic virtue. The misdemeanors of the purple past of Parrant have been enshrined in legend, along with later ones having to do with Nina Clifford, the noble courtesan of the nineties, and along also with the riotous moment of the racketeers. The municipal government of St. Paul today is scrupulously honest, inexhaustibly efficient, and ad-mirably liberal. St. Paul is both proud of its reform and relieved that the uncertainties of the past need not be expected to appear luridly from behind a false front of innocence.

Still, it rather likes to recount the mischievousness of the bad, mad, sad days of its youth. St. Paul is just Irish enough to love a joke even at its own expense; fortunately it is also Anglo-Saxon enough to know when the joke has misfired.

One of the things that the literal-minded always say of St. Paul is that it is a maze of narrow streets. This is partly true. Streets that are supposed to run parallel have a way of turning corners and meeting in what seems almost like clandestine guilt. All efforts at order are abandoned at Seven Corners, where there is a riot of unexpected meetings. An old resident who was once asked how to get to Junior Pioneer Hall made several attempts at explanation and then admitted in despair: "There is only one way to reach it. Get into an accident and ask to be taken to St. Joseph's Hospital. Then you are just across the street."

But in St. Paul's paradoxical way it manages also to produce many splendid vistas and an air of spaciousness. From the high west bank of the Mississippi River one looks down on the genuinely impressive skyline of modern St. Paul. It is pierced, first, by the dome of the Cathedral on the hill, then by the chic modern line of the new Courthouse and City Hall, next by the dome of Cass Gilbert's Capitol, after that by the towering First National Bank Building, and finally by the blunt, functionalist modernity of the Post Office. At the feet of these lofty guardians of church, city, state, and Federal government the business district disposes itself gracefully and attractively. Kellogg Boulevard, a wide and handsome highway, sweeps along the brow of the cliff, giving a dignified approach to a newly developed section. This is the re-born Third Street, which, only a few years ago, had degenerated into a welter of second-hand clothing stores and pawnshops. But its regeneration is now complete. Below Kellogg Boulevard the high, white cliffs, in honor of which the Indians called this place Innijiska, descend to the river level.

As gateway to the Northwest, St. Paul thrives today in its solid and unchallengeable right to exist. Not all cities that have sprung up in the course of America's fabulous development can claim as much. They have been left stranded, by-passed by progress. But as the meeting-place of nine railway systems St. Paul is the natural distributing center for the region. It busies itself at a variety of other things. Its foundries, machine shops, and shops for the repair of rolling stock have taken on new importance in the war emergency, and its training as a manufacturing center has brought new war industries. By way of demonstrating its adaptability, St. Paul puts its jobbing and wholesale houses at one end of Kellogg

Boulevard, while a fish-packing plant and a firm of distinguished and aristocratic law-book publishers are neighborly at the other. And it has the home office of a great, far-reaching empire of wood.

Part of the paradox of St. Paul lies in the fact that, though it cherishes the idea of itself as old and mellow, its tastes are modern. The Courthouse is not merely a modern shell: it is strictly of our time in every detail. The courtrooms lack the musty quaintness of courtrooms in American comedies. The effluvium of the spittoon has been quite blown away and the Petroleum V. Nasby atmosphere has been eliminated. Beautifully paneled in wood, tasteful in the use of color, and completely comfortable, these courtrooms are distinctive in an even more important respect. They have been designed to reveal the significant relationships of judge, lawyer, and jury so that the drama of the administration of justice is fully and intimately realized.

The Courthouse has another significant attraction, a statue by Carl Milles that towers eighty feet in the beauty of its Mexican onyx. The figure of an Indian, the symbolic pipe of peace in his hand, gives a kind of superb dignity to the entrance of the building. The citizens have not always liked it, because it expresses so little of the traditional notion of the noble savage with strictly Aryan features and an air of fatuous benignity. The blocky mass of the design, dictated by its size and position, has troubled many, and one dear old lady never passes it without murmuring in rueful resentment: "I like a leg to have a calf." But gradually St. Paul has become aware of its beauty, aware also that its magnificence is a kind of protection against the shabby, cracker-box provincialism of past city administrations. There is an obligation of an inescapable kind to live up to the Milles Indian. St. Paul takes its visitors to see the statue, and is secretly very proud of it.

It is proud of its other public buildings which lack the bleakness that is associated with their very names. American satirists from Robert Benchley to William Saroyan have agreed that the public library is a place of woeful charmlessness in which the disenchanted abandon themselves to the higher learning in despair of finding anything more lively. The St. Paul Public Library is so beautiful in its Tennessee marble exterior, so sympathetic and clean and inviting in its interior, that it has made reading pleasant even to adolescents. The James Jerome Hill Reference Library shares the block and one wall with the Public Library. It shares also the exterior architectural design. The interior is strikingly handsome. A central reading-room, two stories high, dramatizes its function charmingly by showing the decorative backs of books on both the ground floor and the balcony level. Against the gray of the Kettle River sandstone walls stand two huge cloisonné vases of the subtlest blue. The atmosphere is so thoroughly gracious that an afternoon spent with the card catalogues manages to take on some of the gratifying character of a personal encounter with a very great lady. It would not be in the least difficult to conduct a quiet, lifelong love affair with the Hill Reference Library.

There is also in the new development of St. Paul on Kellogg Boulevard a women's club which is an exquisite bijou affair. Architect, interior decorators, all have conspired to take the traditional ideas out and deposit them resolutely in the Mississippi. In place of the fake Renaissance richness and splendor that most clubs end up by having, here is a gleaming, sun-drenched modernity making intelligent use of all the new resources of building and all of the charm that the site, high above the Mississippi, commands.

St. Paul has a self-sufficiency that could easily be, and often is, misunderstood. The same people have dominated its life for many years, through several generations. When a committee is being formed in St. Paul for any instructive, virtuous, or enterprising purpose, the same names invariably appear on it. If a foreign name were miraculously to find its way onto such a letterhead, it would fade away of itself out of sheer chagrin at having made such an inappropriate intrusion.

This tendency to depend on the same group of people should not, however, be put down to a lack of receptivity or hospitality. St. Paul has conducted its affairs on an almost familial basis for a long time and cannot overcome the habit. Any public meeting in the city is bound to seem like a reunion of the clan.

Inevitably this must make the community sound like Marquand's Boston and, indeed, the suggestion of a similarity has been flung at St. Paul's feet as praise and at St. Paul's head as abuse. It is a tight community which has managed to evolve a pattern of homogeneity out of its various European strains, French, English, Scottish, Irish, German. It has lived well for a long time, and continues to live comfortably now without envy or conceit or delusions of grandeur. Its people understand one another well. There have been few labor difficulties, few hints of racial prejudice.

Most visitors find the atmosphere of St. Paul sympathetic. They like its self-respect. They like the fact that it continues to live in the houses established by its grandfathers, even though unfashionable neighbors may have engulfed them. They like the tone of its social life, which has the reticence of New England manners seasoned with the spice of Irish wit. St. Paul has, of course, the defects of its qualities, and these defects have been ascribed by the ungenerous to snobbery rather than to self-sufficiency, and to inertia rather than to self-respect. These criticisms do not, however, take account of the reality, which is that St. Paul lives solidly and comfortably as it wishes to live, feeling no obligation to desert its traditional ways at the urging of any captious transient. To St. Paul a transient is one who has not lived at least a generation within its borders.

Minneapolis is the younger and now the larger twin. Any tension in its attitude toward St. Paul may be related, perhaps, to the fact that it went through an awkward age when it felt its adolescent wrists to be hanging gracelessly out of its coat-sleeves while its relative was already able to present a poised and confident face to the world. Like any brother who grows up in resentful awe of a twin, to find in maturity that he is just as handsome and even more muscular, Minneapolis is sometimes (though not often) tempted to avenge itself for early moments of self-doubt by making family jokes at the expense of St. Paul.

The development of Minneapolis has been amazingly swift and, for the most part, harmonious. There was a lapse of nearly a century and a half between Father Hennepin's discovery of the Falls of St. Anthony and any attempt to exploit their power. But once that usefulness was fully realized, the spinning up of a great city proceeded with a swiftness that makes even the creative effort of Aladdin's genie seem sluggish by comparison. In 1854 there were two hundred inhabitants; in 1944 there are nearly half a million. In many a dramatic way the memory of man spans its whole existence. A philosophic observer, now aged eighty, remembers seeing one of Minneapolis's first inhabitants, the French-Indian Bottineau, gliding down its streets "showing the characteristic walk of a man whose feet were more accustomed to the woods and prairies than to city pavements."

Two communities presently grew up at the Falls. The first, the village of St. Anthony, was laid out by Franklin Steele, sutler from Fort Snelling—who appears to have divided his time, like an enterprising pre-Babbitt, between supplying provisions for the soldiers and planning elaborate real-estate developments. The other sprang up around the succession of flour- and saw-mills that made early efforts to exploit the water power.

Tiny settlements in that day were as jealous of their identities as large cities are in our time. The community that grew up around the mills gave itself a name so that it might be distinguished from the village of St. Anthony and it chose a very fancy one. It barely escaped being "Minnehapolis" when the Indian word Minnehaha, which means "curling water," was rushed into a miscegenetic union with the Greek suffix meaning "city of." The "h" was dropped in the interest of euphony. But Minneapolis has had to answer to many humiliating variations on its name. Quite often it is called "Minneanapolis" by travelers who have a vague feeling that possibly they are in Indianapolis.

St. Anthony and Minneapolis watched each other's growth with appraising anxiety until at last Minneapolis took the lead, and in 1872 they were merged.

It was, of course, the fact that lumber passed through Minneapolis on its way to build the cities of the Middle West and that wheat came to Minneapolis to be made into flour to feed the nation that gave it so fabulously swift a rise. Today it is the executive center of a great milling empire. It has souvenirs of the lumber industry in its sash and door factories and its pulpwood manufacturing plants. It has used its water power to develop other manufacturing interests—furniture, electrical machinery, machine-shop products. It is important as a flaxseed market and producer of linseed oil. It is busy and enterprising and full of inventiveness in the whole field of business, straddling the region in its trading and banking zeal.

Minneapolis lies on a plateau above the Falls of St. Anthony. In the business district its streets are wide and handsome. Many new buildings tower in ornate, sometimes almost Babylonian splendor to impressive heights, giving Minneapolis the look of being a little "big city" just as surely as St. Paul gives the impression of being a big "little city." Minneapolis delights in and cultivates this impression even to the point of imitating the garish vulgarity of the worst stretches of New York and Chicago streets. The design of Hennepin Avenue, which once seemed so graciously urban, is now marred by shops that seem to make outrageous raids on the sensibilities of the passer-by, demanding his pained attention to a tasteless display of far too many objects. Hennepin Avenue, with its profusion of noisy little bars opening directly on the street, its shooting galleries and peep-shows, makes the carnival of life after eleven thirty as absurdly provincial-looking as it is on Broadway.

The great beauty of Minneapolis is its residential district. Few communities have been so fortunate as to have a chain of lakes around which to build its homes. Lake of the Isles, Harriet, and Calhoun, linked a number of years ago in a great civic ceremony, have provided a perfect setting in which Minneapolis can give itself the combined advantages of urban comfort and rural vista. There is a local legend that Sarah Bernhardt once kept a matinee audience waiting two hours to see her play *L'Aiglon* while she drove in rapture around and around these lakes.

The architecture, though it would not satisfy the demand of a propagandist for the future like Frank Lloyd Wright, is for the most part agreeable and dignified. Occasionally the eye comes upon an Italian villa, seeming ludicrously to shiver in the snow-drifts of Minnesota. Occasionally also some paranoid delusion of grandeur in marble and wrought iron has manifested itself along these lakes. In one such instance the ostentation was so quickly rebuked by the depression that the monstrous palace had laboriously to be torn down again because no one was able or willing to pay the taxes. Happily, much the greater number of the homes harmonizes with the variety and grace of the scene. Minneapolis, having lived through the rococo era, when the estate of a gentleman was not complete without an iron deer in the front yard, has developed a taste in its private residences that is as unpretentious as it is comfortable.

In the older residential districts of Minneapolis there were many architectural oddities—earnest approximations of Buckingham Palace, slightly Moorish castles having iron gates that barred nothing from nothing between one room and another. Gradually these are being evacuated to make way for insurance companies, music conservatories, and automobile agencies as the business district expands. The tendency is for the Minneapolis citizens to go deeper and deeper into the surrounding country to live. They commute even from Lake Minnetonka, once regarded as a place for summer homes, but now the location of the permanent residences of many Minneapolitans.

Expansion in Minneapolis seems likely to be endless. The whole community is animated by an inexhaustible fervency of faith in the gospel of getting-on. This may be attributed in part to the fact that Minneapolis is dominated in its civic life by a new set of people in each generation. It might be said with a very considerable degree of justice that the city offers a springboard to the enterprising. They spring to it from places of less prominence and promise; then they spring from it into the great seas of endeavor. All this restless agility has given Minneapolis the continuity only of effort. Someone is always striving mightily within its gates. And the city has preserved the eternity of its youth.

It is the imperishable youthfulness of Minneapolis that gives it both its charms and its defects. Like a strenuous adolescent, it attends fussily to certain aspects of its appearance and then blandly ignores others that are just as conspicuous. It puts on its fine and expensive suit of clothes and then dashes from the house wearing no necktie at all. Only some such boyish impulse can explain the paradox of its fastidiousness and carelessness.

Minneapolis has an Institute of Art housing an important collection. The emphasis is upon standard items, the excellence of which is attested by long-standing tradition. The building itself, designed perhaps a little cautiously in the neo-classic style, has a magnificent setting in fine, parklike grounds. The equally important collection of the Public Library, however, is allowed to remain in a building that is like a perverse monument to the memory of all comfortless, cheerless public libraries that have ever been.

Nowhere in the United States is a more beautiful system of parkways to be found than in Minneapolis. Its natural wealth of lakes started a tradition that has grown into a deep need. The city demands glimpses of green everywhere to relieve the eye from urban monotony, and where nature has provided no lake for a mile or two, Minneapolis has gone to a great deal of work to create artificial ones. A great sorrow to the community is the fact that a control dam at Minnetonka has had the unforeseen effect of drying up Minnehaha Creek, so that for long periods no water flows over the famous Falls about which Longfellow wrote *Hiawatha*. (Oddly enough, Longfellow never saw the Falls; more oddly still, neither did Hiawatha, who lived somewhere else.) There was some reckless thought of directing water artificially over the Falls, but the wisdom of men with a livelier sense of the grotesque prevailed. Minneapolis waits eagerly for those flood seasons when Minnetonka rises high enough to send water over the Falls once more.

Though its office buildings are modern and immaculate, it worries along with a huge, sprawling, ugly, dingy City Hall which should long since have been relegated to memory. Putting its best foot forward, Minneapolis does not always bother to make sure that that foot is neatly shod.

The solid and reliable character of Minneapolis may be related to its Scandinavian inheritance. Of all the peoples who have come to America, the Norwegians and the Swedes are the most idly misinterpreted by those who do not understand them. Nothing could be further from the truth than that their reticence is a symptom of nervelessness, their silence an indication of a lack of ideas, or their tendency to keep the peace a confession of inertia. The Scandinavians have lent themselves resolutely and uninterruptedly to the fulfillment of the essential impulse of the "American dream," but they are visionaries with a gift for dreaming with their eyes wide open. They came to America in the first place because they wished to escape from the rigidities of a system that allowed of neither change nor experimentation. Here they have been leaders in diversified farming, in co-operatives, in all the features of social progress that lack the violent character and color of revolution. Since our Scandinavians came to us the institutions of their native country have tended to catch up with the native psychology. With temperaments as moderate as their minds are receptive, the transplanted Scandinavians of Minneapolis have worked quietly, steadily to help a new city flower and flourish as swiftly as any that has ever taken firm root.

The social life of Minneapolis has the briskness of its inexhaustible youth. There is, of course, a private interchange of courtesies among friends which is selective and personal. The tone of these entertainments, as conducted behind the façades of Minneapolis homes, has the same range between the giddy and the sober, the casual and the formal, that private parties have anywhere. But the social life of Minneapolis tends to splash over also into public view. The equivalent of café society exists in Minneapolis as it can hardly be said to exist in St. Paul. Minneapolis likes to borrow the night-club entertainers of whom Broadway is fond and to sit rapturously at their feet. In every urban civilization there are those who hold that a city is a success, not when it has a place in the sun, but when it has a place in the night-club spotlight. Such people when they visit Minneapolis find themselves at home.

Minneapolis is a beautiful city. Its perennial youthfulness, which is in obvious contrast to the mellow maturity of St. Paul, produces a special kind of charm. This is evident in the delight that it takes in its mounting birth rate; in the engaging garrulity of its talk about its bank account; in short, in the terrific vitality devoted to getting-on. There is an urgency and breathlessness about life in Minneapolis. The whole community wants to try anything at least once, and to try it before nightfall. Tomorrow there will be a great many other things to try, and they will be zestfully crowded into a program the liveliness of which seems inexhaustible.

St. Paul, having tried everything already, is less easily dazzled by the promise of novelty. In its own way it savors the human comedy fully, in enterprise and trade, in old tasks and new tasks, in the endless round of entertainments—lectures, concerts, recitals, improving thinkers, art shows, plays. But it takes its pleasures less giddily than does Minneapolis. St. Paul has the greater poise of its greater age.

It has been said that St. Paul is the last of the East and Minneapolis the beginning of the West. Like all the clichés, this one has an irritating little way of being able to demonstrate that it is true. The first assistant cliché in this department is also smugly correct, for never the twain shall meet. But at least St. Paul and Minneapolis have been able through the years to demonstrate for the edification of a troubled world that it is possible for East and West, if they really wish to do so, to live together in amity.

The other great urban community of the region is buoyant, busy, song-loving, beer-loving Milwaukee. Oldest of this trio of cities, it celebrated its hundredth anniversary in the 1930's.

There is something soothing and uncluttered about the early history of Milwaukee. Its settlement and its brisk beginnings may be told almost as the record of one amiably persistent man. The French-Canadian Solomon Juneau went in the year 1818 to the handsome site of the city at the mouth of the Milwaukee River on Lake Michigan, to establish there a trading post of the American Fur Company. He found in the neighborhood one white man's dwelling, that of Jacques Vieau, who had married the daughter of a Menominee chieftain. In 1820 Juneau married Josette Vieau, who showed her Indian background in her gift for protracted and dignified silences. In 1833 other settlers arrived, the most important among whom were Morgan Martin and Michael Dousman. With Juneau they began to brood about the possibility of establishing a town. In 1836 there was a tremendous land boom, ably furthered by these same efficient men. Into the rest of that decade Juneau crowded the activity of a dozen workers. He tossed off a bank with one deftly creative hand, a newspaper with another. In 1852 his silent wife spoke long enough and effectively enough to persuade him to retire to the country, for to her way of thinking Milwaukee was already a place of bustling enterprise where it was impossible to find a moment's peace. She and her husband moved to the town of Theresa, which Juneau had created in a moment of idleness and named for his mother. But if Josette Juneau expected her husband to rest at Theresa she had underestimated his irrepressible creativity. Presently he had thought up a sawmill, a gristmill, and a general store. He served the community also as postmaster.

He was entirely worthy of his Christian name, this Solomon. His granddaughter remembered him as standing six feet four inches in height. He had curly brown hair, clear-cut features, light gray eyes. "While of a jovial temperament, he never for a moment lost his dignity; of a kind benevolent nature, he was the confidant of all." He was not too softly benevolent, however, to refrain from doing his obvious duty when a well-planted boot and a sizzling "*Sacré!*" were needed to eliminate undesirables from his settlement. When Solomon Juneau was through with Milwaukee, there was little that needed to be done but just to go on from there.

One finds an inexhaustible fascination in the little dramas of the rise of frontier cities. In 1834 Solomon Juneau established the first school. It was made up entirely of his and the dutiful Josette's children, of whom there were seventeen in all. In 1836, in the midst of the land boom, a boat on which Harriet Martineau was a traveler stopped in the port to deliver more newcomers. Miss Martineau thought that these men were unnecessarily rough and vulgar (why they must curse and spit so much was more than she could understand!), but it pleased her to be visited by a delegation of eight women from the settlement. They made up the entire female population of a community that had a total of two hundred souls. A century later there were some six hundred thousand people living in Milwaukee.

Even in its early days the city began to attract distinguished visitors, and all of them liked it greatly. Carl Schurz arrived shortly after Juneau had looked upon his work and found it good and so retired. Schurz declared that no American city had made so favorable an impression upon him. He was particularly delighted with its physical situation.

"At dusk," he wrote, "I came upon a height above the lake where the white light tower stands visible from afar. From a distance the lake made itself audible with a subdued roar and suddenly I stood upon the precipitous edge of a cliff above the light green, sail-dotted endless expanse. The appearance of the lake there is not much different from that of the ocean only the colors are not so darkly sombre."

Anthony Trollope made a pilgrimage in 1868, and found that affairs were going ahead nicely in Milwaukee. He thought it "a pleasant town," though he was unable to say why he found it much more agreeable than Detroit. He was pleased to record that he had heard nothing but what was good of the townsmen. "Praises of their morals, their thrift, and their new patriotism" made a mighty chorus in his ears. Father Solomon Juneau could rest in peace.

Economically Milwaukee has moved forward in a free, unbroken stride, and today its people are energetically employed in making everything from silk stockings to turbines and hydraulic electric units, from toilet soaps and doll carriages to automobile frames and excavators.

Milwaukee's chief attraction is still its lake front. The city owns much of this land, the greater part of which has been given over to commerce—to harbor facilities and airports, warehouses and railroads. Many a European visitor has grieved over the fact that America, beginning to build its country with a high degree of scientific and technological skill, has neglected beauty in its treatment of lake fronts and rivers. But such a man, in the rapture of abstract analysis, forgets to explain how such facilities could be used without looking as though they were being used. Milwaukee unapologetically employs its natural advantages of water and employs them fully.

Yet much of the lake front has been turned over to impressive sweeps of park-land boulevard. The handsome homes that Carl Schurz admired so much have been replaced by much less ornate apartment buildings. But these present to the world the same fine reassuring look of housing people who know how to live with dignity and comfort.

The rivers contribute less in the way of charm. Navigable into the heart of the business district, they give Milwaukee the appearance of a city that had half made up its mind to be Venice and then given up the effort in panic at the idea of trying to challenge so notable an achievement. Along the streams that flow through the busy streets the buildings rise in unbroken rows, but they do not greatly resemble the *palazzi* in which Byron and Wagner petulantly wooed their genius.

A city's individuality is often embodied in a citizen whom it chooses to be its leader. Milwaukee seems to have had a special gift for finding such men to speak its collective mind. Just as Solomon Juneau represented the time of its robust youth, so Victor Berger represented its maturity.

By the time of Berger's arrival from Austria, the life of Milwaukee had begun to be dominated by its German immigrants. They needed and enjoyed newspapers printed in their native tongue. In 1890 Berger took over the editorship of the *Volkszeitung* and changed its name to the *Wisconsin Vorwaerts*. Into it he poured the stream of his liberal beliefs, carrying his community along with him to such convictions as that labor should have an eight-hour day, that children should be protected against exploitation by employers, that the Federal government should grant farm relief, and that pensions should be provided for the aged. From the background of an unusually rich education in philosophy and political science at universities in Budapest and Vienna, Victor Berger drew an inexhaustible wealth of argument. He was no simple immigrant on the make, trying to build up a journalistic following by flattering the prejudices of his neighbors. He was a leader who told them what to believe. After telling them for many years in German, he began to tell them in English. His paper, called first the *Social Democratic Herald* and then the *Milwaukee Leader*, had an eloquent voice. It ran through all the repertory of the emotions of personal journalism, with the accent on ferocious contempt for illogic and for thinking that was either loose or drawn tight with cunning.

As a very young man Victor Berger had convinced himself of the wisdom of Socialism. His conversion, he once said, occurred when he was debating against it. He won the debate, but the sterner jury of his own conscience told him that he had lost, and he began a systematic study of social questions. In his younger days he often went hungry, preferring a book to a meal, and at the end of his life he had a library of eight thousand volumes, one of the most complete collections on Socialism in private hands.

But those missed meals did not leave him devitalized. He was tall and well made. As a young man he had a ruddy complexion, a rolling gait like that of a sailor, and a head of fine black hair which he liked to toss as an accompaniment to his denunciations of folly and cynicism. Even as an old man when he had no hair at all, he was still awesome to those who worked with him. When he strode into his composing-room to rewrite an editorial that was already in proof, wanting to make it a little more fierce and uncompromising, the printers, who as a race are hard people to intimidate, shrank away from the splendor of his approach. He slashed and edited with a fine frenzy that earned their respect as well as their terror.

Berger's ability to shape the minds of his neighbors is dramatically indicated in the figures of election returns. In 1898, 2,400 people voted for his Socialist candidates; in 1902, 8,400 had been persuaded to follow him; in 1906, he had doubled his following again; and in 1910, when he made his own debut as a candidate for office, he won by polling 27,622 votes.

In and out of public office Victor Berger continued to work for the principles of honest government. Milwaukee became a center of Socialist councils and experiments. The whole country sent formal and informal delegates to inspect what was going on. Under a succession of Socialist mayors a city government had been established that was not only scrupulously honest, but as imaginative and enterprising in the service of the people as the ordinary man of initiative is resourceful in furthering his private interests.

There were many dramas in Victor Berger's life. Like other conscientious men who had left the Old World to help create a new one, he hated to see the quarrels and hostilities of the society from which he had escaped introduced into the society where he had taken refuge. Like the elder Lindbergh, Berger protested against America's entry into the first World War. When he was subsequently elected to Congress in 1918, he was refused admission on the ground that his speeches against national policy amounted to espionage. He was tried on such charges before Judge Kenesaw Mountain Landis (later the baseball czar) and sentenced to Federal prison for twenty years. Milwaukee stubbornly reaffirmed its faith in him at a special election held in 1919. But the threat of prison hung over him through many appeals.

In the midst of this uncomfortable period of waiting, a typical group of Job's comforters gathered about him, pointing out how noble a thing it is to suffer for a cause, how the flames of Jeanne d'Arc's pyre had glorified her tortured flesh and given her immortality in place of a mere physical wholeness. Berger listened to them patiently, but when they came to a pause at last, the genius of common sense that had gone into all his writing and planning asserted itself. "That's all very well," he said, "but I don't want to go to jail." He lacked the temperament of the martyr; yet out of less loose and specious gifts he had managed to shape some small, firm, tangible results.

He did not go to jail. Charges that he had conspired to obstruct recruiting during the war were dismissed. He was elected to Congress still another time in 1926 and defeated at last in 1928 by a narrow margin.

At sixty-nine he still worked actively as editor of the *Milwaukee Leader*. Leaving his office one evening in July 1929 to walk to his home, he was struck by a streetcar. He died of the injuries that he had received from the blind, flurried force of the city in a great hurry to get home. It seems a little ironic that he should have been struck down by the impetuous drive of a community that he had done so much to create. But it may be considered a good death because it found him still in possession of his full strength, still humorous of eye, incisive of mind, sharp of tongue. With a kind of filial awe, Milwaukee filed past his body lying in state in the City Hall. Farmers and workers, printers and politicians, seventy-five thousand people made the pilgrimage in acknowledgment of their belief that Berger had been the just and incorruptible, the lively and enlivening father of his community.

The political life of Milwaukee seems to have been dominated in a casual and comfortable way by a succession of conscientious parents. The same familial atmosphere is noticeable from an early period in its social life. Unchallenged leaders set themselves up in the several sections of the city, and a kind of rivalry for pre-eminence existed among them. But within these smaller groups the spirit of camaraderie appears to have been easy and gracious. Friendly relations were soundly based on song and beer.

Being German in its background, Milwaukee very soon had

singing societies in each of its large and small communities, setting waves of melody washing back and forth across the city in a fine harmonious storm. A Christian of orthodox and fundamentalist views might have been excused for imagining when he entered early Milwaukee that he had been translated unexpectedly into heaven, so very nearly uninterrupted was the program of singing that the city conducted around its own small, but quite adequately glassy inland sea.

The ubiquitousness of beer was also the result of German background. It played a significant part in all social life. In an earlier day men and women bicycled together out to places like the Whitefish Bay resort, where on high bluffs upon a great expanse of grass, toadstool tables spread themselves out as far as the eye could reach. At them sat the thirsty, well-exercised citizens, justly drinking their beer. The steamer *Bloomer Girl* also served the resort, bringing other customers by water. There were great parties at Whitefish Bay, and for one of them Charles K. Harris wrote his undying song, *After the Ball*.

There were beer gardens everywhere in the city. One of them offered the gratuitous but magnificent attraction of summer opera along with beer. Indeed, the combination of music and drink seems to have been regarded as sacred. Arthur Pryor's famous band made one of the beer gardens of Milwaukee the setting for some of its most notable experiments with American song.

Whatever his favorite sport or pastime might be, the true man of Milwaukee liked to have in the background a fountain of beer. When the citizens went out to shoot, wearing funny hats complete with feathers, they took heroic quantities of beer along. Appreciation of beer encouraged appreciation of art, at least of a kind. Behind the Empire Bar hung a huge painting by Mikowsky, *The Judgment of Paris*, which revealed with the utmost candor the details of a legendary beauty contest. At Ma Heiser's the Milwaukee Philatelic Society held all of its meetings. Ma Heiser had a beautiful inspiration, which contemporary bars might well follow. For the boys in the back room she created a reference library where all those points of difference about fact and theory which inevitably arise out of deep, beer-drenched conversation could be settled.

The well-planned Milwaukee bar had mountains of free lunch: cheese, pickles, olives, anchovies, ham, haunches of beef, stacks of bread. It also had certain theatrical properties for the frequently recurring bits of horseplay that belonged to its mood. When a customer came in wearing a new derby hat, it was snatched immediately from his head. As it seemed to him, in his fury of rage and anxiety, his property was tossed from hand to hand, kicked, trampled upon, used as a football. Then finally it was returned unharmed. Only the sensibilities of the owner had really been assaulted. The hat that had been kicked about was a special one, kept under the bar for just such emergencies.

The spirit of Milwaukee in its developing years was genial and boyish. No one thought it very remarkable when a high-spirited young man rode into a bar mounted on a fine mare and demanded to be served in the saddle. The drive-in restaurant of our time seems drab by comparison. Ingenuity matched high spirit in those days. When "Honest John" Callahan had an unwanted visitor in the violent Mrs. Carrie Nation, he was inspired to save his bar by a really beautiful bit of recourse to poetic justice. Before she could begin operating with her hatchet, "Honest John" had resourcefully baffled one of America's most resolute women by directing full in her face the fine spray of a seltzer bottle. The attack so humiliated Mrs. Nation that she abandoned her plan for reforming Milwaukee and left town hurriedly.

The boyishness of the city was once personified in a mayor who, having taken an intense dislike to certain signs and street clocks, went out after dark with a rope and derrick and pulled them down with his own resolute, if quite unauthorized hand. Milwaukee woke next morning to find that its leading conscript father had given the streets the look of the day after Hallowe'en.

The importance that beer has always played in its life is made dramatically clear in an episode out of another mayor's career. This latter gentleman once announced in the public prints that on election day no wine or "bier" was to be served until four o'clock. After that hour, his announcement declared, slipping jovially into a still less formal style, "you can let her go."

Milwaukee today is still genial, casual, well-informed about its own briskly and efficiently managed affairs. After a recent tour of one of the great breweries, where I admired the huge expertness of the whole project, the Gargantuan size of the casks, the cleanliness and sweetness of the pervasive malty smell, my guide and I wound up in the taproom. The official escort was as nice and friendly an old gentleman as I have ever met, and he introduced me to one of the most conversable of companions, a traffic cop who had just dropped in for a glass of free beer. The three of us had a satisfying talk about the fine, cheap water supply of Milwaukee, taken from Lake Michigan at two pumping stations, the entire cost of which has been paid out of earnings, and about the excellent sewage-disposal plant where a commercial fertilizer is produced by the activated sludge process. It pays two thirds of the cost of operation. After the third glass of beer my Milwaukee cop gave me a brisk and intelligible dissertation on the advantage of a city's owning its own institutions and of operating through officials who have acquired the habit of honesty. When we walked out of the taproom together, I felt that I had learned something new about good beer and something new about good democracy.

The individuality of Duluth, on the north shore of Lake Superior in Minnesota, might be said to be that of the unexhausted pioneer. While other communities of the region have settled down to follow a destiny that they take to be permanently fixed, Duluth looks for new ways of creating a new heaven and a new earth. It will not surrender the idea that it lives on a frontier the possibilities of which are still boundless.

It manages to look a little like a pioneering town though its streets are sleek and urban, its hotels modern, and its stores chic. Duluth is a svelte and youthful city, lying thirty miles long and a mile wide along the lake shore. From the promontories above it, city and harbor present a spectacular view of crowded ore docks and shipbuilding works, elevators and port facilities. It looks both beautiful and enormously busy. But at any point the distance between the most urban of its interests and the green (or white) wild country is dramatically short. A man with an adequate heart and respiratory system can climb the high Duluth hills and be in the open within a half hour.

THE VILLA LOUIS AT PRAIRIE DU CHIEN, WISCONSIN
Top—Drawing Room
Bottom—Library, with Portrait of Hercules Dousman

THE CAPITOL AND LAKE MENDOTA, MADISON, WISCONSIN

Duluth is the point from which tourists launch themselves on their flight into the wilderness of the Arrowhead country. Before they pass on up the north shore of the lake, they like to pause and swank about in the rough finery of their costumes as *voyageurs* or lumberjacks. But they are not as noticeable as they would like to think themselves, for the real lumberjacks are there too, the real hunters and trappers, and workers from the mines. Duluth is the center to which the wilderness men come, and there is no self-consciousness at all to their pageant-making as they pause, in the costumes of their professions, to glance in at shop windows, buy tickets for a movie, or sit down for a malted milk at a drugstore counter.

More surprising still, the country all about Duluth is the refuge of wild animal life. You need not travel far from Main Street to get a deer in season. It is one of the gratifying little commonplaces of the community to see a bear, sometimes acting as escort to a convoy of cubs, playing in one's front yard. This is not a thing that happens every day, to be sure, but often enough to be a part of the curious pageant of the place.

There is something hearty and audacious about Duluth's very site. It is underscored by the fact that the height of the cliffs above the city is a threat to an automobile's weak brakes. Not infrequently the newspapers report that a truck, quite out of control, has plunged through the main thoroughfares, to be brought to rest at last in a vacant lot. Always a greatly gratified troop of little boys, hoping fervently for the worst, pelt strenuously along behind.

It is only eighty-five years or so since Duluth was baptized and launched upon its formal career, though its site was visited by Radisson, by Father Allouez, and by Daniel Greysolon, Sieur du Lhut, in the seventeenth century. It was from this last explorer that the city took its name, though it insists upon using its own modified spelling.

From the days of early settlement, the men who came to this strategic site on the shore of the great inland sea were ruddy, sanguine, ebullient creatures. They hoped to do well for themselves, first, in the fur trade; then in the quest for copper and gold; then in the search for iron; then in the handling of lumber and grain. Sometimes their hopes ran thin. The fur trade exhausted itself; the men who rushed in looking for gold had to be contented with iron. Twice, as Duluth thought itself snugly settled on the knee of destiny, it was unceremoniously dislodged by the whimsical behavior of Eastern financiers. There were the national panic of 1857 and the Jay Cooke failure of 1873. Both toppled all of the city's hopes momentarily into chaos. After the second of these humiliations Duluth was so desperately poor that it dwindled down into a village once more. Not until 1887 did it regain permission of the legislature to regard itself as a city.

But the heartiness and hopefulness that kept it alive through all these vicissitudes are its allies today. Busier than ever with its shipping duties, Duluth scans the future eagerly, seeing itself as an ever more and more important city strategically situated on a water route stretching from the Atlantic Ocean through the St. Lawrence and the chain of Great Lakes to its perfect landlocked harbor. As Duluth looks at the great world, deep calls to deep, and the city on the shores of Lake Superior feels its comradeship with the mightiest seaport cities of the world.

It is this fine, audacious feeling that the "best is yet to be" that gives Duluth, more than any other city of the region, its atmosphere of preserving the mood of the frontier. Minneapolis seems young because of its unappeasable appetite, its adolescent craving for growth. Duluth seems young because it assumes itself to be an infant of destiny with all needed nourishment at its disposal for a development that it is sure will take place in the future.

Duluth is full of garrulous self-congratulation. It calls itself the "air-conditioned city," and with good reason if the endorsement of the victims of hay fever may be accepted as unprejudiced testimony. In all the neighboring countryside there is a panic-stricken rush for its shelter the moment the pollen count becomes dangerously high. Even the healthy are likely to respond to this air of the "vintage class" distilled by the beneficent influence of the lake.

The climate parallels but modifies the general characteristics of the region's weather. Summer is cooler, autumn lingers longer, winter invites the hardy to a full enjoyment of pleasures, with the special advantages of the lake added. Duluth lives out of doors in all seasons.

This is not to say, however, that Duluth neglects the urban tastes and appetites. It has good schools, a good library, an enterprising little theater, and a well-trained symphony orchestra. It has also Margaret Culkin Banning, high-spirited public citizen as well as high priestess of the women's magazines, to see that they are all run properly.

Madison, Wisconsin, as even Frank Lloyd Wright admits, is a beautiful city. He might be expected to disapprove of it on general principles, since it is a university city and he dislikes American universities only a little more thoroughly than he dislikes American cities. But it was the setting of his boyhood days, and perhaps he sees it with an unusual indulgence. Any untutored eye, however, must see that he is right. Madison has great charm.

It is unique among the communities of the region in that it neither bustles after success nor seems, as some of the small towns do, ruefully to have surrendered all hope of achieving it. Madison is the serene intellectual, brooding on a comfortably withdrawn stretch of land, an isthmus lying between two lakes. The city is not, however, completely indifferent to industry. It manufactures plows and other farm machinery. But the interests of the mind are what really concern it. As in Springfield, Illinois, another capital city, the people seem to live a uniform sort of existence with no great contrasts in comfort between the richest and the poorest. To a visitor Madison seems like Utopia on a modest scale. The eye relaxes comfortably in following its vistas, finding nothing that is distressing in the scene and little that is inharmonious.

The Capitol, which looks very much as capitols seem required to look by tradition, occupies a dominating position in the very center of the business district and all the streets ray out from it. The symbolism of this design seems appropriate, and it pleases one's fancy to discover that a chief thoroughfare leads directly from the Capitol to the campus of the University of Wisconsin.

Everywhere the use of the natural advantages of water has been thoughtful and appreciative. The frequent recurrence in the landscape of bits of park land seems to rhyme on the theme that this is a place where it is legal, and even reputable, to take one's ease. The people have built themselves comfortable homes, many of modern design, which seem to gather up the vistas of the rolling country and take them indoors to beautify well-planned living-rooms.

Since Madison lives to study and experiment, it has attracted other institutions besides the state government and the university, which have similar interests. The United States Forest Products Laboratory (where the ladder of the Lindbergh case was analyzed, to give up its secrets) is there, and so is a United States Weather Bureau.

Because it is small, because its interests are concentrated upon abstract and intellectual matters, because it has a uniform way of life, Madison seems much less torn by vehement impulses, much less harried by insistent needs, than other cities. Its individuality is that of a slow-spoken, contemplative, good-humored, and rather undemanding professor of law.

Winona might be regarded as a sort of retired capitalist among Minnesota communities. It is like a highly cultivated and sophisticated old gentleman, living in a father's Victorian house and spending a father's money.

During the latter half of the nineteenth century this town, beautifully situated on the banks of the Mississippi beneath the granite cliffs of the valley wall, had a moment of grandeur. Its New England settlers, followed by industrious Poles, found themselves in the very midst of all the booms in lumber and in wheat. The shrewd leaders amassed fortunes. They built great houses that looked reassuringly like those of English estates; they beautified their grounds and the grounds of the city itself.

Then with a *pop!* which may have sounded very loud in the ears of those nearest, but which had little real violence, the boom came to an end. Diversification in farming ended the tremendous importance of wheat, and Winona could live no longer by shipping great quantities of it. The year 1915 saw the very end of the long-dwindling importance of the lumber industry. But like the shrewd and cultivated people in novels by Edith Wharton, the citizens of Winona had known how to preserve their fortunes. Nothing so distressing or vulgar as a city-wide collapse occurred. Though they were deserted by their industries, they were not deserted by good fortune. Winona simply retired from business and prepared to live a graceful private life.

Presently other industries grew up. Most important of all, there was the tremendous development of a patent-medicine business which had been begun in a modest way with the selling of soaps and lotions and cough syrups from farmhouse door to farmhouse door, all out of a little brown wagon. Presently this infant industry grew to lusty proportions and there were new millionaires to build palaces (with gold fixtures in the bathroom) near those of the nineteenth-century crop.

But Winona can afford to loaf and invite its soul in the leafy shade of its quiet streets and in the splendor of its castles. There are twenty millionaires living among the twenty thousand citizens of the city. Unlike the situation in Madison, the range in comfort between the way of life on the estates and that of the back streets is wide. But the citizens of Winona meet in many activities—in those of the colleges of St. Mary and St. Theresa, and in those of the Anvil Theater, an extremely enterprising little-theater group where intelligent efforts have been made to develop a local literature of drama by the production of original scripts.

The poet, Byron, once observed that "the hum of human cities" was to him a "torture." If he managed to be so grievously afflicted in his sensibilities by the urban centers of his time, he would certainly have suffered far more under the impact of the modern industrial city of America. But today's child of the pavements cannot understand this snobbish rejection of the charm of the way of life he has always known. It seems to be merely another Byronic pose. There is stimulation, excitement, and friendliness to the music of the cities. Each of them has its characteristic tone and accent—the clamor of Milwaukee's waterfront life, muted by the wind; the roar of the falls and the throb of the dynamos in the Minneapolis mills; the purr of railroad traffic in St. Paul, become quite completely subdued and feline under the influence of modern technique; the judicial academic murmur of Madison; the courteous hospital-whisper of Rochester. All these variations on the theme of urban living blend into a song of great intricacy and interest. If the symphony of cities really gave him only pain, Byron must have had a badly tutored ear.

21

MAIN STREET REVISITED

᚛

IN THE YEAR 1920, when Sinclair Lewis published *Main Street*, he was deeply concerned with the problem of the meagerness of life in the small community. The man who had read a book was suspected of having other vices practiced in secret to the shame of his pretense to masculinity. The lover of music was a pale æsthete whom the robust shunned in fear of having to suffer both contamination and boredom. Ideas were alien to Main Street, and its values were those of the full stomach, the tongue whose wit followed the familiar formulas for ribaldry, and the body reasonably were exercised in the authorized sports of the arena.

The desire of Mr. Lewis and his favorite character of the moment, Carol Kennicott, was that the more abundant life should be transported to Main Street. Mrs. Kennicott had some notions of how this was to be done, which today seem very odd indeed. One was to serve chow mein at an evening party and invite the yokels to put on crepe-paper costumes suitable to the international spirit of the occasion while the hostess herself ran upstairs to put on a wondrous affair of silk and embroidery. As an arbiter of taste Mrs. Kennicott in her priggish exhibitionism left a great deal to be desired.

It is curious to realize that only a quarter of a century has passed since *Main Street* so startlingly appeared and divided Minnesota into two bitterly opposed camps. In one were the people who delighted in the unflattering picture of the world in which they lived, either because they were masochists at heart or because what they took to be Mr. Lewis's spite expressed the resentment they themselves had felt for neglect of their talents. In the other camp were the defenders of the local tradition, who raced off to the Chamber of Commerce for facts and figures in defense of the thesis that theirs was the best little town in the world. If they felt themselves to be thrown back violently from this first line of defense, the anti-Lewis contingent resorted to the tearful declaration that "kind hearts are more than coronets." Perhaps the small town was made up of "just folks," but at least they knew the values of family pride and hospitality, which was more than many a treacherous highbrow could say.

But the dust of the battle has settled, and now it is no longer clear why there should ever have been so much heat and anger. Main Street revisited does not seem very much like the community that Sinclair Lewis described. Perhaps he should have credit for calling attention to its *gaucherie* with such humiliating emphasis that Main Street has made haste to change. But that seems questionable. Main Street simply has had twenty-five years in which to grow more mature.

It will take longer than that to make the small towns of the region beautiful to look at. Their business districts were run up in the greatest haste in response to completely utilitarian need. Modern architects have demonstrated that adaptation to use is the soundest æsthetic principle of building. But the improvisers of the small towns were not expert in architectural form, and they did not know how simplicity and beauty could be combined. They simply slapped up shelters for their enterprises. Later, when they came to a pause and began to yearn vaguely after ornamentation, their ideas were naïve and muddled. They tried to mask the ugliness of what they had built with false fronts and brick veneers. But their disguises served no better than do the veils and necklaces that a vain old woman drapes about herself in an effort to conceal her lack of youth. Such towns and such women lack chiefly the awareness that there can be charm in old age.

The American town was thrown together by energetic men who did not care how it looked. They were anxious only to get about the business of exploiting the natural resources of the neighborhood. They were not concerned with the fact that, to be beautiful, towns must grow slowly out of the needs of the people who live patiently and permanently on their soil. Time helps to mellow their defects and to cover their gross angularities with vine and moss. The small town of our region has had no such help. It stands exposed in the rawness if its youth. Only time and the widespread interest in city planning can improve it.

But the people themselves have passed Carol Kennicott's ambitions for them by a very long way. The tone of life in a small town today is very little different from that of a larger community. The teachers who have gone out from the University of Minnesota, pre-eminent in its department of education, have taken to Ely, Minnesota, the standards that prevail in St. Paul. Their individual culture is quite likely to be as broad and their methods of instruction as modern as those to be found in the most progressive academy. The library is no longer run by a fussy eccentric out of *Cranford* who lets the arid meagerness of her private taste control the reading of the community. She has not been assigned to her job in desperation by a community that can think of no other way to care for the aging spinster daughter of a deceased civic leader. The librarian also has had standardized training, and she knows how to throw open the facilities of instruction to the inquiring.

The young Methodist minister on Main Street may easily be as well informed as he is earnest. He mines the material of his Sunday morning sermon not from the clichés of rudimentary ethics, but from the bulletins of the Foreign Policy Association, perhaps, or from a study of hidden hostilities contained in a recent work on psychoanalytical method. Because the priests of Catholic churches are appointed by the ecclesiastical authorities, without the competitive influence of congregations, there is no reason at all why the representative of Rome in a tiny obstruction on the prairie should not be a man of deep cultivation as well as of broad human compassion. Such a man in such a town may have a living-room so small that there is space in it for little besides a grand piano. But when the right visitors are with him he will play the sonatas of Mozart on the violin as they have seldom been played "this side of paradise." The vicar-general of another diocese in our region is a Parisian-born man of the world who seems to have strayed absent-mindedly out of a seventeenth-century romance when he elegantly helps himself to snuff from an elaborately carved silver box.

Novels of the past made much of the bitter feuds between the religious leaders of different sects in the small town. If that ever truly represented the spirit of Main Street, it represents the prevailing mood no longer. Priest and rector sit together on local boards for the improvement of practically everything. In the privacy of their close friendship they sometimes laugh together about how easily life could degenerate into a process of going from one public meeting to another. But the important thing is that they are friends.

The radio has been a great leveler. If it has leveled taste downward in certain respects, the tendency has certainly been in the other direction as far as music is concerned. In proportion to their size, the towns along Main Street are quite as well represented as are the great cities in the audience that spends Sunday afternoon in a musical orgy with Rodzinski and Toscanini. One of the really admirable radio stations of the region is presided over by the appointees of a Lutheran college in a small town. From it comes such a splendid tide of Grieg and Sibelius that one turns to it with perfect confidence at hours when the cosmopolitan networks are completely surrendered to the hoarse anxieties of the soap operas.

Main Street no longer feels in the least obliged to be furtive about its pleasures. Perhaps men like doctors, who are everywhere required by their communities to be above suspicion, will carefully draw the shades of their houses before pouring highballs for their guests, but the community as a whole shows no hesitancy about strolling into the little neon-lighted bar between the hotel and the general store. A visitor in such a place may find himself eavesdropping upon an intelligent conversation between middle-aged men who are extremely earnest and troubled about Spain and the State Department. Presently one of the men disappears from the bar and in a moment reappears behind it, wearing a white coat. He is the bartender, as he begins very competently to demonstrate by stirring up an admirably dry Martini. Yet though he lives on Main Street and spends his life among people who have come to him merely in search of relaxation, he is not cut off from the world. He does not have to hunger hopelessly for stimulation as did the lost æsthetes of the world of Zona Gale and Sinclair Lewis. Somehow he has managed to take from life what he needs, and as he stands there in his white coat pouring out a jigger of bourbon for the drummer who is his customer, he seems still to be thinking about grave and absorbing matters.

In a Minnesota resort one stumbles into the company of a group of local young people who are celebrating the last moment of civilian life that remains to one of their number who will go the next day into the Army. This amazing young man, a basketball-player of fabulous achievement (partly by virtue of the fact that he stands six feet six inches tall), has had a very considerable amount to drink. But that does not prevent him from demanding quite vehemently to know why many of his treasured French artists seem so sycophantically to have become collaborationists. Seeking to escape the intellectual exactions of this conversation at midnight, one makes for the dance floor of the great barnlike pavilion in the company of a pretty girl. The experiment is going quite well until suddenly the orchestra breaks down. One's partner explains that the musicians are fourteen-year-olds, replacements for the members of the original group, all of whom are in the Army. These earnest but inadequate children saw at their violins and blow into their saxophones wearing expressions of tense determination. Legs are wound about the legs of their chairs; shocks of hair fall into their eyes; lips are parted to let the tips of tongues show in the way that is universal among people who strive innocently with tasks beyond their capacity. The group looks as though it had been drawn by Norman Rockwell as a cover for the *Saturday Evening Post* and then had magically come to life.

Yes, this is Main Street, one thinks, as one gives up the effort to dance and seeks out a quiet corner.

But presently one's companion is off on a discussion as earnest as that which the basketball-playing ex-admirer of France had launched. Don't write about B—, she urges, naming her town. Not after knowing it just for twenty-four hours. It is too complicated for that, she insists. You cannot really understand it without coming to know the whole truth about old Mrs. Grimes, whose father built the town; and about the private tragedy in the life of Editor

O'Hara, who seems so childish and absurd, but who is really a complex and delightful person; and about Congressman Olson, who was elected on the Farmer-Labor ticket and who has lately been through hell trying to decide whether he is really a Republican or a Democrat.

Before she has come to a pause this unpretentious young woman, who is not writing a novel and who has never ever thought of writing one, has done a sort of offhand *Spoon River Anthology* for her town. And she has made her point. Main Street is no longer peopled (if indeed it ever really was) by hollow men childishly and jovially unaware of their emptiness or achingly conscious of wanting something that their community cannot give them.

The small town is a microcosm of the great world, containing all of its possibilities for good and evil, wisdom and stupidity, fine achievement and foolish futility. And the men of Main Street know that they are not hollow but whole, or at least as nearly whole as it is possible to become on such a diet as the world's present standards of intellectual nourishment allow.

22

THE OLD COMPLAINT

𝒯

DISRAELI, that gifted exponent of diplomacy as drama of intrigue, once confessed that whenever he found himself confronted by a man whose identity he should know but did not, he would launch a conversation bravely with the question: "And how is the old complaint?" It never failed to happen that the unidentified acquaintance would expand in the warmth of this surprising sympathy and straightway begin a spirited description of his favorite symptoms. In the course of unfolding the secrets of his suffering he would unfold also, for the benefit of the cunning diplomatist, the secret of his name.

Everyone, as Disraeli knew, has an old complaint. Everyone in America has at some time or other brooded about the possibility of taking his old complaint to Rochester, Minnesota, home of the famous Mayo Clinic.

Rochester, more than any other city in the region, is a place of lively contrasts. It is a small community with the transient population of a huge center. The skyscraper of the clinic raises itself high above the rolling prairie country so that it is visible far off, like an urban mirage, in the midst of the agricultural country that stretches away on every side. Lying in the midst of this rural district, it has the atmosphere of a metropolis, with hotels, theaters, dress shops, book shops that might have been transplanted *en bloc* from a city of half a million people. Health is its business; wheel-chairs are everywhere more in evidence than any other means of conveyance; yet it has a smiling and cheerful look about it.

People who take "the old complaint" to Rochester soon learn, in the midst of a population whose occupation is illness, to be at once candid and casual about their trials of the flesh. Like the beginner in medical school who protects his startled sensibilities by assuming a humorous style of grim audacity, the beginner in invalidism hides what may actually be apprehension behind a mask of jaunty amusement at his plight.

It helps enormously to keep the tone of the Rochester drama urbane and impersonal that the huge cast of characters represents a broad cross-section of the human race. It is so interesting to find that one's neighbor in the waiting-room is a Bolivian novelist or a Brahmin whose most intimate friend is the Pandit Nehru or Madame Chiang Kai-shek's private secretary that one is almost able to forget the gnawing of the ulcers, the pinching of the sacroiliac joint, or indeed the whole onslaught of thrusts, stabs, grindings, and torments arranged by one's army of internal devils.

In Rochester, during normal times, you will hear snatches of every known language spoken on the street and the chatter in a hotel dining-room is blended of all the accents that philologists have ever identified. The woman from Montgomery, Alabama (who used to go to school with Tallulah Bankhead), joins up for a cozy seminar on the symptomatology of gallstones with an understanding soul from Kennebunkport, Maine, who firmly removes the letter "r" from every syllable where it belongs and rivets it, with her fiery tongue, to some syllable where it does not belong at all. Such a scene, no matter how deep the undercurrent of personal tragedy may run, cannot fail to translate itself into the terms of artificial high comedy.

The hotels of Rochester used to display signs reading: "Please do not talk about your operation"; but more recently there has been a tendency to make peace with the inevitable preoccupation of the place. Conversation never departs for long or far from the familiar line, the length and scope of which is measured by the dimensions of one's own abdominal incision. But it is the sporting tone that dominates talk in and about the clinic. To require of a new acquaintance that he force his interest in one's own case to pass from the level of decent friendly curiosity to the level of pity would be a serious violation of the code of the place.

To go through the clinic is a little like taking an examination for some fantastic co-educational army. Patients travel en masse through the great building visiting one set of examiners, one set of technicians after another. To be sure, one's costume is not so informal as that which the Army requires for mass examinations, but the variety of the inspections is similar. Everything of possible significance about girth and weight, everything that blood tests or metabolism tests can show about the secret drama of one's functioning, is known before the diagnosis of an individual complaint is offered.

Medical ethics are so sensitive and they register so emphatically any deviation from discretion on the part of a layman attempting to describe the work of doctors that it is unwise even to offer the formulas of praise that a place like the Mayo Clinic so obviously deserves. Sentimentalists are always prompted to regard Rochester as a shrine and to force a kind of sainthood upon its scientists. This attitude can only alienate conscientious men who know that the sole magic they have to offer is the patient application of knowledge that other patient men, collaborating over the centuries, have slowly acquired. A doctor at the Mayo Clinic is never so unhappy as when a patient gets to imagining that he sees a nimbus behind his head.

No one who is quite well balanced could ever persuade himself to believe that a group of men like those at Rochester have established a corner on a superlatively high grade of wisdom. Jealous only of their reputations as scientists among scientists, the men of the Mayo Clinic have studiously rejected all extravagant claims. The institution that they serve grew up in a perfectly natural way; no miracle was "passed" to call the clinic into being on the Minnesota prairie.

As has happened so often in the history of man's progress toward a good society, it was a catastrophe, shared by the whole community, that inspired the first step toward the building of the clinic. In 1883 a tornado swept through the neighborhood, killing twenty-six people and injuring twice as many more. That was a very large number of people to require medical care all at one time in so small an ill-equipped a place. The memory of this distress prompted the Sisters of St. Francis who had opened a convent in Rochester two years earlier to think of setting up a hospital. In 1889 St. Mary's Hospital was opened, with Dr. William W. Mayo, the conscientious country doctor, as consulting surgeon, and with his two sons, Dr. William J. and Dr. Charles H. Mayo, as attending surgeons. The elder Mayo was a pioneer from England who had experimented with pharmacy, tailoring, and farming before he settled down to a career as a doctor. The defenders of New Ulm, wounded in the Indian massacre, had been his first large group of patients, and their plight had given him an early glimpse of mass suffering.

The Mayo men were a close-knit group and they collaborated well. More and more people from the immediate environment began to consult them. Then their influence and reputation spread beyond the county, beyond the state, finally beyond the nation.

Facilities had constantly to be expanded. A second and third hospital supplemented the first and a hotel-hospital made a fourth addition. But these facilities today are not sufficient. Plans, which await the conclusion of the war to become a reality, are even now being thoughtfully prepared. Architects are designing a still larger center for the clinic.

Other distinguished men like Dr. E. Starr Judd and Dr. Louis B. Mallet came to join the organization. In 1915 the Mayo Foundation was established, and entered into a collaboration with the graduate school of the University of Minnesota. The clinic began an institute for instruction and research as well as for the active practice of medicine.

All of these opportunities inevitably have attracted excellent men. The prestige of the clinic and, what is far more important, its usefulness have steadily grown. The clinic itself performs operations by the tens of thousands, and the various facilities in the fields of medicine, dentistry, and nursing that the Mayo Foundation and the University of Minnesota together make available have established the Twin Cities as a kind of health center.

Typical of the way in which the pioneering example of the Mayos has attracted other pioneers is the American chapter in the history of Sister Elizabeth Kenny, the Australian nurse who created the Kenny treatment of infantile paralysis. Her ideas have revolutionized medical theory and written a new chapter in the history of healing.

Sister Kenny is a blunt, direct, and decisive woman. She had a fight on her hands in persuading doctors to accept her conviction that their own theories about poliomyelitis were elaborately and exactly wrong. When she found that she was making slow headway against tradition in her own country, and that the preoccupation of the entire British Commonwealth of Nations with the problems of the war was likely to put further obstacles in her way, she set out for America, determined to put her ideas before the orthopedic surgeons of what she calls "the world famous Mayo Clinic."

Through Dr. Melvin Henderson of Rochester, Sister Kenny was given an opportunity to demonstrate her methods before the doctors of the University of Minnesota and the Minneapolis General Hospital.

Her quarrel with tradition has been stated as often as she could persuade anyone to listen to her. The core of the difference is that orthodox treatment calls for immobilization, rest, and shortening of the affected muscles, while the Kenny system calls for abandonment of immobilization, active treatment to restore as soon as possible the brain path to the affected area, and "a special effort to keep the muscles affected with spasm from being shortened and normal muscles from being lengthened and atrophied from disuse."

Sister Kenny (her title is the one given by the British to nurses) began her study of polio when she was a young nurse struggling with all the turbulent aspects of life and death in an obscure corner of the Australian bush. To her one day was brought a very sick child. Alarmed by the symptoms, she dramatically risked death by invading the sacred privacy of a native "corroboree" to find a savage who would run for her with a telegraph message. To the distant doctor who was her mentor she described the child's condition. "Infantile paralysis," he wired back, "no known cure. Do the best you can."

The best that she could do was to make the miserable child comfortable by wrapping strips of blanket soaked in hot water about

TEN CHIMNEYS
Home of Alfred Lunt and Lynn Fontanne at Genesee, Wisconsin

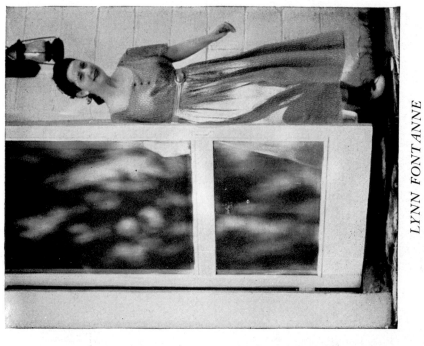

LYNN FONTANNE
at the kitchen door of Ten Chimneys

ALFRED LUNT
in the garden of Ten Chimneys

the painful legs. She also urged the patient to try to restore normal functions by making experimental movements. All this was directly contrary to established method, which required that legs be put in splints to keep them absolutely immobile. The idea of this heroic inactivity was to let the pain exhaust itself in the hope that patience alone might reduce the eventual degree of crippling.

Everything about the Kenny method seemed disastrously wrong to those who clung stubbornly to orthodox ideas. But Sister Kenny's patients had a curious way of getting well just at the moment when, according to the rules, they should have succumbed to either death or crippling.

The Minnesota doctors believed in her method. Dr. John F. Pohl reported to the Hennepin County Medical Society that "to those who have watched her work, there is no doubt but that her methods in the acute stage of the disease offer greater hope for recovery than do those previously employed."

Dr. Wallace H. Cole of St. Paul and Dr. Miland E. Knapp of Minneapolis collaborated on a report in which they stated: "We have been favorably impressed with this work both as a rationale of therapy and as to results. . . . We personally . . . believe that this method will be the basis of the future treatment of infantile paralysis."

But Sister Kenny had not fought her last battle by many and many a campaign. Her blunt and uncompromising habits of speech appear to attract defiance as metal attracts lightning. She is a woman in the grip of an idea and has trained herself to consider nothing but the defense of her convictions.

The fight has been long and bitter. In December 1941 the American Medical Association through its *Journal* seemed to give full recognition to the Kenny method. But in June 1944 a special committee, after devoting two years to research into the treatment, reported that quite as many patients recover under other kinds of care as recover in Sister Kenny's hands, that her concept of the disease is wrong, and that her theories are neither new nor unique. With characteristic fervor Sister Kenny declared the report to be "the most cruel thing that ever happened in America." It is certain that Sister Kenny has not said her last word, and it is much more than probable that the American Medical Association has not given its final judgment.

Meanwhile the Minneapolis Public Welfare Board has dedicated a handsome building to Sister Kenny's use and created an institute which bears her name.

Sister Kenny has said that she would much rather have married than have become a sort of evangelist of medical method. She would rather have devoted her private time to raising fine horses than to the constant service of her faith. But her destiny was determined long ago by her own temperament. When she was a girl in her teens she became troubled by the fact that a favorite younger brother was a physical weakling. She felt an obligation of the heart or of the head to do something about it. Slyly or openly, she laid her hands on every book within reach that might help her to understand the muscular system. In three years she had acquired an expert knowledge of all its intricacies, and out of that knowledge she created a system of exercise that transformed her brother from a weakling into one of Australia's strongest men and one of its heroes in the first World War.

Out of that knowledge, too, came the insight that made her understand the problem of polio better than anyone has understood it before.

It was inevitable that a woman of such intellectual hardihood should find an idea to serve; and it was inevitable that a woman of such delight in strength should have battered down all resistance to her idea.

Now that man has pushed back the horizon of his world as far as physical limits will permit him to go, any pioneering that he hopes to accomplish in the future must be made vertically, into the realm of ideas, toward higher and higher levels of intellectual service to the race.

The men who developed the Mayo Clinic and all the supporters of the Kenny method are pioneers of that sort. It is interesting that the region, where the story of the conquerors of physical distances has been completed so recently, should have been found a sympathetic place in which to begin the new pioneering and to start on their careers the conquerors of the pyschological distance between our own and an ideal world.

23

SOUVENIRS OF PIONEER
SPLENDOR

THE WELL-ESTABLISHED LITERARY CONCEPTION of the Western frontiersman is that he was an unlettered fellow who was able to survive the boredom of his mean and meager way of life solely because he possessed a rude and insensitive quality, unattractively called grit. To challenge this notion is to run the risk of being considered both a heretic and a poseur. Yet Wisconsin and Minnesota retain many souvenirs of pioneer energy showing clearly that the most resourceful of the frontiersmen made themselves both comfortable and contented in their wilderness world. The houses in which they lived, refitted today with their own possessions, are proof that they knew much about the art of translating repose into charm, and leisure into grace.

Hercules Louis Dousman and his descendants created such a house near the confluence of the Wisconsin and Mississippi Rivers at Prairie du Chien. Dousman was the eldest of a family of energetic men who came into the region from Mackinac Island early in the nineteenth century. Among them were the co-founders of Milwaukee. Hercules, justifying his name, proved to be the most vigorous of all. He came to the wilderness as a confidential clerk of the American Fur Company, with additional assignments to study the region and send back geographical information about its design. He stayed on to become one of the creators of a new world.

He was a good man of affairs because he was also a man of good will. The Indians trusted him deeply—in part, perhaps, because he took the trouble to learn several of their tribal languages. When serious disputes threatened, Dousman was the one for whom all the embroiled parties sent to act as mediator. In a turbulent realm Hercules Dousman appears to have been the cheerful adviser of every faction. He was the universal guide, counselor, and friend.

A tremendous amount of wealth passed through the Prairie du Chien market, and Dousman acquired a reasonable share of it. In 1831 he began buying land on what the people of the neighborhood called the "mound." This was an elevation, two hundred feet high, believed to have been built by a prehistoric race of moundbuilders and used by the Fox Indians as a burial place. It had been the site of a succession of fortresses—first Shelby, then McKay (as the British called it after they had seized it in the War of 1812), and finally Crawford. Later still, Fort Crawford, a picturesque and important military stronghold where such men as Zachary Taylor and Jefferson Davis served, was moved a little distance away, and Dousman took possession of the mound. There he built a "baronial mansion in which he lived the life of a country gentleman."

It was in 1844, after he had married Jane Fisher Rolette, widow of his former partner Joseph Rolette, that the hospitality of the "house on the mound" reached a height of graciousness. Madame Dousman was a vivacious and beautiful woman who was delighted to receive the roaming representatives of the fur interests. In the midst of their well-tended farm, vineyards, and gardens the Dousmans lived spaciously.

Dousman births and deaths affected the destiny of the house, but always for the better as a monument to ease and comfort. Madame Dousman enlarged it a first time; her son, Hercules II, and his bride, Nina Sturgis, helped her to impose a new house upon the old. After Madame Dousman's death when Hercules II came into possession, it was given the name Villa Louis and decorated as a visitor sees it today.

Villa Louis represents an excellent period in American taste. Lacy gray woodwork envelops the severity of the brick structure. There is nothing aggressive about its grandeur. The size of the house is not imposing; it seems not to demand obeisance as the stern magnificence of later American architectural designs seemed determined to do. Indeed, the exuberance of the display of porches and balconies seems cozy, even confiding. It is as though Villa Louis, dominating its site in a kind of casual, hospitable embrace, expected life to be a long, uninterrupted house party.

Inside, it is grand enough to satisfy the most aristocratic taste. But the general plan of decoration was devised in a moment before Americans had begun to confuse the abundant life with the cluttered one. A decade or two after Villa Louis took its final design, wealth began to translate the yearning for expression into a welter of unrelated impulses and objects. Villa Louis, as one sees it restored today, shows that taste in the wilderness of 1872 was good. Indeed, it was far better then than it was later to be in the most sophisticated of urban centers when the imaginative abandoned themselves to a passion for Moorish nooks and to frenzied imitations of anything thought to be quaint and picturesque. Villa Louis represents an unconfused, uncluttered, unadulterated American style.

There is, to be sure, nothing of false reticence about its declaration in favor of the spacious life. The family portraits are huge; the panel mirrors framed in gold reach from floor to ceiling of the lofty rooms. But every item of decoration has its use, and every one is well designed. The chairs and sofas of the carved rosewood set, made in Philadelphia in 1850, look as inviting today as they must have looked to Madame Dousman's guests, hot from long rides across the prairie. The bronze lamps of the style named for George Washington shone none the less brightly for being beautifully made.

The decorators of the Dousman house patronized the craftsmen and artists of the time who made objects of use which were also handsome. Their chandeliers were of Waterford glass. They covered their floors with the subtle designs of Aubusson rugs, and their walls with paper of hand-blocked design. In their dining-room they had plates painted by Audubon and glassware that sang under the flick of a finger with the authentic accent of its maker, "Baron" Stiegel. Hercules II traveled east to have his portrait done by Eastman Johnson. In their walnut bookcases the Dousmans kept fine editions of Audubon's *Birds* and Schoolcraft's *Indians*. Canopy bedsteads, made at a time when nails were a luxury and wooden pegs were far easier to come by, where created for the Dousmans by craftsmen who obviously loved the stately designs with which they worked and were in no hurry to be finished with their intricate carving. There were spreads of Brussels lace to give the final touch of regality to beds so noble. And Nina Sturgis Dousman, who was chiefly responsible for the look of Villa Louis as one sees it reproduced today, needed no professional decorator to tell her that draperies of deep yellow velvet would bring out the rich tones of her mahogany dining-room table.

Hercules II loved fine horses, and he built brick stables to house a large stock of the finest Kentucky breeds. He installed an artesian well and fountain, and from it piped water to all the paddocks. He laid out a cork-surfaced race track, the outlines of which can still be seen from the porch of Villa Louis.

All of these glittering activities were being carried on during the infancy of the region as the home of white men. In the "howling wilderness" there were shelters where civilization spoke with the grace of the well-bred and the authority of the well-informed.

In what was presently to become Minnesota, Hercules Dousman I had a friend and partner, Henry Hastings Sibley. The latter had settled, as an agent of the American Fur Company, near the confluence of the Minnesota and Mississippi Rivers. The Indians, with their superb indifference to vowels, called the place Mdote, meaning "mouth of the river." The white men modified the word to suit their own lingual prejudice, making it Mendota.

Here in 1835 Sibley built himself a house. More than a hundred workmen helped him to put it together out of the materials available in the immediate neighborhood. From the bluffs they took a fine quality of yellow stone to form the outer walls. These blocks were put together with mud from the river. The roof was covered with "shakes" or clapboards, split by hand. The boards for the floor were hand-hewn. The partitions for rooms were made by hewing out beams for studding and by setting heavy timbers some eighteen inches apart. Small willows were woven into this curious but serviceable plan and packed into place with mud and hay. Over this base the walls were lathed and plastered. Again, willows wrapped with hay were used for laths. To save nails, cleats were fastened around the willows. When Henry Sibley's house was finished, the owner looked upon his work and found that it was good. Today, after a century and more, it looks rather more fresh and far more permanent than most of the five-year-old bungalows in the brand-new residential district near by.

Sibley confessed in an unfinished autobiography that he had been the bad boy, "the black sheep" of the family born at Detroit to his distinguished father, Chief Justice Solomon Sibley. That half-humorous sense of guilt clung to him, no doubt, because he had disappointed his father's hopes of having a son to follow him in the law. The young Sibley had had two years of training in Greek and Latin and another two in law when he decided stubbornly to go off on his own into the wilderness. But his father would not have been displeased with the career that his son finally made out of nothing but his own sturdy qualities of initiative, generosity, and courage.

Like Dousman, Sibley got on admirably with the Indians. The top story of his house was maintained as a kind of dormitory for them. The outside stairway that led to it was never locked. Whenever an Indian, passing by, felt the impulse, he was free to take advantage of Sibley's casual hospitality.

Those years of Latin and Greek and law had put the mark of their discipline on Sibley's mind. No matter how much he may have wanted as a boy to escape from the exactions of the intellectual world, the life of the mind kept reabsorbing him into its pattern. A letter written by Sibley from Mendota asked a friend to buy and send to him these books: Prescott's *Conquest of Mexico*, Hallam's *Middle Ages*, Thier's *French Revolution*, and Froissart's *Chronicles*. One of the first bits of furnishing that Sibley required for his house was a piano.

In 1843 Sibley married Sarah Steele, and their house, in the very center of the fur industry's thriving market, became, like Dousman's "house on the mound," an embassy of civilization in the wilderness. It was perhaps at this time that Sibley ordered from Cincinnati the handsome walnut bedroom set which is among the furnishings that the Daughters of the American Revolution, present owners of the house, have returned to it. "H. H. Sibley" is stamped on one of the bureau drawers. The bureau and commode are topped by slabs of Italian marble. The drawer handles have the charming form of bunches of grapes. By far the most engaging feature in the decoration of the bed are the carved knobs on the two sides of the head. One is so much larger and sturdier than the other that when the set was rediscovered, these were thought not to be mates. A cabinetmaker pointed out, however, that the theory of the time was that the paterfamilias needed a firmer and stouter knob by which to lift his tired bulk into bed. The woman, though the frailer vessel, required a much less substantial knob.

The house at Mendota was the background of all of Sibley's early activities. As fur-trader he conducted his affairs from an office on the ground floor. From it he went out as a delegate to Congress from Wisconsin Territory. In it he met with other patriots of the region to work out a campaign for the creation of Minnesota Territory. Finally his house became the first executive mansion of the newly formed state when Sibley put by his title as major general of the Volunteers to become the first Governor of the state.

This "prince of pioneers," as Sibley has been called, exercised both the prerogatives and the responsibilities of his native prince-liness. He lived very well, in an atmosphere of preoccupation with the things of the mind, and he shared his comfort with everyone about him, excluding not even the least worthy member of the un-deserving poor who trudged daily to rest in his attic room. In that fine solid house Sibley lived as a democratic leader should live, a model of energy both physical and mental, but a model of toler-ance, too.

It was in 1857 that Ignatius Donnelly reached the banks of the Mississippi. He had been persuaded to come on from Philadelphia by John Nininger, who, as brother-in-law of the great Alexander Ramsey, had an already established position in the community. Nininger and Donnelly, out of their youthful hope and audacity, created a town to which they gave the name of the elder partner. They had mighty plans for it and suddenly "mills, factories, schools, stores, saloons sprang out of the sod." Donnelly had a superb imagination, as he demonstrated in such of his novels as *Atlantis*, in which he re-created the whole of a "lost continent," and in *Cæsar's Column*, which anticipates many of the events of the twentieth century. But his eager mind permitted him to anticipate just a little too extravagantly as far as the town of Nininger was concerned. When the railroad decided to route itself through near-by Hastings, Nininger faded. Most of the citizens surrendered to the inevitable and scrambled across the deep ravine to join forces with the successful rival. They took their houses with them, contriving even to transport a large hotel through the gulley. From a population of five hundred, Nininger fell off to nothing but the family of that splendid and unyielding die-hard, Ignatius Donnelly.

He had built himself a house, and it still stands among the yawning, weed-filled cellars of the ghost town. When people speak of Nininger today, they mean the house of Donnelly, which under the supervision of a committee of admirers of "the Sage" survives as a monument to his reputation.

The frame house is sadly weather-beaten. A porch which once ran around two sides of the building has crumbled away and has been removed. The fence that the old prints show has disappeared and so has the windmill. But the essential features of the building and its site are indestructible. The house surveys a splendid sweep of river valley and, though it stands now looking a little bleak and exposed on its promontory, all the essentials of a fine monument to the past are there, awaiting the interest of the right enthusiast.

Living in an isolated spot in the heart of what the Indians, despite all discouragements, persisted in regarding as their country, Donnelly built his house with a dramatic appreciation of its potential dangers. He topped his dwelling, not with a dormitory for tired Indians such as Sibley maintained, but with an "Indian lookout." This was a squared-off and railed section of the roof from which a guard could discover the far-off approach of Indians. Since there were still to be massacres in Minnesota when Donnelly built, he clearly had the right of the matter. Carrying the logic of his position one step further, he let into the wall, just under the roof, narrow, slitlike windows through which guns could be fired in case of an Indian siege. The Donnelly house at Nininger is the only structure in the region where these architectural features are still to be seen.

The library remains as it was in the owner's time. Two rooms, opening into each other, both paneled in oak and both lined with bookshelves, were the workroom of the "Sage of Nininger." Here are his easy chair, his desk, his picture taken in England by the Queen's own photographer. Here Donnelly sat dreaming his extraordinary variety of dreams—plans for a new campaign to win the presidency, plans for a novel like *Atlantis*, plans for further demonstrations of his staunch belief that Bacon wrote the plays attributed to Shakespeare. Here, in the midst of a thinking man's version of comfort and splendor, surrounded by his pictures, his books, his old family furniture, carried all the way from Philadelphia, he conducted his voluminous correspondence with the makers and shakers of the world of his time. At the age of seventeen Donnelly had written and published a volume of verse that had brought a long, friendly letter from Oliver Wendell Holmes. And to Nininger his later work kept bringing him messages from all over the world—a letter from Gladstone about his *Atlantis*, letters from Baconians everywhere, each offering his own cryptic proof that Shakespeare was an ignorant factotum masquerading as a playwright while Francis Bacon was a playwright masquerading as a gentleman.

Scattered along the rivers of Wisconsin and Minnesota are these souvenirs of pioneer splendor. Memories of the Dousmans and the Sibleys and the Donnellys help to give to our perception of the past mellowness and range and depth. Indeed, the past of the region shows something of the grace, something of the charm, as well as something of the oddity that any little segment of the past, taken from any way of life, would show.

TEN CHIMNEYS

ȝ

THE HEADING ON Alfred Lunt's stationery reads, in red letters: "The Farm, Genesee Depot, Wisconsin." But he has decided to change the name to Ten Chimneys. There are only nine now, but when the war is over, Lunt intends to erect one more structure on his farm, and then the place will have earned its name.

Genesee Depot has the most typical little station shed that ever existed outside of an early comedy by Winchell Smith or George M. Cohan. It has the wooden benches, the stove in the corner, the cobwebs, the atmosphere of neighborliness and geniality. Now that stations in other Wisconsin towns like La Crosse are radiant with glass brick, colorful with murals, and comfortable with modern chairs of the plumbing school of design, this one at Genesee should be lovingly taken down, bit by bit, and sent to the Smithsonian Institution as an item of Americana.

Along with the station should go the country road and all the houses that line it. There is about them a village placidity that is passing. It is difficult to think that behind the façades of these little frame houses radios are telling the news of our angry world writhing over all its surface in the anguish of war. This little community seems lost out of time in a quiet fold of earth to which change has never penetrated.

Yet up this road only a quarter of a mile from Genesee Depot lies the plot of ground to which Alfred Lunt and Lynn Fontanne, the most distinguished acting partners of the English-speaking stage, make as many returns each year as their engagements in

New York and London and the whole broad expanse of America will permit.

It is no whimsey that has brought them here. Alfred Lunt fits the description "citizen of the world" as well as anyone in our American society. His wife, born in London, an American by adoption, is also a completely cosmopolitan creature. Yet Genesee is Alfred Lunt's home, the place of ineradicable boyhood memories. He lived in the village as a child. From it he went out to school and college at Waukesha, only a few miles away. And to it he returns with the perennial interest and enthusiasm of a native. It is an almost universal impulse with men whose early days have been happy to try to recover the past, to rebuild the childhood home, to reclaim the soil of their beginnings. That is what Alfred Lunt has done at Genesee.

By the mystical process of identification that occurs in all successful marriages, it has become Lynn Fontanne's home as well. Once when she met Frank Lloyd Wright of Spring Green, Wisconsin, at a party in Walt Disney's Hollywood studio, she said to him quite without self-consciousness: "We're neighbors, you know."

The Lunts were in England, playing *There Shall Be No Night*, when I made a pilgrimage to their farm to explore a unique aspect of the local culture. Mr. Lunt's mother, Mrs. Sederholm, was away, too. But Jules was there and so was Ben. Jules is Mr. Lunt's "dresser," a gleaming and radiant alien from Broadway whose racial gift of hospitality asserts itself in his dark face quite as readily on this foreign field as it does in a theatrical dressing-room. Jules had been left behind on this trip because of the military problems of transportation. But with a young man's lively curiosity he gropes his way into the unfamiliar practices of farm life. The day of my visit he had just left a gate open, so that some capons had got in among the chickens, and the outraged hens were forced to spend much of their valuable time chasing the pathetic and grotesque creatures into corners. But Jules was trying to do himself over dutifully into a farmer.

Ben is a native of the neighborhood and has been a resident of the Lunt farm since his boyhood. He is a reticent but friendly young man, so poised and well informed that he would seem as well able to cross the psychological bridge between Genesee and Broadway as Lunt himself is able to cross from Broadway back to Genesee.

The buildings of Ten Chimneys represent liveliness of imagination and an uninhibited taste for many styles, periods, racial traditions, and impulses. The place seems above all else to represent an experiment in internationalism. The basic notion is, of course, that this is a Swedish farmhouse. The theory is pleasantly underscored in many details of decoration—the brightly painted cupboards, the gingerbread frames for mirrors, the elaborate and often beautifully designed stoves, each of which can be made to function. (The central heating system functions, too, but Mr. Lunt, being a conscientious and an exacting artist, is opposed to degrading objects of use into objects of decoration merely.) In the kitchen there is a pleasant and orderly profusion of Swedishness in the shining pots and pans that hang on the wall, in the open dresser with its brilliantly colorful designs, in the quaint stove set into a whitewashed brick alcove. In the Lunts' charming and spacious living-room the Swedish motif is echoed again in the mural decorations by Clagett Wilson. The themes are Biblical. Over the fireplace, Elijah rises to heaven in a chariot of fire. A whirlwind offers a kind of early version of the police escort. Over the piano and the chessboard and the tea tables, other sternly just figures of the Judaic mythology go about being stern and just with the unabated fervor of a vital tradition. What contributes greatly to their vitality is the fact that, just as the Madonnas of the Renaissance wore Italian dress and the prophets of *The Green Pastures* wore blackface, these saints of the murals are impressive in Swedish ceremonial dress. They ascend to heaven, preach redemption, offer their burnt sacrifices against a background of neat Swedish villages.

A cheerful uprush of the farmhouse influence greets one everywhere in the pleasantly gaudy scrolls that decorate doors, in the pewter plates, the rag rugs, clipped sheepskin rugs, the striped curtains, the red-and-white-checked covers of furniture in guest rooms. It is only when one later recalls this welter of comfort and coziness—so warm, enveloping, gay—that one thinks of obvious contradictions of style. Probably few farmhouses, even in Sweden, where they have practiced the middle way profitably and peacefully, are decorated with crystal chandeliers, portraits of Lynn Fontanne by fashionable painters, portraits of Alexander Woollcott by fashionable artists in pastel, upholstered divans, hoopskirt dressing-tables, boudoir poufs, and, in the bathroom, mirrors circled by glass flowers illuminated by tubes of fluorescent light.

It is a Swedish farmhouse out of Hollywood by *Vogue*. It is a Swedish farmhouse with a neat, though tiny bathing pool in the yard. It is a Swedish farmhouse on the Wisconsin prairie with the Union Jack and the Stars and Stripes flying side by side overhead. Ten Chimneys is as cosmopolitan as Monte Carlo. That this should happen in the midst of country that is supposed to be dedicated monotonously to the interests of the dairy farm is an indication of how varied, vital, and surprising is the life of America. Genius can be born anywhere, but when it is born in agricultural Wisconsin it need not look frantically about and despair of appreciation and encouragement. Genius can go out from Wisconsin and enroll the world as its admirers; then it can return to Wisconsin and feel comfortably at home.

Ten Chimneys, with its bright souvenirs of many lives and many arts, is the proper home for an actor who has interpreted the fervors of Russian philosophers, Viennese ex-princes, Finnish scientists, and American song-and-dance men. It is equally appropriate as a setting for an actress who in her time has played many parts—resourceful Cockney girls, American neurotics, matrons of high esteem, and once, as she was never played before, England's greatest queen. The Lunts' home offers a curious reflection of the multiplicity of their own interests, affections, and sympathies.

Adding a few more to the congress of chimneys at the farm are those that top the separate establishment built by Alfred Lunt for his mother. This house echoes the Swedish motif of the larger dwelling, rather more intensely, and it echoes also the interest in murals that derive their themes from the Old Testament. Mr. Lunt made the decorations on these walls himself. His chief triumphs are the figures of Adam, complete with sense of guilt, and Eve, complete with apple. He has somewhere made the family confession that Miss Fontanne posed for both Adam and Eve, adding: "You know how vague these old pictures are, so it didn't matter in the least!"

Mrs. Sederholm's house, one suspects, is a mere gesture of independence. She has a large room in the main house as well, and here no doubt she really lives. Like any right-thinking mother of sons and daughters she has her family portraits about her there— Alfred as a little boy in sailor suit, wearing ears that seem bigger than the same ears seem today; Alfred in all the phases of his development down to the present one. But it is never Alfred the most distinguished actor of the American stage. It is Alfred of Genesee, resting for a moment on the terrace and laughing with his handsome, hearty mother in an inextinguishable burst of spontaneous hilarity. Few mother-and-son portraits have ever suggested more appealingly the gusto that sometimes belongs to the relationship.

There is no Petit Trianon pretense about the Lunt farm. Miss Fontanne has not cast herself in the role of Marie Antoinette to play at making butter, even in this dairy country, where it might so easily prove tempting to a *poseuse*. At Ten Chimneys, Miss Fontanne says, she sews and studies French and cultivates her flowers and her neighbors. But the place is honestly and uninterruptedly farmed by Alfred Lunt and Ben and whatever hired men they can come by.

It is not the most gracious land in all abundant Wisconsin. Perched on the rim of a kettle moraine, the farm is pitted with depressions left by the receding glacier. Densely wooded, this uneven land is more inviting to a man who wants to wander idly in its shade than to one who wishes to work its soil. None the less, one hundred acres of meadow have been put under intense cultivation, and the crops run through the list of those appropriate to dairy country. Alfred Lunt has, besides, a very large truck garden which is his particular labor and delight. It has been given every advantage in which a gardener with capital can indulge. In bad seasons when the peas and string beans might otherwise surrender to the austerity of drought, a spray from a permanently established water system like that of a nursery sweeps with languid but persistent grace back and forth over the whole stretch.

"Mr. Lunt cares for the truck garden alone," Ben explains.

"When he is through with his day's work it looks as though he had gone through it with a vacuum cleaner."

It is Alfred Lunt's determination that, at least in the war years, the farm shall be a real contribution to the economy of the community, not something that drains its resources to please the vanity of a gentleman farmer. When Ben needed more room for his hay, Alfred Lunt gave up his studio, had the piano moved to the house and his miniature theaters packed away. There is a proper and pervasive agricultural smell to the place where, in the two-story room with an attractive balcony, the guests from Broadway used to make music and play games.

In these years the farm has justified itself as a fully functioning agricultural unit. Perhaps it has been able to do so on somewhat unpromising land because the artistic temperament has presided over its destiny. Never have there been farm animals more handsome, better cared for, better groomed. Only an actor would have thought to provide costumes so dazzling. The coats of the Jersey cows show a tawny gloss that would have made Rosa Bonheur nearly swoon with ecstasy as she rushed for palette and brush. Anyone who has ever wondered whether Homer was really being the perfect gentleman when he referred to the goddess Hera as "ox-eyed" would wonder no longer after meeting the serene gaze of Alfred Lunt's cow Lily. The limpidity of this creature's eye shows that cattle can have a beauty of orb that quite surpasses any petty standards set up on the basis of intelligence. Lily of Ten Chimneys possesses a charm that is positively regal in its bland acceptance of superiority. Similarly, the Plymouth Rocks have a satiny luster of feather that never was in barnyard or chicken run. Unlike the cows they are not washed every day, yet such is the effect of proper food on their general look of well-being that they seem just to have been removed from the tissue paper of the dry-cleaner's box.

It is dangerous to permit oneself to brood about the names that imaginative people give their animals. But as I looked at Alfred Lunt's Jersey cow named Lily and thought how much more beautiful she is than are most creatures of her kind, a small bit of biographical information about the actor kept popping into my mind. One of the first important assignments that Alfred Lunt had as a young actor was to appear as leading man in a vaudeville skit with the beautiful Mrs. Langtry, whose name was Lily and who because she was born in the Isle of Jersey was called "The Jersey Lily." Coincidence, of course, I told myself rather sharply. But the idle thought, with the grinning shiftlessness of all such memories, kept crowding impudently in upon me.

At Genesee, when times are normal, Alfred Lunt likes to join in the ceremonial of the Friday night dance, participating in revivals of the very athletic predecessors of today's gymnastic jitterbugging. At its dances Genesee alternates exhibitions of galops, reels, glides, and slides with samples of contemporary rug-cutting.

When the owners must leave Ten Chimneys and go away to England, the departure, according to Miss Fontanne, is "positively Russian." It does sound rather like the last scene of *The Cherry Orchard* as she describes it. "We cried, all the maids cried. We waved and they all waved. Somebody tried to give us a pie to eat on the train. It was extremely harrowing. . . ."

Harrowing, that is, in the actor's best sense of the word, which means productive of the richest mixture of strong and contrasted emotions.

Ten Chimneys is a curious and interesting monument to the imagination of man. It is a kind of microcosm of the world, into which the audacious hand of an actor has crowded all the cosmopolitan quality of his experience along with the native character of his heritage. It is dedicated to work and pleasure; to study and escape from duty; to sobriety and giddiness. The farm lies a few miles out of Milwaukee—and right in the heart of the human experience.

POSTSCRIPT AND PREDICTION

AND NOW, after only a century of history as states, Wisconsin and Minnesota have emerged into full maturity. They have been forced to come of age quickly, as individual men and groups of people always do under the spur of critical conditions.

For these states experience has been one long, uninterrupted crisis. Emergency has tumbled so fast upon the heels of emergency that there has seemed scarcely to be a moment in all the hundred years when the character of life has been less than tense, better than uncertain.

Great pervasive influences have shaken the society of our region in the very midst of its coming into existence. Those swaggering demigods, the pioneers, while they created with one hand, destroyed with the other. Cyclonic storms of panic, rising in the East, ripped through the flimsy economic structure of the cities and toppled them into collapse, so that they had to begin to build all over again with less than nothing. Before Wisconsin was in its teens, and when Minnesota was exactly two years old, they were invited to send men to their first war. While they were assimilating their first generation of immigrants from Europe, they found themselves under the necessity of finding volunteers or drafting citizens to fight against two foreign powers, Spain in 1898 and Germany in 1917. During the war years Wisconsin and Minnesota worked strenuously to provide wheat and iron for a nation that seemed to have an inexhaustible need for those resources, and when the wars were over at last, they felt their full share of the effects of economic depression.

It has been a crowded century for these young states, with either the hot breath of panic or the cold breath of depression ever blowing over them as they have been pushed and prodded out of their frontier psychology into the complex responsibilities of modern states.

Two important psychological developments have been packed away into the short history of the region. In the first phase neither Wisconsin nor Minnesota was at all sure of its identity. The pioneers regarded the region as merely a storehouse of resources. They came on a gigantic treasure hunt to work the richest veins of iron and take the tallest, broadest trees. For the soil itself they cared little, or at least they felt no close identification with it. Immature and exploited, these communities were like vigorous but slightly bewildered children, unable to say precisely who they were.

In the second phase of their development, Wisconsin and Minnesota turned egocentric. Like young men in their pride, they took a deep breath and set about the business of pulling their world together after the riot of the pioneering days. They counted their resources and began to preserve them. The popular ideas of the time sprang out of an awareness of duty toward their own place. They did not like very well to be interrupted by war in the midst of that preoccupation. The political leaders wished to continue with their experiments in government. The artists were absorbed in getting their first impressions of their own realm down clearly on paper or on canvas. But they accepted the great interruption of 1917–18 stoically in the end, and when the fighting was over, they returned to the absorbed contemplation of their own images. In the decades between 1920 and 1940 the men of Wisconsin and Minnesota, like Americans in almost all other regions, felt intimately close to their own soil. They were preoccupied with their own problems and absorbed by their own interests. If the love of a man and woman is a "dual egotism," then the love that the people of Wisconsin and Minnesota felt for their region was a multiple egotism.

Now an end has come to that phase, too. Waiting, along with the rest of the world, for the future to be born out of the shocking travail of the present war, these states have recognized another obligation, their own obligation toward the world.

There will be, this time, no turning away from the problems of society as there was after the first World War. Isolationism as a philosophy is dead. It may flare fitfully in a stubborn mind here and there, but it has burned itself out in the thinking of the people.

Wherever one travels in Wisconsin and Minnesota, one finds the same patient commitment to an exacting belief that out of this war must come a society that is willing to accept its destiny as a unit, a society based on the idea of the fellowship of all mankind.

There is no escaping the evidence that this is true. The leaders of the region express their belief freely and unreservedly; the people subscribe to it in every action of their daily lives. A public man with a Scandinavian name, who has just exchanged his task as Governor of his state for that of an officer in the Navy, rejects isolationism when, in his last official utterance, he offers a blueprint for world co-operation. A husky little Finnish lumberjack rejects isolationism with touching, tacit eloquence when he puts most of his wages into war bonds, holding back only what he needs for tobacco. A college president sweeps isolationism away when he organizes a committee to spread the gospel of internationalism. So do the grandsons of the German immigrants in New Ulm when they oversubscribe their Red Cross quota. A leader of the flour industry in Minneapolis repudiates the philosophy of "America first" when he urges that this country be ready to feed the world and speaks out for free trade in the society of tomorrow. So do the élite marines of the Scout and Sniper Platoon who take to Tarawa their Wisconsin training as expert riflemen and who employ their skill in the self-conscious determination to wipe out arrogant international gangsterism.

If, as Bernard De Voto believes, the Middle West is the heartland of America, there is no reason to fear that that heart will not work generously in the crisis of the peace which must follow the crisis of war. Once more our region has "heard from the people." What Wisconsin and Minnesota now declare with unmistakable emphasis is that they wish to stand with the rest of human society for world co-operation and international order.

INDEX

Acetic acid, wood product, 95
Adams, James Truslow, 17
Agrarian crusade, 113–34, 167, 182, 184
Agricultural College, Wisconsin, 54
Agricultural Experiment Stations, 52
Agricultural Extension Services, 53, 56
Albinson, Dewey, 200
Aldrich, Darragh, 182
Alfalfa, 50
Allouez, Father Claude Jean, 277
American Fiction, 1920–1940, 169
American Fur Company, 268, 295, 298
Anti-Monopoly Party, 114
Anvil Theater, Winona, 281
Apples, 50
Appleton, Wisconsin, 148, 189
Arrowhead Region, 73, 277
Arrowsmith, 117. *See also* Lewis, Sinclair
Atlantis, 300
Atlas of American History, 17
Austrians, 34, 75

Babbitt, 177. *See also* Lewis, Sinclair
Babcock, Stephen Moulton, 161–5
Baker, Ray Stannard, 190
Ball, Senator Joseph, 134
Balsam, 88, 239
Banning, Margaret Culkin, 181, 279

Banvard, John, 193, 194, 196
Barley, 50
Beach, Joseph Warren, 169–71
Beach, Warren, 203
Bear, 40, 89, 239, 245, 246, 277
Beard, Dr. Charles, quoted, 166
Beaver, 40, 89, 239
Beck, Warren, 189
Beecher, Catherine, 149
Beers, Lorna Doone, 182
Being Respectable, 181
Beloit, Wisconsin, 148
Beloit College, 148
Beltrami, G. C., 11
Bemidji, Minnesota, 230
Bentley, Lester, 203
Berkman, Alexander, 77
Berger, Victor, 271–3
Bethel Merriday, 177. *See also* Lewis, Sinclair
Beyer, Thomas, 148
Birch, 88
Birling, 90
Birth, 166, 185. *See also* Gale, Zona
Bobleter, Lowell, 148, 201
Bohemians, 235
Bohnen, Roman, 142
Bonga, Pierre, 35
Booth, Cameron, 200
Border, The, 182
Bottineau, Pierre, 262
Briggs, Lucia Russell, 149
Broadacre City, 209, 213, 214, 246
Brown, Bob, 201

i

Bryce, James, 72
Bunyan, Paul, legend of, 92, 99, 202, 230, 241
Burton, Marion Leroy, 144
Business Enterprise, The, 152. *See also* Veblen, Thorstein
Butler, Pierce, 28

Cæsar's Column, 300. *See also* Donnelly, Ignatius
Callahan, "Honest" John, 275
Canada, 26, 27, 48, 240
Canadian jay, 42
Cantilever principle, 207. *See also* Wright, Frank Lloyd
Capitol, Madison, 279
Capitol, St. Paul, 220, 259
Carleton College, 146, 154
Carnegie, empire of, 77, 78
Carnegie Steel, 77
Carpenter, Elbert, 93
Carroll, Gladys Hasty, 189
Carroll College, 149
Carver, Jonathan, 11
Cathedral, St. Paul, 257
Catlin, George, 193, 194, 196
Cedars, 239
Cellophane, wood product, 95
Cellulose, wood product, 95
Center for Continuation Study, University of Minnesota, 141
Charcoal, wood product, 95
Chase, Mary Ellen, 189
Chinese, 34
Chippewa River, 91, 93, 195
Christensen, Chris L., 137
Christiansen, F. Melius, 148
City Hall, Minneapolis, 266
City Hall and Courthouse, St. Paul, 259, 260
Civil service, 30, 157
Civil War, 48, 63, 73, 112, 143, 161, 209
Clemens, Paul, 203
Cloquet, Minnesota, 96
Coffey, Walter, 144
Coffman, Lotus Delta, 144
Coffman Memorial Hall, University of Minnesota, 139

Cole, Dr. Wallace H., 293
College of St. Catherine, 147
Come and Get It, 187. *See also* Ferber, Edna
Commons, John R., 156–61
Concept of Nature in Nineteenth-Century English Poetry, The, 169. *See also* Beach, Joseph Warren
Conservation, 30, 130, 240
Conservation, Department of, Minnesota, 95
Contour farming, 214
Cooke, Jay, 278
Corn, 50, 54
Cornishmen, 75
Cortissoz, Royal, quoted, 219
County agents, 53
Coureurs de bois, 26, 40
Cousin Jacks, 79
Cowling, Donald J., 146
Croats, 34, 87
Crosley lifter, 104
Crystalline glucose, wood product, 95
Curry, John Steuart, 137, 203
Cut-over land, 19, 97, 130. *See also* Logging
Cuyuna Range, 70, 81. *See also* Mining
Cyrus Northrop Memorial Auditorium, University of Minnesota, 222
Czechs, 33, 246

Dane County, Wisconsin, 116
Davis, James W., 119
Davis, Jefferson, 296
Dawn O'Hara, 187. *See also* Ferber, Edna
Deer, 40, 42, 89, 245, 277
Dehn, Adolph, 201
Dells of Wisconsin, 15
Department of Agriculture: University of Minnesota, 144; University of Wisconsin, 137
Derleth, August, 188
Des Groseilliers, 25
Devil River, 89

De Voto, Bernard, 6, 312
Diary of a Freshman, 178. *See also*
Frandrau, Charles
Dietrich, Tom, 200
Doneghy, Dagmar, 182
Donnelly, Ignatius, 113–15, 118, 124, 124, 128, 175, 300–2
Dousman, Hercules, 29, 295
Dousman, Hercules, II, 296
Dousman, Michael, 268
Dousman, Nina Sturgis, 296
Dr. Huguet, 15. *See also* Donnelly, Ignatius
Du Lhut, Daniel Greysolon, Sieur, 25, 277
Duluth, Minnesota, 71, 74, 77, 181, 276–9
Dusk at the Grove, 189
Dutch, 33, 51

Earth Never Tires, 182
Eastman, Seth, 193
Ely, Minnesota, 202, 284
Embree, Edwin R., quoted, 137, 146
English, in Wisconsin and Minnesota, 25, 262
Ethyl alcohol, wood product, 96

Faint Perfume, 186. *See also* Gale, Zona
Falls of St. Anthony, 58, 68, 262, 264
Farm Bureau, 53, 56
Farmer-Labor Party, 125
Farmers' Alliance, 114
Farmington, Wisconsin, 26
Fearing, Kenneth, 190
Fellowship of Taliesin, 208
Ferber, Edna, 97, 187–8, 189
Festival of Nations, St. Paul, 34, 236
Finns, 33, 40, 75, 81, 86, 98, 182, 241, 246, 248
Firkins, Oscar, 183
First National Bank Building, St. Paul, 259
Fishing, 101–8, 239
Fitzgerald, F. Scott, 179–80, 186
Flambeau River, 15
Flandrau, Charles Macomb, 178–9, 182

Flandrau, Grace, 181
Flax, 54
Flora Shawn, 189. *See also* Rogers, Samuel
Flower, Forrest, 200
Folwell, William Watts, 143
Folwell Hall, University of Minnesota, 138
Fontanne, Lynn, 137, 301, 307
Ford, Guy Stanton, 144
Forest fires, 19, 94. *See also* Logging
Fort Crawford, 194, 195, 295
Fort Snelling, 194, 195, 256
Fossum, Syd, 201
Fox River, 13
French, 25, 40, 134, 257, 262
Frick, Henry Clay, 77
Frost, Robert, 52

Gale, Zona, 166, 184–5, 286
Galtier, Rev. Lucian, 256, 258
Garland, Hamlin, 184
General Mills, 67
Genesee, Wisconsin, 303
Germans, 23, 29, 223, 257, 262, 273
Giants in the Earth, 32, 146, 183. *See also* Rölvaag, O. E.
Gideon Planish, 177. *See also* Lewis, Sinclair
Gilbert, Cass, 139, 148, 217–21
Gill, Captain John, 75
Gill nets, 103
Glacier, effects of, 13, 72, 92, 307
Glass Mountain, 170. *See also* Beach, Joseph Warren
Glendale, Minnesota, 236
Godfrey, Mike, 75
Gogebic Range, 70, 78, 81. *See also* Mining
Golden Gophers, 142
Good-bye, Wisconsin, 186. *See also* Wescott, Glenway
Goodhue, J. M., 20
Goodykoonz, Colin B., quoted, 38
Goodly Heritage, A, 189
Gág, Flavia, 202
Gág, Wanda, 202
Gopher Prairie, 6
Grand Marais, 101

Grand Portage, 39
Grasshopper plagues, 48, 65
Grasty, Charles H., 174
Great Cryptogram, The, 113. See
also Donnelly, Ignatius
Great Gatsby, The, 179. *See also*
Fitzgerald, F. Scott
Greeks, 34, 235
Greenbackers, 114
Greenman, Frances, 202
Gregory, Horace, 190
Gridiron Club, Washington, D.C.,
123
Groom, Emily, 203
Grotenrath, Ruth, 203
Guardian Angel, 186
Gunflint Trail, 16
Gustavus-Adolphus College, 148

Hamline University, 148
Harris, Charles K., 274
Harvard Episodes, 178. *See also*
Flandrau, Charles M.
Hastings, Minnesota, 301
Haupers, Clement, 200
Hauser, Alonzo, 203
Havighurst, Walter, 189
Heiser, "Ma," 274
Hemlock, 88
Henderson, Dr. Melvin, 292
Hennepin, Father Louis, 25, 58, 68,
262
Hennepin Avenue, Minneapolis,
264
Hennepin County Medical Society,
293
Henry, A. W., 163
Hiawatha, 195, 266
Hibbing, Frank, 75
Hibbing, Minnesota, 78, 85
Hillside School, 209
Hinckley, Minnesota, 94
Hoard, William D., 51
Homestead Law, 48
House of Vanished Splendor, The,
182
Hudson's Bay Company, 27
Hull-Rust-Mahoning Mine, 78. *See
also* Mining

Humble Lear, A, 182
Hungarians, 23

Indeed This Flesh, 181
Indians: Algonquins, 24; Chippewa,
24, 35, 39, 48, 73, 236; Cree, 24;
Dakota, 24, 38; Fox, 24, 59, 295;
Menominee, 24, 268; Potawatami,
24; Sac, 24; Sioux, 11, 37, 38, 236;
Indian culture, 5; mounds, 24;
subjects of portraiture, 193; way
of life, 37
Innijiska, 259
Instinct of Workmanship, The, 153.
See also Veblen, Thorstein
Institutional Economics, 157
Insulation materials, wood prod-
ucts, 9, 97
International Institute, St. Paul, 236
Ireland, Archbishop John, 147
Irish, 23, 27, 122, 134, 257, 258, 262
Isaak Walton League, 240
It Can't Happen Here, 177. *See also*
Lewis, Sinclair
Italians, 33, 75
Itaska, Lake, 16

Jack-pine savage, 43
James Jerome Hill Reference Li-
brary, St. Paul, 261
Jansen, Richard, 203
Jemne, Elsa, 202
Job, Thomas, 146
Johnson, John A., 123–5, 131
Johnson, Magnus, 31, 109, 128
Johnson Floor Wax Company,
building at Racine, Wisconsin,
207
*Journal, American Medical Associa-
tion,* quoted, 293
Judd, Dr. E. Starr, 291
Juneau, Solomon, 197, 268–9
Jurka, Antonin, 33

Kelley, Oliver H., 113–14
Kellogg, Frank Billings, 111, 146
Kellogg, Louise P., quoted, 25
Kellogg Boulevard, St. Paul, 259
Kelm, Karlton, 186

Kenny, Elizabeth, 291–4
Kerfoot, Justine, 46
Kerfoot, William, 46
Kinkel, Johann Gottfried, 30
Knapp, Dr. Miland E., 293
Koehler, Robert, 198
Krasman, Ann, 202
Krause, Herbert, 182
Křenek, Ernst, 148

La Crosse, Wisconsin, 63, 303
Lac Qui Parle, 26
Lactic acid, wood product, 96
La Follette, Philip, 131, 133
La Follette, Robert M., Jr., 131
La Follette, Robert M., Sr., 30, 109, 115–20, 122, 124, 127, 135, 157, 175
La Salle, René Robert Cavelier, Sieur de, 58
Last Tycoon, The, 129. See also Fitzgerald, F. Scott
Latimer, Margery, 186
Lawrence College, 148
La Vérendrye, Pierre Gaultier, Sieur de, 239
Lend-Lease shipments, flour, 68
Leonard, William Ellery, 189
Le Sueur, Mac, 201
Le Sueur, Meridel, 181
Lewandowski, Edmund, 200
Lewis, Henry, 193, 195
Lewis, James Otto, 193
Lewis, Sinclair, 6, 8, 176–7, 282, 286
Lichtner, Schomer, 201
Lignin, wood product, 95
Lin Yutang, 72
Lincoln, Abraham, 10, 30
Lind, John, 31, 120–1, 124
Lindbergh, Charles Augustus, Jr., 132–3
Lindbergh, Charles Augustus, Sr., 125–6, 127, 272
Little Crow, 195
Little Falls, 126
Little Gallery, University of Minnesota, 141
Lloyd-Jones, Jenkin, 209
Locomotive God, The, 189

Loftus, George Sperry, 109, 121–2, 127
Logging, 88–100; building the cities of the Middle West, 93; Chippewa River activity, 91; Cloquet disaster, 96; Companies: Bovey, Brooks, Carpenter, De Laittre, Shevlin, Walker, 93; exploitation of forests, 50; first sawmill, 89; forest fires, 94; importance of logging today, 98; loggers' lives, early days, 91, today, 100; Mississippi Logging Company, 93; Weyerhaeuser, Frederick, 91; Weyerhaeuser, Rudolph, 96; veteran loggers, 40; wood products, 99
Longfellow, Henry Wadsworth, 89, 195, 266
Loquacities, 179. See also Flandrau, Charles Macomb
Loran, Erle, 203
Lumberjack Festival, Stillwater, 232
Lunt, Alfred, 136, 301–9
Lutz, Josephine, 201

Macalester, 148, 217
Mackenzie, Alexander, 246
Mad Carews, The, 182
Madison, Wisconsin, 30, 64, 135, 137, 154, 156, 279–80
Main Street, 177, 282. See also Lewis, Sinclair
Main Travelled Roads, 184
Mairs, Clara, 202
Mallet, Louis B., 291
Manahan, James, 109, 121–3
Manship, Paul, 203
Many a Green Isle, 182
Marine-on-the-St. Croix, 8, 29
Marquette, Father Jacques, 25
Marquette University, 146
Marr, Carl, 198
Martin, Morgan, 268
Martineau, Harriet, 269
Mayer, Frank, 193, 195
Mayo, Dr. Charles, 291
Mayo, Dr. William J., 291

Mayo, Dr. William W., 291
Mayo Clinic, 288–91, 292
Mayo Foundation, 291
McLoughlin, Dr. John, 72
McNally, William J., 182
Me, 182
Meat-packing, 50
Meek Americans, 170. *See also* Beach, Joseph Warren
Mendota, Lake, 136
Menominee Range, 70
Menominee Mine, 73
Merritt, Leonidas, 75, 76
Merritt, Lewis, 74
Merritt family, 74
Methyl alcohol, wood product, 95
Mexicans, 33, 235
Michigan, Lake, 200
Milles, Carl, 260
Milling, 58–69; bleaching of flour, 68; cleanliness of mills, 60; explosion, 62–3; leadership of J. S. Pillsbury, 65; of C. C. Washburn, 63; Lend-Lease shipments, 68; "middlings purifier," 61; organization of General Mills, 67; "revolution," 61; technique of, 60; vitamins in flour, 68; world markets, 68–9
Milwaukee, 31, 136, 146, 187, 197, 198, 228, 268–76
Milwaukee-Downer College, 149
Milwaukee Leader, 271
Milwaukee River, 268
Mining, 70–87; beneficiating ore, 84; Carnegie Steel, 77; Cooke, Jay, 78; Cousin Jacks, 79; Cuyuna Range, 70, 81; discovery of iron, 72; development of mines, 73; engineering problems, 80; formation of iron deposits, 70–2; Frick, H. C., interest in, 77; glacier, effects of, 72; Gogebic Range, 70, 78, 81; Hull-Rust-Mahoning mine, 78; laboratories, 85; lawsuits regarding mines, 77; low-grade ores, 84; Menominee Range, 70; Merritt family, 74; Missabe, 70, 72, 74, 76, 77, 81; Mountain

Iron, 76, 84, 85; Nichols, Captain J. A., share in discovery of mines, 75; open-pit mines, 75–9; Ramsey, Alexander, share in development of mines, 72; Range cities, 86; Rockefeller interests, 77, 78; Stone, George, share in development of mines, 73; Stuntz, George, share in discovery of deposits, 73; Tower, Charlemagne, interest in mines, 74; underground mining, 83; Vermilion mine, 73, 78, 81; Vermilion Range, 70
Minneapolis, 31, 60, 65, 66, 76, 93, 109, 128, 129, 133, 181, 183, 197, 199, 200, 223, 262–7
Minneapolis Aquatennial, 235
Minneapolis General Hospital, 292
Minneapolis Institute of Arts, 196
Minneapolis Public Welfare Board, 294
Minneapolis School of Art, 198
Minneapolis Symphony Orchestra, 93, 141, 222–6
Minnehaha Creek, Minneapolis, 266
Minnesota Progressive Republican League, 122
Minnesota River, 11, 13, 148
Minnesota State Executive Council, 84
Minnesota State Fair, 227
Minnesota State Historical Society. 195, 196
Minnetonka Lake, 191
Missabe Range, 70, 72, 74, 76, 77, 81
Mississippi Logging Company, 93
Mississippi River, 13, 16, 58, 90, 193, 194, 195, 300
Mitropoulos, Dimitri, 225
Moccasin Telegraph, 46
Moose, 239, 248
Moynihan, Monsignor Humphrey, 147
Moynihan, Rev. James, 147
Muir, John, 184
Myself, 156. *See also* Commons, John R.

Nation, Carrie, 275
National Grange, 114
Native American, 190
Nelson, Knute, 114
New Ulm, 29, 291
Nicollet, Jean, 25
Nichols, Captain J. A., 75
Night Outlasts the Whippoorwill, 190
Nininger, John, 300
Nininger, town of, 113, 300
Nokomis, Lake, Minneapolis, 183
Nonpartisan League, 112
North, Sterling, 190
North country, 37, 76, 92, 239
Northfield, Minnesota, 146, 148, 156
Northrop, Cyrus, 143
Norwegians, 42, 75, 184
Nuthatches, 142

O River, Remember! 182
Oak, 88
Oats, 50
Oberhoffer, Emil, 223
Oliver, Henry W., 76
Oliver Mining Company, 78
Olson, Floyd B., 109, 128–31
Open-pit mining, *see* Mining
Ormandy, Eugene, 224–5
Ostenso, Martha, 182
Ottawa Indians, 24
Otter, 40

Pace, Dr. Charles Nelson, 148
Panorama painting, 194
Panic: of 1850, 65; of 1857, 278; of 1873, 278; of 1893, 77
Parrant, Pierre, 256, 258
Parsons, David, 203
Parsons, Mrs. William, 149
Patrons of Husbandry, 114
Peavey, 91
Peculiar Treasure, A, 187. *See also* Ferber, Edna
Peder Victorious, 183. *See also* Rölvaag, O. E.
Pegler, Westbrook, 191
Pembina, 27
Pepin, Lake, 14

Peshtigo, 94
Pilgrim Hawk, The, 186
Pillsbury, Charles, 65
Pillsbury, J. S., 63, 65
Pine: jack, 88, 97, 187, 239, 244; red, 88; white, 88
Pipestone, 236
Plastics, wood products, 95
Ploughing on Sunday, 190
Pohl, Dr. John F., 293
Poles, 33, 280
Poliomyelitis, 292–4
Pond, Samuel, quoted, 38
Poplar, 88
Populist, or People's, Party, 114, 121
Porcupine, 89, 239, 245
Portage, Wisconsin, 165, 185, 190
Post Office Building, St. Paul, 259
Potatoes, 50
Pound net, 108
Prairie, 17
Prairie du Chien, 17, 194, 295
Prairie Fires, 182
Prairie Folk, 184
Priebe, Karl, 202
Prejudices, 179. *See also* Flandrau, Charles Macomb
Progressive Movement of Wisconsin, 120, 136
Prokosch, Frederick, 190
Pryon, Arthur, 274
Public Library, Minneapolis, 265
Public Library, St. Paul, 260
Pulpwood, 9, 95, 97
Pyrites, 73

Quetico National Park, 240

Radisson, Pierre Esprit, 15, 25, 277
Racine, Wisconsin, 207
Rainy Lake, 239
Ramsey, Alexander, 29, 72, 300
Rawlings, Marjorie Kinnan, 160, 191
Rayon, wood product, 95
Recollect Order, 58
Red River: ox carts, 28; valley, 48, 53, 160
Reeves, Elizabeth, 182

Regionalism, 5, 175, 200
Resler, George, 201
Richland Center, 217
Ripon, Wisconsin, 149
Ripon College, 149
Roberts, Kenneth, 64
Rochester, Minnesota, 18, 131, 288–91
Rockefeller, business empire of, 77, 78
Roofs of Elm Street, The, 182
Rogers, Major Robert, 11
Rogers, Samuel, 189
Rollette, Jane Fisher (Madame Hercules Dousman), 296
Rollette, Joseph, 296
Rölvaag, O. E., 32, 148, 183–4
Roumanians, 34
Russians, 34
Rust, Ezra, 75
Rye, 50

Sac Indians, 24
St. Anthony, village of, 65, 263
St. Croix River, 13, 15, 29, 50, 195, 232
St. John's Abbey, 147
St. Mary, College of, Winona, 281
St. Mary's Hospital, Rochester, 291
St. Olaf's College, 148, 184
St. Paul, city of, 22, 26, 29, 31, 34, 93, 200, 217, 220, 223, 256–62, 267, 284
St. Paul Figure Skating Club, 234
St. Peter, Minnesota, 124
St. Theresa, College of, Winona, 281
St. Thomas' Academy and Military College, 147
Saratoga Trunk, 187. See also Ferber, Edna
Salute to Spring, 181
Sauna, 249–250
Scottish people, 27, 40, 262
Schorer, Mark, 189
Schurz, Carl, 29, 269
Selkirk, Lord, 27
Serbs, 34, 235
Sessler, Alfred, 202
Seward, William H., 21

Seymour, Samuel, 193
Shipstead, Senator Henrik, 128
Sibley, Henry Hastings, 29, 298
Sinclair, Gerrit, 200
Sioux Indians, 11, 37, 38, 236
Siscowet, 103
Slovenes, 75, 87
Smith, Glanville, 182
Smith, John J., 51
Social Democratic Herald, 271
Somerset, Wisconsin, 26
Sophomores Abroad, 178. See also Flandrau, Charles Macomb
South St. Paul, 50
Spring Green, Wisconsin, 56, 205, 304
Spring wheat, 62
Spruce, 88, 97, 239
Stassen, Harold, 131, 134
Steele, Franklin, 263
Steele, Sarah (Mrs. Henry Hastings Sibley), 299
Steffens, Lincoln, quoted, 125
Stillwater, Minnesota, 15, 201, 232
Stoll, E. E., 171–4
Stone, George, 73
Streiff, Fridolin, 51
Stuntz, George, 73
Submarginal lands, 43
Sugar maple, 88
Sullivan, Louis, 207
Summit Avenue, St. Paul, 257
Superior, Wisconsin, 74
Superior, Lake, 13, 17, 70, 92, 101, 193, 200, 239, 276, 278
Superior National Forest, 98
Superior National Park, 240
Supreme Court Building, Washington, D.C., 218
Swedes, 23, 31, 40, 75, 81, 98, 123, 134, 183, 223, 235, 266–7
Swiss, 28, 51
Swiss cheese, 51

Taliesin, 205
Tamarack, 42, 88
Taylor, Zachary, 296
Tenant farmers, 54
Then I Saw the Congo, 181

This Is My Body, 186
This Side of Paradise, 179. *See also* Fitzgerald, F. Scott
Thomas, Howard, 201
Thwaites, Charles, 202
Tickanoggin, 39
Timber cruisers, 74
Tower, Charlemagne, 74, 76, 78
Townley, A. C., 127–9
Traverse des Sioux, 26, 195
Trollope, Anthony, quoted, 270
Trout, 103
Turner, Frederick Jackson, 165–9
Twentieth Century Novel, The, 169. *See also* Beach, Joseph Warren
Twin Cities (St. Paul and Minneapolis), 141, 222, 223, 227, 255–6, 291
Two Harbors, 74
Two Lives, 189

Ueland, Brenda, 182
Ukrainians, 34, 235
Under the Sun, 181
Underground mining, *see* Mining
Underground Railroad, 49
United States Bureau of Mines, 85
U. S. Department of Agriculture, 53, 68
U. S. Forests Products Laboratory, 280
U. S. Steel, 78
U. S. Weather Bureau, Madison, 280
University of Minnesota, 66, 122, 138–46, 170, 171, 186, 190, 222, 284, 296
University of Wisconsin, 64, 116, 121, 122, 135–8, 185, 186, 189, 190, 205, 279
Upson, Arthur, 182
Usonian architecture, 209. *See also* Wright, Frank Lloyd

Van Hise, Charles Richard, 138
Veblen, Thorstein, 146, 152–6, 197
Verbrugghen, Henri, 223
Vermilion Lake country, 73

Vermilion mine, 73, 78, 81
Vermilion Range, 70
Vianden, Henry, 197
Vieux, Jacques, 268
Vieux, Josette (Madame Solomon Juneau), 268
Villa Louis, 296–300
Vincent, George Edgar, 143
Viva Mexico! 178. *See also* Flandrau, Charles Macomb
Volkszeitung, 271
Von Neumann, Robert, 200
Voyageurs, 7, 25, 40, 244, 277

Walker, T. B., 93
Wanagan, 100
Warren, Robert Penn, 190
Washburn, C. C., 63, 65
Washburn-Crosby Company, 67
Watertown, Wisconsin, 30
Watrous, James, 202
Watson, Forbes, quoted, 200
Waukesha, Wisconsin, 149, 304
We Are Incredible, 186
Weed trees, 9, 42, 96
Wescott, Glenway, 186–7
West Salem, Wisconsin, 184
Weyerhaeuser, Frederick, 91, 93
Weyerhaeuser, Rudolph, 97
Wheat, 9, 48, 60, 61
White, Helen Constance, 189
Whitefish Bay, Milwaukee, 274
Whitman, Walt, 10, 49
Whitney, Dan, 89
Wilder, Thornton, 191
Wilderness country, 9, 14–15, 16, 22, 46, 99, 184, 193, 195, 239–53, 277, 295–302
Willard, Frances, 149
Williard, James F., quoted, 38
Wilson, Clagett, 305
Wilson, Woodrow, 120, 121, 136
Wind over Wisconsin, 188
Wind without Rain, 182
Winholtz, Caleb, 201
Winnebago Indians, 24, 89
Winona, Minnesota, 280–1
Winter Carnival, St. Paul, 233–4
Wisconsin Historical Society, 196

Wisconsin "idea," 136, 159
Wisconsin River, 8, 13, 89, 205
Wisconsin State Fair, 227
Wisconsin Vorwaerts, 271
Wolfe, Thomas, 5
Wolves, 239
Wood cotton, 95
Wood wool, 95
Woolworth Building, New York, 217

Working People's Nonpartisan Political League, 128
WPA, 193, 202, 204
Wright, Frank Lloyd, 205–16, 264, 274, 304

Xylose, wood product, 96

Zaturenska, Marya, 190
Zingale, Santos, 200